Todd G. Morrison, PhD
Editor

Eclectic Views on Gay Male Pornography: Pornucopia

Eclectic Views on Gay Male Pornography: Pornucopia has been co-published simultaneously as *Journal of Homosexuality*, Volume 47, Numbers 3/4 2004.

Pre-publication
REVIEWS,
COMMENTARIES,
EVALUATIONS . . .

"It's about time that writers and scholars take up gay pornography as a serious subject of discourse. One of the most important contributions is editor Todd Morrison's examination of how gay male viewers interpret pornography. The book's high point is Paul Hallam's deeply personal and illuminating essay on the role pornography has played in his life and the value it has had. Hallam's almost Proustian account of the role of pornography in stimulating personal and historical memory is an important and original perspective."

Jeffrey Escoffier
Author of American Homo: Community and Perversity; *Editor of* Sexual Revolution

Eclectic Views
on Gay Male Pornography:
Pornucopia

Eclectic Views on Gay Male Pornography: Pornucopia has been co-published simultaneously as *Journal of Homosexuality*, Volume 47, Numbers 3/4 2004.

The *Journal of Homosexuality* Monographic "Separates"

Below is a list of "separates," which in serials librarianship means a special issue simultaneously published as a special journal issue or double-issue *and* as a "separate" hardbound monograph. (This is a format which we also call a "DocuSerial.")

"Separates" are published because specialized libraries or professionals may wish to purchase a specific thematic issue by itself in a format which can be separately cataloged and shelved, as opposed to purchasing the journal on an on-going basis. Faculty members may also more easily consider a "separate" for classroom adoption.

"Separates" are carefully classified separately with the major book jobbers so that the journal tie-in can be noted on new book order slips to avoid duplicate purchasing.

You may wish to visit Haworth's website at . . .

http://www.HaworthPress.com

. . . to search our online catalog for complete tables of contents of these separates and related publications. You may also call 1-800-HAWORTH (outside US/Canada: 607-722-5857), or Fax 1-800-895-0582 (outside US/Canada: 607-771-0012), or e-mail at:

docdelivery@haworthpress.com

Eclectic Views on Gay Male Pornography: Pornucopia, edited by Todd G. Morrison, PhD (Vol. 47, No. 3/4, 2004). "An instant classic. . . . Lively and readable." *(Jerry Zientara, EdD, Librarian, Institute for Advanced Study of Human Sexuality)*

The Drag Queen Anthology: The Absolutely Fabulous but Flawlessly Customary World of Female Impersonators, edited by Steven P. Schacht, PhD, with Lisa Underwood (Vol. 46, No. 3/4, 2004). *"Indispensable. . . . For more than a decade, Steven P. Schacht has been one of the social sciences' most reliable guides to the world of drag queens and female impersonators. . . . This book assembles an impressive cast of scholars who are as theoretically astute, methodologically careful, and conceptually playful as the drag queens themselves." (Michael Kimmel, author of* The Gendered Society; *Professor of Sociology, SUNY Stony Brook)*

Queer Theory and Communication: From Disciplining Queers to Queering the Discipline(s), edited by Gust A. Yep, PhD, Karen E. Lovaas, PhD, and John P. Elia, PhD (Vol. 45, Nov. 2/3/4, 2003). *"Sheds light on how sexual orientation and identity are socially produced–and how they can be challenged and changed–through everyday practices and institutional activities, as well as academic research and teaching. . . . Illuminates the theoretical and practical significance of queer theory–not only as a specific area of inquiry, but also as a productive challenge to the heteronormativity of mainstream communication theory, research, and pedagogy." (Julia T. Wood, PhD, Lineberger Professor of Humanities, Professor of Communication Studies, The University of North Carolina at Chapel Hill)*

Gay Bathhouses and Public Health Policy, edited by William J. Woods, PhD, and Diane Binson, PhD (Vol. 44, No. 3/4, 2003). *"Important. . . . Long overdue. . . . A unique and valuable contribution to the social science and public health literature. The inclusion of detailed historical descriptions of public policy debates about the place of bathhouses in urban gay communities, together with summaries of the legal controversies about bathhouses, insightful examinations of patrons' behaviors and reviews of successful programs for HIV/STD education and testing programs in bathhouses provides. A well rounded and informative overview." (Richard Tewksbury, PhD, Professor of Justice Administration, University of Louisville)*

Icelandic Lives: The Queer Experience, edited by Voon Chin Phua (Vol. 44, No. 2, 2002). *"The first of its kind, this book shows the emergence of gay and lesbian visibility through the biographical narratives of a dozen Icelanders. Through their lives can be seen a small nation's transition, in just a few decades, from a pervasive silence concealing its queer citizens to widespread acknowledgment characterized by some of the most progressive laws in the world." (Barry D. Adam, PhD, University Professor, Department of Sociology & Anthropology, University of Windsor, Ontario, Canada)*

The Drag King Anthology, edited by Donna Jean Troka, PhD (cand.), Kathleen LeBesco, PhD, and Jean Bobby Noble, PhD (Vol. 43, No. 3/4, 2002). *"All university courses on masculinity should use this book . . . challenges preconceptions through the empirical richness of direct experience. The contributors and editors have worked together to produce cultural analysis that enhances* *our perception of the dynamic uncertainty of gendered experience." (Sally R. Munt, DPhil, Subject Chair, Media Studies, University of Sussex)*

Homosexuality in French History and Culture, edited by Jeffrey Merrick and Michael Sibalis (Vol. 41, No. 3/4, 2001). *"Fascinating. . . . Merrick and Sibalis bring together historians, literary scholars, and political activists from both sides of the Atlantic to examine same-sex sexuality in the past and present." (Bryant T. Ragan, PhD, Associate Professor of History, Fordham University, New York City)*

Gay and Lesbian Asia: Culture, Identity, Community, edited by Gerard Sullivan, PhD, and Peter A. Jackson, PhD (Vol. 40, No. 3/4, 2001). *"Superb. . . . Covers a happily wide range of styles . . . will appeal to both students and educated fans." (Gary Morris, Editor/Publisher, Bright Lights Film Journal)*

Queer Asian Cinema: Shadows in the Shade, edited by Andrew Grossman, MA (Vol. 39, No. 3/4, 2000). *"An extremely rich tapestry of detailed ethnographies and state-of-the-art theorizing. . . . Not only is this a landmark record of queer Asia, but it will certainly also be a seminal, contributive challenge to gender and sexuality studies in general." (Dédé Oetomo, PhD, Coordinator of the Indonesian organization GAYa NUSANTARA; Adjunct Reader in Linguistics and Anthropology, School of Social Sciences, Universitas Airlangga, Surabaya, Indonesia)*

Gay Community Survival in the New Millennium, edited by Michael R. Botnick, PhD (cand.) (Vol. 38, No. 4, 2000). *Examines the notion of community from several different perspectives focusing on the imagined, the structural, and the emotive. You will explore a theoretical overview and you will peek into the moral discourses that frame "gay community," the rift between HIV-positive and HIV-negative gay men, and how Israeli gays seek their place in the public sphere.*

The Ideal Gay Man: The Story of Der Kreis, by Hubert Kennedy, PhD (Vol. 38, No. 1/2, 1999). *"Very profound. . . . Excellent insight into the problems of the early fight for homosexual emancipation in Europe and in the USA. . . . The ideal gay man (high-mindedness, purity, cleanness), as he was imagined by the editor of 'Der Kreis,' is delineated by the fascinating quotations out of the published erotic stories." (Wolfgang Breidert, PhD, Academic Director, Institute of Philosophy, University Karlsruhe, Germany)*

Multicultural Queer: Australian Narratives, edited by Peter A. Jackson, PhD, and Gerard Sullivan, PhD (Vol. 36, No. 3/4, 1999). *Shares the way that people from ethnic minorities in Australia (those who are not of Anglo-Celtic background) view homosexuality, their experiences as homosexual men and women, and their feelings about the lesbian and gay community.*

Scandinavian Homosexualities: Essays on Gay and Lesbian Studies, edited by Jan Löfström, PhD (Vol. 35, No. 3/4, 1998). *"Everybody interested in the formation of lesbian and gay identities and their interaction with the sociopolitical can find something to suit their taste in this volume." (Judith Schuyf, PhD, Assistant Professor of Lesbian and Gay Studies, Center for Gay and Lesbian Studies, Utrecht University, The Netherlands)*

Gay and Lesbian Literature Since World War II: History and Memory, edited by Sonya L. Jones, PhD (Vol. 34, No. 3/4, 1998). *"The authors of these essays manage to gracefully incorporate the latest insights of feminist, postmodernist, and queer theory into solidly grounded readings . . . challenging and moving, informed by the passion that prompts both readers and critics into deeper inquiry." (Diane Griffin Growder, PhD, Professor of French and Women's Studies, Cornell College, Mt. Vernon, Iowa)*

Reclaiming the Sacred: The Bible in Gay and Lesbian Culture, edited by Raymond-Jean Frontain, PhD (Vol. 33, No. 3/4, 1997). *"Finely wrought, sharply focused, daring, and always dignified. . . . In chapter after chapter, the Bible is shown to be a more sympathetic and humane book in its attitudes toward homosexuality than usually thought and a challenge equally to the straight and gay moral imagination." (Joseph Wittreich, PhD, Distinguished Professor of English, The Graduate School, The City University of New York)*

Activism and Marginalization in the AIDS Crisis, edited by Michael A. Hallett, PhD (Vol. 32, No. 3/4, 1997). *Shows readers how the advent of HIV-disease has brought into question the utility of certain forms of "activism" as they relate to understanding and fighting the social impacts of disease.*

Gays, Lesbians, and Consumer Behavior: Theory, Practice, and Research Issues in Marketing, edited by Daniel L. Wardlow, PhD (Vol. 31, No. 1/2, 1996). *"For those scholars, market researchers, and marketing managers who are considering marketing to the gay and lesbian community, this book should be on their required reading list." (Mississippi Voice)*

Gay Men and the Sexual History of the Political Left, edited by Gert Hekma, PhD, Harry Oosterhuis, PhD, and James Steakley, PhD (Vol. 29, No. 2/3/4, 1995). *"Contributors delve into the contours of a long-forgotten history, bringing to light new historical data and fresh insight. . . .*

An excellent account of the tense historical relationship between the political left and gay liberation." (People's Voice)

Sex, Cells, and Same-Sex Desire: The Biology of Sexual Preference, edited by John P. De Cecco, PhD, and David Allen Parker, MA (Vol. 28, No. 1/2/3/4, 1995). *"A stellar compilation of chapters examining the most important evidence underlying theories on the biological basis of human sexual orientation." (MGW)*

Gay Ethics: Controversies in Outing, Civil Rights, and Sexual Science, edited by Timothy F. Murphy, PhD (Vol. 27, No. 3/4, 1994). *"The contributors bring the traditional tools of ethics and political philosophy to bear in a clear and forceful way on issues surrounding the rights of homosexuals." (David L. Hull, Dressler Professor in the Humanities, Department of Philosophy, Northwestern University)*

Gay and Lesbian Studies in Art History, edited by Whitney Davis, PhD (Vol. 27, No. 1/2, 1994). *"Informed, challenging . . . never dull. . . . Contributors take risks and, within the restrictions of scholarly publishing, find new ways to use materials already available or examine topics never previously explored." (Lambda Book Report)*

Critical Essays: Gay and Lesbian Writers of Color, edited by Emmanuel S. Nelson, PhD (Vol. 26, No. 2/3, 1993). *"A much-needed book, sparkling with stirring perceptions and resonating with depth. . . . The anthology not only breaks new ground, it also attempts to heal wounds inflicted by our oppressed pasts." (Lambda)*

Gay Studies from the French Cultures: Voices from France, Belgium, Brazil, Canada, and The Netherlands, edited by Rommel Mendès-Leite, PhD, and Pierre-Olivier de Busscher, PhD (Vol. 25, No. 1/2/3, 1993). *"The first book that allows an English-speaking world to have a comprehensive look at the principal trends in gay studies in France and French-speaking countries." (André Bèjin, PhD, Directeur, de Recherche au Centre National de la Recherche Scientifique [CNRS], Paris)*

If You Seduce a Straight Person, Can You Make Them Gay? Issues in Biological Essentialism versus Social Constructionism in Gay and Lesbian Identities, edited by John P. De Cecco, PhD, and John P. Elia, PhD (cand.) (Vol. 24, No. 3/4, 1993). *"You'll find this alternative view of the age old question to be one that will become the subject of many conversations to come. Thought-provoking to say the least!" (Prime Timers)*

Gay and Lesbian Studies: The Emergence of a Discipline, edited by Henry L. Minton, PhD (Vol. 24, No. 1/2, 1993). *"The volume's essays provide insight into the field's remarkable accomplishments and future goals." (Lambda Book Report)*

Homosexuality in Renaissance and Enlightenment England: Literary Representations in Historical Context, edited by Claude J. Summers, PhD (Vol. 23, No. 1/2, 1992). *"It is remarkable among studies in this field in its depth of scholarship and variety of approaches and is accessible." (Chronique)*

Coming Out of the Classroom Closet: Gay and Lesbian Students, Teachers, and Curricula, edited by Karen M. Harbeck, PhD, JD, Recipient of Lesbian and Gay Educators Award by the American Educational Research Association's Lesbian and Gay Studies Special Interest Group (AREA) (Vol. 22, No. 3/4, 1992). *"Presents recent research about gay and lesbian students and teachers and the school system in which they function." (Contemporary Psychology)*

Homosexuality and Male Bonding in Pre-Nazi Germany: The Youth Movement, the Gay Movement, and Male Bonding Before Hitler's Rise: Original Transcripts from Der Eigene, the First Gay Journal in the World, edited by Harry Oosterhuis, PhD, and Hubert Kennedy, PhD (Vol. 22, No. 1/2, 1992). *"Provide[s] insight into the early gay movement, particularly in its relation to the various political currents in pre-World War II Germany." (Lambda Book Report)*

Gay People, Sex, and the Media, edited by Michelle A. Wolf, PhD, and Alfred P. Kielwasser, MA (Vol. 21, No. 1/2, 1991). *"Altogether, the kind of research anthology which is useful to many disciplines in gay studies. Good stuff!" (Communique)*

Gay Midlife and Maturity: Crises, Opportunities, and Fulfillment, edited by John Alan Lee, PhD (Vol. 20, No. 3/4, 1991). *"The insight into gay aging is amazing, accurate, and much-needed. . . . A real contribution to the older gay community." (Prime Timers)*

Monographs "Separates" list continued at the back

Eclectic Views on Gay Male Pornography: Pornucopia

Todd G. Morrison, PhD
Editor

Eclectic Views on Gay Male Pornography: Pornucopia has been co-published simultaneously as *Journal of Homosexuality*, Volume 47, Numbers 3/4 2004.

Harrington Park Press®
An Imprint of The Haworth Press, Inc.

Published by

Harrington Park Press®, 10 Alice Street, Binghamton, NY 13904-1580 USA

Harrington Park Press® is an imprint of The Haworth Press, Inc., 10 Alice Street, Binghamton, NY 13904-1580 USA.

Eclectic Views on Gay Male Pornography: Pornucopia has been co-published simultaneously as *Journal of Homosexuality*, Volume 47, Numbers 3/4 2004.

© 2004 by The Haworth Press, Inc. All rights reserved. No part of this work may be reproduced or utilized in any form or by any means, electronic or mechanical, including photocopying, microfilm and recording, or by any information storage and retrieval system, without permission in writing from the publisher. Printed in the United States of America.

The development, preparation, and publication of this work has been undertaken with great care. However, the publisher, employees, editors, and agents of The Haworth Press and all imprints of The Haworth Press, Inc., including The Haworth Medical Press® and Pharmaceutical Products Press®, are not responsible for any errors contained herein or for consequences that may ensue from use of materials or information contained in this work. Opinions expressed by the author(s) are not necessarily those of The Haworth Press, Inc. With regard to case studies, identities and circumstances of individuals discussed herein have been changed to protect confidentiality. Any resemblance to actual persons, living or dead, is entirely coincidental.

Cover design by Marylouise E. Doyle

Library of Congress Cataloging-in-Publication Data

Eclectic views on gay male pornography : pornucopia / Todd G. Morrison, editor.
    p. cm.
    "Eclectic Views on Gay Male Pornography: Pornucopia has been co-published simultaneously as Journal of Homosexuality, Volume 47, Numbers 3/4 2004."
    Includes bibliographical references and index.
    ISBN 1-56023-290-0 (hard cover)–ISBN 1-56023-291-9 (soft cover : alk. paper)
    1. Pornography. 2. Gay erotic videos. 3. Gay men–Sexual behavior. I. Morrison, Todd G. II. Journal of homosexuality.
HQ471.P6469 2004
363.4'7'086642–dc22
                                                                                         2004015699

Indexing, Abstracting & Website/Internet Coverage

Journal of Homosexuality

This section provides you with a list of major indexing & abstracting services. That is to say, each service began covering this periodical during the year noted in the right column. Most Websites which are listed below have indicated that they will either post, disseminate, compile, archive, cite or alert their own Website users with research-based content from this work. (This list is as current as the copyright date of this publication.)

Abstracting, Website/Indexing Coverage	Year When Coverage Began

- *Abstracts in Anthropology* 1982

- *Academic Abstracts/CD-ROM* 1989

- *Academic ASAP <http://www.galegroup.com>* 2000

- *Academic Search: database of 2,000 selected academic serials, updated monthly: EBSCO Publishing* 1995

- *Academic Search Elite (EBSCO)* 1993

- *Applied Social Sciences Index & Abstracts (ASSIA) (Online: ASSI via Data-Star) (CD-Rom: ASSIA Plus) <http://www.csa.com>* 1987

- *ATLA Religion Database. This periodical is indexed in ATLA Religion Database, published by the American Theological Library Association <http://www.atla.com>* 1983

- *ATLA Religion Database with ATLASerials. This periodical is indexed in ATLA Religion Database with ATLASerials, published by the American Theological Library Association <http://www.atla.com>* 1983

(continued)

- *Book Review Index* 1996
- *Business Source Complete: coverage of nearly 3,350 quality magazines and journals; designed to meet the diverse information needs of corporations; EBSCO Publishing <http://www.epnet.com/corporate/bsource.asp>* 1974
- *Cambridge Scientific Abstracts is a leading publisher of scientific information in print journals, online databases, CD-ROM and via the Internet <http://www.csa.com>* 1993
- *Contemporary Women's Issues* 1998
- *Criminal Justice Abstracts* 1982
- *Current Contents/Social & Behavioral Sciences <http://www.isinet.com>* 1985
- *EMBASE/Excerpta Medica Secondary Publishing Division. Included in newsletters, review journals, major reference works, magazines & abstract journals <http://www.elsevier.nl>* 1974
- *e-psyche, LLC <http://www.e-psyche.net>* 2001
- *Expanded Academic ASAP <http://www.galegroup.com>* 1989
- *Expanded Academic Index* 1992
- *Family & Society Studies Worldwide <http://www.nisc.com>* 1996
- *Family Index Database <http://www.familyscholar.com>* 2002
- *Family Violence & Sexual Assault Bulletin* 1992
- *GenderWatch <http://www.slinfo.com>* 1999
- *GLBT Life, EBSCO Publishing <http://www.epnet.com/academic/glbt.asp>* 2004
- *Health & Psychosocial Instruments (HaPI) Database (available through online and as a CD-ROM from OVID Technologies)* 1986
- *Higher Education Abstracts, providing the latest in research and theory in more than 140 major topics* 1997
- *HOMODOK/"Relevant" Bibliographic Database, Documentation Centre for Gay & Lesbian Studies, University of Amsterdam (selective printed abstracts in "Homologie" and bibliographic computer databases covering cultural, historical, social & political aspects) <http://www.ihlia.nl/>* 1995

(continued)

- *IBZ International Bibliography of Periodical Literature*
  <http://www.saur.de> 1996
- *IGLSS Abstracts* <http://www.iglss.org> 2000
- *Index Guide to College Journals (core list compiled by integrating 48 indexes frequently used to support undergraduate programs in small to medium sized libraries)* 1999
- *Index Medicus (National Library of Medicine)*
  <http://www.nlm.nih.gov> 1992
- *Index to Periodical Articles Related to Law* <http://www.law.utexas.edu> 1986
- *InfoTrac Custom* <http://www.galegroup.com> 1996
- *InfoTrac OneFile* <http://www.galegroup.com> 1996
- *International Bibliography of the Social Sciences*
  <http://www.ibss.ac.uk> 2003
- *Internationale Bibliographie der geistes- und sozialwissenschaftlichen Zeitschriftenliteratur ... See IBZ* 1996
- *ISI Web of Science* <http://www.isinet.com> 2003
- *ITER-Gateway to the Middle Ages & Renaissance*
  <http://iter.utoronto.ca> 1974
- *LegalTrac on InfoTrac Web*
  <http://www.galegroup.com> 1990
- *Lesbian Information Service*
  <http://www.lesbianinformationservice.org> 1991
- *MasterFILE: Updated database from EBSCO Publishing* 1995
- *MEDLINE (National Library of Medicine)*
  <http://www.nlm.nih.gov> 1992
- *MLA International Bibliography provides a classified listing & subject index for books & articles published on modern languages, literatures, folklore, & linguistics. Available in print and in several electronic versions. Indexes over 50,000 publications*
  <http://www.mla.org> 1995
- *National Child Support Research Clearinghouse*
  <http://www.spea.indiana.edu/ncsea/> 1998
- *OCLC Public Affairs Information Service* <http://www.pais.org> ... 1982

(continued)

- *PASCAL, c/o Institut de L'Information Scientifique et Technique. Cross-disciplinary electronic database covering the fields of science, technology & medicine. Also available on CD-ROM, and can generate customized retrospective searches* <http://www.inist.fr> 1986
- *Periodical Abstracts, Research I (general and basic reference indexing and abstracting database from University Microfilms International [UMI], 300 North Zeeb Road, PO Box 1346, Ann Arbor, MI 48106-1346)* 1993
- *Periodical Abstracts, Research II (broad coverage indexing and abstracting database from University Microfilms International [UMI], 300 North Zeeb Road, PO Box 1346, Ann Arbor, MI 48106-1346)* 1993
- *PlanetOut "Internet site for key Gay/Lesbian Information"* <http://www.planetout.com/> 1999
- *Psychological Abstracts (PsycINFO)* <http://www.apa.org> 1995
- *Psychology Today* 1999
- *PubMed* <http://www.ncbi.nlm.nih.gov/pubmed/> 2003
- *RESEARCH ALERT/ISI Alerting Services* <http://www.isinet.com> 1985
- *Sage Family Studies Abstracts (SFSA)* 1986
- *Sexual Diversity Studies: Gay, Lesbian, Bisexual & Transgender Abstracts (formerly Gay & Lesbian Abstracts) provides comprehensive & in-depth coverage of the world's GLBT literature compiled by NISC & published on the Internet & CD-ROM* <http://www.nisc.com> 1999
- *Social Science Source: coverage of 400 journals in the social sciences area: updated monthly; EBSCO Publishing* 1995
- *Social Sciences Abstracts indexes & abstracts more than 460 publications, specifically selected by librarians & library patrons. Wilson's databases comprise the peer-reviewed & peer-selected core journals in each field* <http://www.hwwilson.com> 1999
- *Social Sciences Citation Index* <http://www.isinet.com> 1985
- *Social Sciences Full Text (available only electronically)* <http://www.hwwilson.com> 1991
- *Social Sciences Index (from Volume 1 and continuing)* <http://www.hwwilson.com> 1991
- *Social Scisearch* <http://www.isinet.com> 1985
- *Social Services Abstracts* <http://www.csa.com> 1982
- *Social Work Abstracts* <http://www.silverplatter.com/catalog/swab.htm> 1994
- *Sociological Abstracts (SA)* <http://www.csa.com> 1982
- *Studies on Women and Gender Abstracts* <http://www.tandf.co.uk/swa> . 1987

(continued)

- SwetsNet <http://www.swetsnet.com> 2001
- *Violence and Abuse Abstracts: A Review of Current Literature on Interpersonal Violence (VAA)* 1995
- *Wilson OmniFile Full Text: Mega Edition (available only electronically)* <http://www.hwwilson.com> 1987

Special Bibliographic Notes related to special journal issues (separates) and indexing/abstracting:

- indexing/abstracting services in this list will also cover material in any "separate" that is co-published simultaneously with Haworth's special thematic journal issue or DocuSerial. Indexing/abstracting usually covers material at the article/chapter level.
- monographic co-editions are intended for either non-subscribers or libraries which intend to purchase a second copy for their circulating collections.
- monographic co-editions are reported to all jobbers/wholesalers/approval plans. The source journal is listed as the "series" to assist the prevention of duplicate purchasing in the same manner utilized for books-in-series.
- to facilitate user/access services all indexing/abstracting services are encouraged to utilize the co-indexing entry note indicated at the bottom of the first page of each article/chapter/contribution.
- this is intended to assist a library user of any reference tool (whether print, electronic, online, or CD-ROM) to locate the monographic version if the library has purchased this version but not a subscription to the source journal.
- individual articles/chapters in any Haworth publication are also available through the Haworth Document Delivery Service (HDDS).

∞ ALL HARRINGTON PARK PRESS BOOKS
AND JOURNALS ARE PRINTED
ON CERTIFIED ACID-FREE PAPER

ABOUT THE EDITOR

Todd G. Morrison, PhD, is a social psychologist at the National University of Ireland–Galway. He is founder of the Canadian Psychological Association's Section on Sexual Orientation and Gender Identity Issues and has a longstanding interest in gay and lesbian studies. Dr. Morrison conducts research on pornography, male body image and homonegativity, and has published in a variety of journals including *Psychology of Men and Masculinity*, *Youth and Society*, and the *Journal of Social Psychology*.

Eclectic Views on Gay Male Pornography: Pornucopia

CONTENTS

Acknowledgments	xvii
Eclectic Views on Gay Male Pornography: Pornucopia *Todd G. Morrison, PhD*	1
Memoir and Performance: Social Change and Self Life-Writing Among Men Who Are Gay Pornography Producers and Actors *Bertram J. Cohler, PhD*	7
Body Image, Eating Disorders, and the Drive for Muscularity in Gay and Heterosexual Men: The Influence of Media Images *Scott J. Duggan, PhD (cand.)* *Donald R. McCreary, PhD*	45
If You Look at It Long Enough . . . *Paul Hallam*	59
Homecoming: The Relevance of Radical Feminism for Gay Men *Robert Jensen, PhD*	75
Educating Gay Male Youth: Since When Is Pornography a Path Towards Self-Respect? *Christopher N. Kendall, SJD*	83
The Queer Sensitive Interveners in the *Little Sisters* Case: A Response to Dr. Kendall *Karen Busby, LLM*	129

In the Slammer: The Myth of the Prison in American Gay
   Pornographic Video   151
     John Mercer, PhD

"He Was Treating Me Like Trash, and I Was Loving It . . ."
   Perspectives on Gay Male Pornography   167
     Todd G. Morrison, PhD

Sex Pigs: Why Porn Is Like Sausage, or The Truth Is That–
   Behind the Scenes–Porn Is Not Very Sexy   185
     Benjamin Scuglia

Alterity and Construction of National Identity
   in Three Kristen Bjorn Films   189
     Clare N. Westcott, MA

Porn Again: Some Final Considerations   197
     Shannon R. Ellis
     Bruce W. Whitehead

Index   221

Acknowledgments

First, I would like to thank all of the individuals who contributed to this anthology: Karen Busby, Bertram J. Cohler, Scott J. Duggan, Shannon R. Ellis, Paul Hallam, Robert Jensen, Christopher N. Kendall, Donald R. McCreary, John Mercer, Benjamin Scuglia, Clare N. Westcott, and Bruce W. Whitehead. Their receptivity to reviewers' (oft times lengthy) comments and patience with the editorial process were certainly appreciated. As well, I would like to thank John De Cecco, William Haver, Sarah Hill, Melanie A. Morrison, A. Mary Murphy, Dave Reed, Rod Schumaker, Joe Thomas, Gerald Walton, Gregory Wells, and Bruce W. Whitehead. Without their various queries, suggestions, and editorial observations, this anthology would not have been possible. A special note of gratitude is extended to Shannon R. Ellis, who spent countless hours proofreading contributors' work, and JoEllen A. Morrison, for things too countless to list. Finally, I want to acknowledge the "silent" contribution of L.D.M. Many years ago, I was fond of arguing that gay male pornography "isn't erotic because it decontextualises sexual activity." Fortunately, L.D.M. knew a porn aficionado when he saw one, and wasn't convinced by my feigned disinterest in this medium. It was through his "tutelage" that I discovered Scott Baldwin, Ryan Idol, Joey Stefano, and the rest of the "boys"–discoveries that played an integral role in the creation of this book.

Eclectic Views on Gay Male Pornography: Pornucopia

Todd G. Morrison, PhD

National University of Ireland-Galway

Pornography that targets heterosexual consumers (hereupon called heterosexual pornography) has received substantial attention from social scientists. For example, according to the electronic database PsycINFO, 407 journal articles were published on this topic between 1980 and 2003. (It should be noted that this figure excludes doctoral dissertations and articles not published in English.) Other databases such as the Social Science Index (SSI) reveal similar levels of scholarship (i.e., using pornography as a keyword, 337 entries appear between February 1983 and April 2003).

While numeric indicators of knowledge production denote interest in a given topic, they do not illuminate *why* that interest exists. The attention directed toward heterosexual pornography likely reflects the importance some academics have accorded this medium, both at the individual and societal levels. For example, some argue that heterosexual pornography eroticises men's fear and loathing of women and encapsulates a sexual political system that reflects and strengthens andrarchy (Dworkin, 1997; Russell, 1998). Conversely, others contend that heterosexual pornography is not necessarily oppressive or exploitive of women, and in fact may serve to enhance individuals' sexual self-determination (Chapkis, 1997; Nagle, 1997). Still others recommend moving beyond the condemnatory/celebratory impasse. They maintain that a binary

---

Correspondence may be addressed: Department of Psychology, National University of Ireland, Galway, Ireland (E-mail: psychology@nuigalway.ie).

[Haworth co-indexing entry note]: "Eclectic Views on Gay Male Pornography: Pornucopia." Morrison, Todd G. Co-published simultaneously in *Journal of Homosexuality* (Harrington Park Press, an imprint of The Haworth Press, Inc.) Vol. 47, No. 3/4, 2004, pp. 1-5; and: *Eclectic Views on Gay Male Pornography: Pornucopia* (ed: Todd G. Morrison) Harrington Park Press, an imprint of The Haworth Press, Inc., 2004, pp. 1-5. Single or multiple copies of this article are available for a fee from The Haworth Document Delivery Service [1-800-HAWORTH, 9:00 a.m. - 5:00 p.m. (EST). E-mail address: docdelivery@haworthpress.com].

http://www.haworthpress.com/web/JH
© 2004 by The Haworth Press, Inc. All rights reserved.
Digital Object Identifier: 10.1300/J082v47n03_01

analysis of pornography is simplistic and that neglected features of pornography exposure such as cross-gender identification should receive greater attention (Wilcox, 1999).

There is no logically compelling reason to argue that sexually explicit material directed toward gay men is less meaningful or influential than its heterosexual counterpart. Yet, despite the apparent ubiquity of gay pornography, and gay men's evident familiarity with the medium, academics–particularly those in the social sciences–have been curiously mute on this topic.

Inspection of the limited published work that is available reveals that much of it falls into one of two categories: (a) biographic accounts of an individual's experience in the gay pornography industry (e.g., Isherwood, 1996; O'Hara, 1997; Poole, 2000); and (b) analyses of gay pornographic magazines, films, and/or performers, usually–though not exclusively–from a cultural/film studies perspective (Burger, 1995; Celline & Duncan, 1988; Duncan, 1989; Dyer, 1985, 1994; Merk, 1997). Unfortunately, in the midst of "self-reflexivity," "illusionism," "meta-discursive analysis," "assimilability," and the "frenzied will to see," the latter category seldom provides insight into the nature of the relationships among gay male pornography, its consumers, and gay culture in general. (See Harris [1997] for a notable exception.) The abstruseness of much of this work divorces the medium from any pragmatic context, lending it an air of unreality. Consequently, myriad questions about gay male pornography remain unexamined. For example, what is the relationship between exposure to gay male pornography and self-assessments of attractiveness? What are viewers' perceptions of this medium in terms of the messages it disseminates about gay male sexuality, masculinity, femininity, the ageing process, and safer sex? Does gay male pornography serve an important educative function? And how important is this medium to gay male culture?

The purpose of this anthology is to address these kinds of questions using an interdisciplinary and multi-method perspective. Due to the eclectic nature of the contributors' work, no attempt has been made to organize their papers by category or theme. With the exception of Karen Busby's response to Christopher N. Kendall's paper and a question and answer piece edited by Shannon R. Ellis and Bruce W. Whitehead, the authors are presented in alphabetical order.

Bertram J. Cohler's piece, "Memoir and Performance: Social Change and Self Life-Writing Among Men Who Are Gay Pornography Producers and Actors," uses the autobiographies of Wakefield Poole, Scott O'Hara, and Aaron Lawrence to illustrate the ways in which gay identity is responsive to social variables (specifically gay and lesbian liberation and the AIDS epidemic). This article suggests that changes in the content and production of gay male pornography offer insight into the larger society's attitudes toward homosexuality.

The next article, written by Scott J. Duggan and Donald R. McCreary, is entitled, "Body Image, Eating Disorders, and the Drive for Muscularity in Gay and Heterosexual Men: The Influence of Media Images." Although some writers have blamed gay male pornography for the "body fascism" that is (purportedly) rife in gay culture (e.g., Harris, 1997; Signorile, 1997), few social scientists have investigated the veracity of this assumption. Duggan and McCreary's article represents one of the first attempts to *empirically* assess the relationship between exposure to gay male pornography and individuals' perceptions of their body.

Paul Hallam's essay, "If You Look at It Long Enough . . ." is a self-described "tribute to pornography and pornographers." The author suggests that one of pornography's important functions (albeit one that has been overlooked by most academics) is its ability to trigger reminiscences–"a trace of someone met, a one-night stand . . . haircuts and pullovers and wallpapers past." The essay is written in a deceptively confessional tone, and it is up to the reader to determine which elements are autobiographical and which ones "denote the voice of a character speaking."

Written from a radical feminist framework, both Robert Jensen's "Homecoming: The Relevance of Radical Feminism for Gay Men" and Christopher N. Kendall's "Educating Gay Male Youth: Since When Is Pornography a Path Towards Self-Respect?" excoriate gay male pornography. In Jensen's article, the author explores the difficulty he experienced attempting to integrate his radical feminist beliefs with participation in gay male culture–a culture that not only accepts, but also celebrates, objectification of the body. Using examples from commercially available gay male pornography, Kendall argues that this medium is not a source of liberation for gay men but, rather, one of oppression. He suggests that it idealizes hegemonic masculinity, which may, in turn, contribute to self-loathing in gay men.

In "The Queer Sensitive Interveners in the *Little Sisters* Case: A Response to Dr. Kendall," Karen Busby provides an alterative interpretation of the *Little Sisters* litigation. She argues that the case was about more than same-sex pornography; that, ultimately, it concerned the right of a sexual minority to have access to materials–both sexual and nonsexual–that are self-affirmative. Busby reveals that Canada Customs has a history of detaining gay and lesbian books and magazines that are clearly nonpornographic. She maintains that Kendall fails to explore the implications of such detainment in terms of the messages it transmits about the "value" of non-heterosexuals and the potential threat it poses to gay and lesbian culture.

John Mercer's "In the Slammer: The Myth of the Prison in American Gay Pornographic Video," explores the "manifest content and formal characteristics" of this medium. Based on a textual analysis of 110 commercially available gay pornographic videos (released between 1987 and 2002), the author identifies and describes six broad categories that operate in the narratives of gay pornography. Focusing on the prison scenario, Mercer attributes the popularity and longevity of this "motif" to its ability to incorporate a number of these categories.

Todd G. Morrison's " 'He Was Treating Me Like Trash, and I Was Loving It . . .' Perspectives on Gay Male Pornography" uses a focus group methodology to better understand individuals' attitudes toward this medium. The author suggests that discussants see gay male pornography in utilitarian terms; it does not resonate with sociocultural significance but, rather, functions as a masturbatory aid, and little else. Finally, Morrison reports that, although capable of identifying ways in which gay male pornography may "harm" viewers, participants appear to minimise their own vulnerability to the medium.

"Sex Pigs: Why Porn Is Like Sausage, or The Truth Is That–Behind the Scenes–Porn Is Not Very Sexy" by Benjamin Scuglia provides a brief behind the scenes look at the adult video industry. The author suggests that few consumers are motivated to divorce themselves from the fantasies surrounding pornographic production–fantasies that are created and maintained by consumers and producers of this medium.

Clare N. Westcott's article, "Alterity and Construction of National Identity in Three Kristen Bjorn Films," explores celebrated gay pornography director Bjorn's use of alterity or "otherness" as an erotic device. The author contends that Bjorn achieves alterity through exotic locations, national stereotypes, and linguistic signifiers. She also maintains that, despite their patina of exoticism, the three films examined do not really challenge the predominant discourse surrounding gay male sexuality.

Finally, in an epilogue entitled, "Porn Again: Some Final Considerations," Shannon R. Ellis and Bruce W. Whitehead present contributors' responses to seven questions examining various aspects of gay male pornography. Ellis and Whitehead suggest that, when reading this article, the reader should imagine that he/she is eavesdropping on a group of individuals having a conversation about this topic.

REFERENCES

Burger, J.R. (1995). *One-handed histories: The eroto-politics of gay male video pornography*. New York, NY: Harrington Park Press.

Celline, H.B., & Duncan, D.F. (1988). Homosexual pornography: Trends in content and form over a twenty-five year period. *Psychology: A Journal of Human Behaviour, 25*, 37-41.

Chapkis, W. (1997). *Live sex acts: Women performing erotic labour*. New York, NY: Routledge.

Duncan, D.F. (1989). Trends in gay pornographic magazines: 1960 through 1984. *Sociology and Social Research, 73*, 95-98.

Dworkin, A. (1997). *Life and death*. New York, NY: The Free Press.

Dyer, R. (1985). Gay male porn: Coming to terms. *Jump Cut, 30*, 27-29.

Dyer, R. (1994). Idol thoughts: Orgasm and self-reflexivity in gay pornography. *Critical Quarterly, 36*, 49-62.

Harris, R. (1997). *The rise and fall of gay culture*. New York, NY: Hyperion.

Isherwood, C. (1996). *Wonder bread and ecstasy: The life and death of Joey Stefano*. Los Angeles, CA: Alyson Publications.

Merk, M. (1997). More of a man: Gay porn cruises gay politics. In M.B. Duberman (Ed.), *Queer representations: Reading lives, reading cultures* (pp. 105-115). New York, NY: Routledge.

Nagle, J. (1997). *Whores and other feminists*. New York, NY: Routledge.

O'Hara, S. (1997). *Autopornography: A memoir of life in the lust lane*. New York, NY: Harrington Park Press.

Poole, W. (2000). *Dirty Poole: The autobiography of a gay porn pioneer*. Los Angeles, CA: Alyson Publications.

Russell, D.E.H. (1998). *Dangerous relationships: Pornography, misogyny, and rape*. Thousand Oaks, CA: Sage.

Signorile, M. (1997). *Life outside: The Signorile report on gay men*. New York, NY: Harper Collins.

Wilcox, R. (1999). Cross-gender identification in commercial pornographic films. In J. Elias (Ed.), *Porn 101: Eroticism, pornography, and the First Amendment* (pp. 479-491). Amherst, NY: Prometheus Books.

Memoir and Performance: Social Change and Self Life-Writing Among Men Who Are Gay Pornography Producers and Actors

Bertram J. Cohler, PhD

The University of Chicago

SUMMARY. Identity may be understood both as a life-story, either told or written as memoir or autobiography, and also as a practice such as producing or acting in gay pornographic film, but always within the context of social and historical change. Study of the memoirs of gay men

---

Bertram J. Cohler is a faculty member in the Committee on Human Development, the Departments of Psychology and Psychiatry, and The College, The University of Chicago. A graduate psychoanalyst, he also is on the faculty of the Institute for Psychoanalysis (Chicago). Dr. Cohler is co-author of the book *The Course of Gay and Lesbian Lives: Social and Psychoanalytic Perspectives*, published in 2000 by the University of Chicago Press. He is completing a book on social change and the expression of desire in the life-writing of men, born between the 1930s and 1980s, who seek sex with other men. The author thanks Professor Henry L. Minton and two anonymous reviewers for their comments on a previous version of this paper. Correspondence may be addressed: The Committee on Human Development, 5730 South Woodlawn Avenue, Chicago, IL 60637-1603 (E-mail: bert@midway.uchicago.edu).

[Haworth co-indexing entry note]: "Memoir and Performance: Social Change and Self Life-Writing Among Men Who Are Gay Pornography Producers and Actors." Cohler, Bertram J. Co-published simultaneously in *Journal of Homosexuality* (Harrington Park Press, an imprint of The Haworth Press, Inc.) Vol. 47, No. 3/4, 2004, pp. 7-43; and: *Eclectic Views on Gay Male Pornography: Pornucopia* (ed: Todd G. Morrison) Harrington Park Press, an imprint of The Haworth Press, Inc., 2004, pp. 7-43. Single or multiple copies of this article are available for a fee from The Haworth Document Delivery Service [1-800-HAWORTH, 9:00 a.m. - 5:00 p.m. (EST). E-mail address: docdelivery@haworthpress.com].

http://www.haworthpress.com/web/JH
© 2004 by The Haworth Press, Inc. All rights reserved.
Digital Object Identifier: 10.1300/J082v47n03_02

who have been actors and/or producers of gay pornographic films across three generation cohorts provides an opportunity for understanding the interplay of social change and life circumstances in making gay identity. This perspective on identity is illustrated through the study of the memoirs of three men from different cohorts who have produced and acted in gay pornographic films: Wakefield Poole, born in 1936; Scott O'Hara, born in 1961; and Aaron Lawrence, born in 1971. Differences in style and content of both memoir and practice in gay pornographic films reflect changing social expectations regarding men who have sex with men following the emergence of the gay rights movement and the AIDS epidemic. *[Article copies available for a fee from The Haworth Document Delivery Service: 1-800-HAWORTH. E-mail address: <docdelivery@haworthpress.com> Website: <http://www.HaworthPress.com> © 2004 by The Haworth Press, Inc. All rights reserved.]*

KEYWORDS. Gay pornography, pornography, life-story, identity, gay culture, AIDS, gay rights movement, gay liberation, autobiography

. . . there is no such thing as an intuitively obvious and essential self . . . Rather we constantly construct and reconstruct ourselves to meet the needs of situations we encounter and we do so with the guidance of our memories of the past and our hopes and fears for the future. Telling oneself about oneself is like making up a story about who and what we are, what's happened, and why we're doing what we're doing . . . Our very memories fall victim to our self-making stories. (Bruner, 2002, pp. 64-65)

Social science deals with problems of biography, of history, and their intersections within social structures . . . The problems of our time . . . cannot be stated adequately without consistent practice of the view that history is the shank of social study, and recognition of the need to develop further a psychology . . . that is sociologically grounded and historically relevant. (Mills, 1959/2000, p. 143)

Questions of self, identity, and the determinants of personal coherence have assumed a preeminent place in much contemporary study of lives within both the social sciences and the humanities. Reflecting a larger concern with consistency of self at a time of significant social change, scholarly study has turned to narratives of personal experience across contrasting historical periods in an effort to understand the interplay of history, social change and particular life circumstances in making a life-story of oneself. This life-story may be told to another or written by one's self. As Bruner (1987, 2002) has observed, the very activity of telling or writing about oneself at any one point across the course of life remakes one's identity. Within contemporary society, considered together with gender, age, ethnicity, and social position, sexual orientation is among the most central aspects comprising personal identity.

Reflecting historical and social influences, over time and across generations, significant change has occurred in what it means both to experience and to realise same gender sexual desire. There has been some study of this interplay of social and historical change and conceptions of same gender sexual desire and identity reflected in stories of self both as written and as told (Cohler, 2002; Holland, 2000; Parks, 1999; Plummer, 1995; Robinson, 1999; Sadownick, 1997; Stein, 1997). However, there has been little exploration of the relationship between social and historical change and the experience of same gender sexual desire both as written in autobiography or memoir and as realised through performance such as in gay pornographic film and video. Contemporary perspectives regarding the study of identity suggest that it is realised through performance (Holland, Lachicotte, Skinner & Cain, 1998). Telling or writing one's life-story is an ideal type of identity work. Enactment of this identity through performance such as in theatre or film further reflects and also fosters an identity such as that of a gay man (Miller, 1997, 2002). Self life-writing and performance alike make public what are often considered the most private moments of lived experience, including sexual fantasies and experiences, and raise important questions regarding what constitutes a private or secret world.

The present paper focuses on the life-writing and identity performance of three men from different generation-cohorts: Wakefield Poole, born in 1936; Scott O'Hara, born in 1961; and Aaron Lawrence, born in 1971. Each of these individuals has performed his gay identity both through writing memoirs of his life and as star and/or producer of films and videos in which men satisfy their desire through sex with other men.[1] Perhaps the best definition of this genre known as gay pornography has been provided by actor and self life-writer Scott O'Hara (1999), who observes that "[in] the considered opinion of a professional: Porn is anything . . . that is created with the intent of sexually arousing someone" (p. 126).[2] The activity of fostering sexual arousal is itself a performance or text which portrays same gender sexual identity in a unique manner and both reflects a present social construction of sexual desire and also influences the manner in which such desire is subsequently portrayed. Performance may remake understanding of the meaning of sexual identity for performer and viewer alike.

Ricoeur (1977) has observed that within our own culture lives are presumed, like all good stories, to have a linear organisation in which there is a beginning, a middle and an end. Autobiographies and memoirs most often follow this linear format. In retelling a life-story, showing how memoir and performance interact with social and historical change in the remaking of a gay identity from childhood through the adult years, I have tried, where possible, to follow the life-writer's own organisation of his life. However, every retelling of a life-story is an interpretation. In order to show the interplay of memoir and performance in gay pornography in a social context, I have necessarily selected some details of each life-writer's recounted story and omitted others. My goal is to provide an understanding of the manner in which aspects of the life-writer's story, together with social and historical changes across the years from childhood through adulthood, might account for the particular life-writer's contributions to the genre of gay pornographic film.

This task has been less difficult in working with the life-stories of Wakefield Poole and Aaron Lawrence than that of Scott O'Hara. O'Hara's often provocative life-story and posthumous collection of essays attempt to underscore the necessity of eliminating the shame so often attached to the experience of sex between men in contemporary society. I have presented O'Hara's life story not always as he presented it in his memoir but rather reorganised in a linear sequence in order to show how the particular experiences of his life and times framed his understanding of his participation in gay pornographic films.

LIFE-WRITING AND SOCIAL CHANGE

Writing about one's own experiences, just like telling others one's life-story, is a means for making sense of a life. While life-stories told to another are necessarily framed in terms of a relationship between teller and listener, self life-writing represents a more extended reflexive activity in which the writer imagines a relationship with a presumed reader who interprets this life-story within the time and place of the reading.[3] There is inevitable tension between the intentions of the writer in telling a life story and those of the reader who makes meaning of the life-story in terms of both own lived experience and social and historical change subsequent to the original account. A complete reading of a life-story must consider both the author's intent in writing the life-story and the reader's necessarily subjective or reflexive reading of this life-story (Iser, 1978; Tierney, 2000).

Further, the life-story itself is most often written backwards from a later point in the course of life recalling a presently remembered past, experienced present and anticipated future. In the present instance, gay pornography director and 1930s generation life-writer Wakefield Poole has written an account of his life from childhood to mid-adulthood from the perspective of a man now in his sixties who has recovered from a long history of drug addiction. The writing project also may be influenced by other life-stories in the genre. For example, 1970s generation gay self-life writer and actor-producer Aaron Lawrence was influenced in his 1999 account by the work of 1960s generation gay writer and gay pornography actor Scott O'Hara who, in turn, was influenced by the life-story of gay author and poet Samuel Delany (1988), who came of age in the turbulent 1960s.

Plummer (1995) has portrayed a "sociology of stories," which are constructed in the context of present understandings regarding what constitutes past, present, and future. Consistent with Mills's (1959/2000) observation in his classic work, *The Sociological Imagination*, Plummer (1995) has suggested that there is a continuing negotiation between life-story and social change. Life-stories both reflect and contribute to social change. For example, Andrew Tobias's (1973/1993) story of his struggle to realise his gay desire, which was first published in 1973 shortly after his graduation from Harvard College, became a "coming out" guide for other men struggling with their own same gender desire. There are significant differences in both the structure and the content of life-stories of men living discreet lives with same gender desire across the first half of the twentieth century (Robinson, 1999), and those of men telling the life-story and coming of age following the Second World War (Sadownick, 1997).

Culture and history both contribute to the structure of these narratives. Following Propp's (1928/1968) account of folktales, Plummer (1995) has suggested that life-stories reflect one or more of the following five plot lines: focusing on a journey, enduring suffering, engaging in a context, seeking transcendence of self, and realising a new identity. These elements of plot are woven in a master or dominant narrative of realising a particular identity using present historical experience. For example, among many gay men, and clearly among the three life-writers considered here, the life-story is one of being *essentially* gay, of knowing their same gender desire from early childhood.

Frontain (2000) has suggested that the genre of gay self life-writing has been shaped by the historical experience of social opprobrium toward gay relationships which effectively forced gay men to have furtive, brief sexual contacts. Gay men remember through coded narratives, which are often portrayed as a kind of confession (Jolly, 2001). Gay self life-writing, including recollections of prior sexual experiences, provides a way of remembering such distorted memories. Films depicting gay sexual activity also provide a means for retrieving the experience of prior sexual encounters that of necessity were suppressed by society. Cinematic representations of gay life may trigger memories of one's own prior sexual encounters albeit recollected as influenced by subsequent personal and shared experiences. An enhanced sense of empowerment is realised from being able to tell the subversive life story of being gay or lesbian (Frontain, 2000; Jolly, 2001).

The life-story provides a unique portrayal of social and historical circumstances at the time the story is written. The very manner in which sexuality is discussed reflects the intersection between social context and the circumstances of a particular life as presently recounted (Barkin, 1976; Mills, 1959/2000). Tobias's (1973/1993, 1998) life-story provides an important account regarding the emergence of a socially visible gay community. Paul Monette (1988, 1994) wrote a powerful account describing the onset of the AIDS epidemic, the response of the gay community to the disease, early efforts at finding a cure, the course of his partner's illness and death, together with his own declining health following his diagnosis as HIVpositive.

Frontain (2000) has noted a shift in gay self-life writing over the past three decades since the emergence of the gay rights movement. Rather than themes of shame and apology, the genre has been marked by themes of coming out, and of struggle to realise an identity as gay or queer. Consistent with Plummer's (1995) discussion of the dominant narrative inherent in stories of becoming gay, realisation of a positive identity as gay represents redemption of oneself following an epiphany (McAdams & Bowman, 2001). The creation of the Internet has made an enormous difference in both reading and writing. For many gay and lesbian adolescents growing up in communities less tolerant of minority sexualities, chat rooms and Web sites for young gay people have helped to diminish their sense of isolation and difference. As well, they have contributed to increased determination to gain acceptance from family and community for their gay identity (www.oasismag.com).

GENERATION AND SOCIAL CHANGE: WRITING AND PERFORMING GAY IDENTITY

Considering differences in political ideologies among adjacent age groups, the social theorist Karl Mannheim (1928/1993) proposed that some number of contiguous birth years could be considered a generation, sharing in common experiences different from those of preceding or following generations. Elder (1974/1998, 1995, 2002) has extended Mannheim's (1928/1993) contribution, noting that successive generation-cohorts travel through the course of life together and experience timing of role transitions in ways different from earlier or later generations. However, Settersten (1999, 2003) has cautioned that there may be considerable variation within a cohort regarding aspects of lived experience, including circumstances fostering emergence of minority sexual identity. For example, adolescents growing up in diverse metropolitan communities such as New York City, where there are opportunities for diverse lifestyles, may find it easier than those residing in less "cosmopolitan" regions to establish a gay or lesbian identity.

Findings reported by Conway and Pleydell-Pearce (2000) and Schuman and associates (1989, 1997) suggest further that events taking place during young adulthood may have particular significance for the manner in which each generation-cohort makes sense of lived experience. These investigators report a "reminiscence bump" in which particular social and historical changes taking place in young adulthood largely shape the manner in which both anticipated and eruptive life-changes are experienced by members of a particular generation-cohort. For example, the generation of young adults participating in the creation of the gay rights movement following the Stonewall Inn riots of June 1969 experienced subsequent historical events and social change across succeeding decades in terms of the need to contest heteronormative society. A later generation of sexual minority young adults growing up in the late 1990s, following development of the Internet and increased social acceptance of a gay lifeway (Hostetler & Herdt, 1998), view their gay sexuality as "virtually normal" (Sullivan, 1995), and as only one aspect of their identity.

While earlier psychological discussion of identity focused primarily upon intra-individual developmental determinants (Erikson, 1968), contemporary social perspectives have emphasised the extent to which identity is realised through performance rather than constituted as an essential attribute realised through psychosocial maturation (Holland et al., 1998; Mishler, 1999). Precisely because a gay identity is a contested one, and was perceived as subversive across much of the post-war period (Loughery, 1998; Sadownick, 1997), gay self life-writing has assumed particular prominence as a genre marked by suffering and struggle to achieve acceptance. From this perspective, both gay self life-writing and enactment of a presently understood life as performance on stage or in film provide important tools for studying the ways in which social change contributes to understandings of what it means to have a gay identity and to satisfy gay sexual desire.

The Internet has provided a similar opportunity for gay men to perform their identity through writing their life story. Websites such as <oasismag.com> have offered a means for telling the story of overcoming such obstacles as opprobrium from family and peers, transcending hostility, and even changing the attitudes of others through forthright acknowledgement of sexual identity. Pornography has provided the opportunity for constructing a new sexual story and reflects social change in a manner similar to writing (O'Hara, 1997; Plummer, 1995). Both Burger (1995) and Harris (1997) have suggested that gay sexual films and videos across the past three decades provide an important historical and social narrative regarding changes in the manner in which gay men have understood their own sexual identity.

Remaking concepts of sexual identity over time has been fostered both by writing and reading the life story of men across generation-cohorts self identifying as gay, and also by watching gay pornography. Over time, video pornography has shown marked changes in plot and characters, and even in the course of the sexual encounter itself; changes which reflect those occurring in the larger social arena. For example, "fisting," which was a form of deliberately outrageous and counter-hegemonic sexual expression appearing in the 1980s, has largely disappeared from gay pornographic film. The advent of AIDS was reflected in gay pornography by increased emphasis on safer sex. Gay videos provide an important means for learning how to be gay and sexual.[4]

These videos have structured the expected sexual encounter for the gay community. The usual sequence is two or more men kiss, undress, engage in fellatio (sometimes followed by anilingus), and then perform anal intercourse. The latter activity typically ends with the "top" withdrawing, shooting a copious load[5] on the "bottom's" face or chest, and then watching while the "bottom" masturbates to orgasm.

Burger (1995) has observed that gay pornographic films sometimes make a political statement. Setting, choice of actor, the sexual activity that is portrayed, and even the actor's tattoos may reflect the producer's own commitment to a variety of issues such as safer sex and the significance of sadomasochistic activity as part of homoerotic life. Burger (1995) notes that the act of translating a supposedly personal and intimate activity into one watched by an audience breaks down the traditional view that same gender sexual desire need necessarily be hidden. This message is reinforced through the use of public spaces such as offices or locker rooms as sites for sexual activities.

The genre of sexually explicit gay film and video emerged in the wake of the gay rights movement following the Stonewall Inn riots of late June 1969 (Burger, 1995; Turan & Zito, 1974). Waugh (1996) has reviewed the genre of male pornography in Europe and the United States from the late nineteenth century to Stonewall. (Waugh reports that as recently as the post-war era, the Kinsey Institute recruited men who were interested in having sex with other men recorded on film. These amateur films were most often explicitly erotic.) Across the post-war period, prior to the advent of the gay rights revolution, gay male pornography was most often disguised as highly stylised physique studies, although Waugh (1996) has found books and films which did show men in sexually explicit scenes with other men. Burger (1995) has comprehensively reviewed the subsequent history of this genre while Waugh (1995) has contrasted setting and action in gay pornographic films with the genre of straight male pornography. Films made earlier than the 1970s were photographed in black and white, using shadows to comply with the requirements of censorship (Waugh, 1996). In the post Stonewall era, and with the advent of video, colour was used and actors were featured in real-life settings such as bedrooms. As Harris (1997) has observed:

> . . . the entire history of gay self-acceptance since Stonewall can be discerned in the changes that have occurred in the lighting of gay films, from the spectral settings of the 1970s to the brilliant, clinical lighting of present-day films which take place in spaces free of guilt, of the erotics of sin. (p. 118)

Prior to the advent of video, gay pornographic films were shown in theatres frequented by gay men seeking furtive sexual encounters (Harris, 1997). Delany (1999) has provided a detailed portrayal of these theatres in New York's Times Square area prior to its later renovation, and argues that these furtive encounters provided a unique sense of community. Both Harris (1997) and Delany (1999) adopt a nostalgic position regarding the loss of the gay pornographic theatre as an element of community, and the creation of videocassette/DVD technology which fosters a kind of solitary sexual release in the "privacy" of one's home.

PORTRAYING GAY IDENTITY AND DESIRE OVER TIME: LIFE-WRITING AND PERFORMANCE ACROSS THREE GENERATIONS

Self life-writing and performance either on stage or in video represent means for making a sexual identity through telling and dramatising the life-story. For example, performance artist Tim Miller has received national recognition for his one-person shows portraying his own struggles as a gay man (Miller, 2002). Much of the material Miller uses in his performances is adapted from his memoir *Shirts and Skins* (1997). His most recent work (Miller, 2002) reverses this effort to portray the life story through performance; in this work, performance has become the basis for his continuing account of his life.

Miller's performances inevitably lead to undressing and appearing naked on stage. Appearing naked reflects both Miller's view of the manner in which gay men experience their own sexuality and also shows the changes that have occurred in gay sexual desire over the past three decades. Gay pornography actor and life-writer Scott O'Hara (1999) has observed that Miller's performance art is clearly not pornography. Reflecting social change across the past three decades, Miller's performance art shows that it is possible to realise gay self-expression in nonpornographic formats.

In addition to the life-writing and performance art of gay activist Tim Miller, there are at least three instances in which life-writing has accompanied performance and/or production of sexually explicit films. These are: (1) Wakefield Poole, born in 1936, and acknowledged as the first producer of gay pornography in the era accompanying the emergence of the gay rights movement; (2) gay pornography actor Scott O'Hara, born in 1961 and later the creator of *Steam*, a journal of gay opinion and listing of gay sexual spaces across the nation; and (3) Aaron Lawrence, born in 1971, and alternately a gay escort, actor, and, more recently, director and producer of his own sexually explicit "amateur" videos.

Poole and O'Hara wrote their story following careers in the pornography industry while Lawrence has written his life-story near the beginning of his career and just as he is making a transition from escort to actor and producer of his own video catalogue. These three men represent three different generation-cohorts. Poole came to adulthood in the post-war era when gay life was largely underground and very much a subversive activity. With a distinguished career as dancer, choreographer, and director in the "legitimate" theatre, Poole makes it clear that public acknowledgement of his sexual identity as gay would have had serious consequences for his future career in Broadway shows. O'Hara grew up in the turbulent years of the late 1960s and came to adulthood just on the cusp of the AIDS epidemic, while Lawrence came of age in the post-AIDS epoch when a gay identity had become "virtually normal" (Sullivan, 1995).

All three men were aware of their gay sexual desire from childhood on and reported first sexual experiences, generally with older men, during mid-adolescence. Growing up at a time of post-war conservatism when the gay lifeway (Hostetler & Herdt, 1998) was highly stigmatised (Goffman, 1963), Poole was understandably more conflicted about his gay sexuality than the other two who grew up later in the post-war era. All three men were literate and well educated (i.e., Poole was a college graduate and Lawrence received an MA degree in higher education administration).

Wakefield Poole and the Gay Journey Through Post-War America

> I've gone beyond shame, but I think when people make love, they are, or should be more vulnerable and open than at any other time. I like to capture that moment of vulnerability in all its eroticism and beauty. (Poole, 2000, pp. 168-169)

For the generation of men born in the mid- to late 1930s, attaining adulthood meant both realisation of unprecedented prosperity in post-war America, and also enhanced conformity. For men aware of their own homoerotic desire, this expectation for a conventional life often meant either estrangement from their own desire or the realisation of that desire through furtive excursions to a hidden gay bar (Brown, 2001; Read, 1973/1980) or exploration of the rest rooms in public parks (Delph, 1978; Humphreys, 1970). Popular and professional commentary alike stressed the importance of a "normal" family life in the wake of the social dislocation which had been characteristic of the war years of the prior decade (Duberman, 1986). This was the era of Leonard Bernstein's *Wonderful Town* in which conventional small-town life was contrasted with the vibrant, bohemian life of the metropolis (D'Emilio, 1998). New York was a magnet for men aware of their same gender desire, as

Wakefield Poole discovered when he was fifteen and was invited there in order to attend an advanced dance class.

Poole is best known for his films *Bijou* and *Boys in the Sand*, which opened in late December 1971, just on the cusp of the gay rights movement. Indeed, *Boys in the Sand*, a formal, carefully posed portrayal of gay desire on Fire Island, New York's legendary holiday playground for gay men, was the first gay sexual film to be shown in a mainstream movie theatre. However, for several decades prior to this low-budget film, Poole was a major figure in the American musical theatre, directing and choreographing numerous Broadway shows.

Poole's life-story, *Dirty Poole: The Autobiography of a Gay Porn Pioneer*, is a classic account of growing up with same gender desire in the post-war American south (Sears, 1997). Poole reports awareness of same gender desire from the age of eight when he was entranced watching an older neighbourhood boy masturbate to orgasm. This desire was intertwined with his love of the theatre with its burlesque, colour, and magic, which he had already experienced by taking part in childhood dance classes. As he observes, from that time on, dancing and sex would occupy most of his time.

Poole's first sexual experience occurred as a young adolescent while visiting his grandparents in a Florida port city. He reports meeting a sailor at a local movie theatre one afternoon and being invited to the sailor's hotel room. He found the sex enjoyable and likened the sailor to a big brother; one who taught him the wonders of gay sexual expression. Following this experience, Poole became a frequent visitor to local men's rooms where he was almost always the one to initiate sexual activity. However, by the early 1950s, public tolerance of "tearooms" decreased, with arrest and prosecution becoming more common. For example, Poole recalls one occasion where police raided a dinner party attended by gay men, and asserts that only his youth kept him from being arrested.

Following the dinner party police raid, Poole realised that he had to leave the conservative South. Just like other young men of his era (Cohler, 2002), Poole was drawn to New York City. While in New York, Poole was simultaneously introduced to Broadway and to sexual experiences with leading men of the Broadway stage. However, frightened by a lover's suicide attempt, Poole returned to the South where, over the next year, he taught dancing. With his talent now well recognised, Poole was invited to join distinguished ballet companies with whom he toured the world.

During this time, he befriended many top-ranking dancers and choreographers; soon, he was invited to perform and direct and became a fixture on the Broadway stage. Poole observes that, during this period, his sex life was almost nonexistent. Occasional affairs with men were less important than maintaining his career, which demanded most, if not all, of his energy. He also observes that he was afraid both of intimacy and of extended relationships, and harboured concerns that these affairs might become public knowledge. One affair, in particular, became public, and Poole found himself embarrassed by his apparently growing reputation as a homosexual.

Left unexplained in Poole's (2000) account is the question of why this man, who had so thoroughly enjoyed sexual encounters during adolescence, became so ashamed and even rejecting of homosexuality during his early adult years. In part, the ethos at the close of the conservative fifties made it difficult for gay men to be explicit regarding their sexuality. However, Poole's (2000) account also suggests feelings of shame regarding his gay desire. Similar to many men struggling with issues of gay sexual identity in the mid-1950s (e.g., Duberman, 1991), Poole believed his gay desire to be evidence of psychological malady. Consequently, he sought psychotherapy, where he was urged by his therapist to become heterosexual. He married a female dancer he had worked with in several musicals and continued his ascent in the theatre. Not surprisingly, the marriage was short lived; at first passionate, the couple gradually drifted apart, prompted by the demands of work and by opportunities in different parts of the country.

A period during which little work was available led to a loss of self-esteem and fear of being unwanted; Poole recognised that his confidence had been built on being desired by other men, and now that admiration had disappeared. Feeling lonely and desperate, Poole sought out anonymous sex at the bathhouses that flourished in the post-war period until the emergence of the AIDS epidemic in the early 1980s. He also turned to drugs, which had become readily available with the advent of the social revolution of the late 1960s. Poole met his lover Peter, also southern, and also passionately involved in his theatre career, at one of these legendary bathhouses. Poole was determined to make this relationship successful, and the couple worked hard at communicating their desires, expectations, and regrets. Soon, they moved in together and developed friendships with several other gay couples with whom they enjoyed sensory illusions while they tripped on acid.

Recognising Poole's fascination with colour and light, Peter gave him a 16-millimeter camera as a gift. Poole's camera accompanied him everywhere, from excursions to gallery openings. One night, after rehearsal for a musical, Poole, Peter, and a group of their friends decided, on a whim, to visit a grungy movie theatre showing the "muscle man" gay pornography acceptable to the censors of that era. Apparently, the movie was boring; Peter even fell asleep. Afterwards, they all asked the same question, "Why can't someone make a good porno film that's not degrading?" (Poole, 2000, p. 148). Since he had become fairly proficient with the camera Peter had given him, Poole suggested that he try making a good gay pornographic film. He had often visited friends with a Fire Island home, and was struck by the sexual tension that pervaded this summer resort. It was clear that Fire Island would be an ideal location for the film. Peter and Poole invited a man named Dino, who worked at a local shop, to participate. He agreed, and the next day, a tense and troubled Poole filmed his partner having anal sex with another man.

The camera's viewfinder provided Poole with a new way of viewing gay sex. He became entranced as Peter and his fellow actor explored each other's bodies in their first sexual encounter. Poole reports that he was never tempted to enter the action. He was entranced by his discovery of watching the world through the camera. He observes, "I've never to this day been aroused while filming. When I look through the camera lens, my ego fades and I almost disappear–so much so that I never directed the actors while shooting" (Poole, 2000, p. 182).

Poole's brief film detailing Peter and Dino's sexual encounter captivated his friends and business manager. Poole was so encouraged by their enthusiastic response, he decided to expand the film to include two other scenes. One of his good friends not only volunteered to do a segment, but also brought along his cute blond friend, charismatic Cal Culver, who would later be known in the world of gay pornography as Casey Donovan. Peter volunteered to do a scene with Cal, who turned out to be a natural and loved "performing" sex on film. With a magnetic personality, Cal was able to recruit others to work on the film with him, including a gay construction worker he had admired. Producing on a low budget and financing with his credit card, Poole put together the classic film *Boys in the Sand*. However, he reports discovering that it was not all fun on the other side of the camera. On at least one occasion, an actor was unable to have an orgasm and Poole had to stand in for him. Although his lover Peter was his partner for this scene, he reports that it took him more than an hour to orgasm. His anxiety may be attributed to the fact that being in front of the camera requires displaying one's self and eliminating the fear and insecurities associated with being gay.

Poole edited the film in his spare time with the help of Peter and another friend, and the final version was soon ready for viewing. Poole suggested taking out ads in the *New York Times*, and his business manager suggested renting an art film theatre in midtown Manhattan. After some hesitation, the *Times* accepted the ad. When the film opened, crowds lined up to see this first film in a new genre. *Boys in the Sand* was the first so-called male pornographic film to be reviewed in the mainstream press (e.g., *Variety* and *After Dark*), and soon reviews and word of mouth led to packed showings. The success of this film inspired Poole to try a second one, *Bijou*, which would follow in the spirit of the first film and affirm the pride the gay community was attempting to establish regarding its sexuality. Much of this movie, including a famous orgy scene featuring Peter and their friends, was shot in their apartment. This second film also opened to rave reviews by the gay and mainstream press.

Making these films did wonders for Poole's struggle with accepting his desire to have sex with other men. Embracing the spirit of the time, as the gay rights movement intensified (Clendinen & Nagourney, 1999), Poole was able to accept his own gay desire, disclose his gay sexuality to his father, and begin to enjoy his new found artistic and commercial success. Wakefield Poole had become "porno chic," as the sexual revolution of the 1970s gained momentum (Burger, 1995). Poole and Peter became part of the fast moving "out of the closet" gay community of New York in the 1970s. Major figures in the world of literature and the arts flocked to see his films, and Poole reports that this was one of the happiest times in his life. With their financial success, he and Peter began collecting pre-Columbian and African art, and the work of their friend, Andy Warhol. However, many of Poole's straight friends in the theatre stopped speaking to him, and soon Broadway job offers vanished. Poole was viewed as "Dirty Poole," although he says he did not feel that way.

In 1974, largely at Peter's urging, the couple moved to San Francisco where, as it turned out, Peter had developed an attachment to another man. The move was part of a plot to be in the same city as his lover. This was a time, following the emergence of gay rights, when San Francisco was celebrating the "gay experience." With the breakup of his relationship with Peter, Poole felt very much alone in a strange city. Even trips to the gay baths did little to brighten his spirits. To make matters worse, cheap copies of his films began to circulate among small, sleazy theatres with mob connections. When he tried to prevent such showings, there were vague threats on his life.

Lonely, losing self-confidence, and unsure about his future, Poole began using cocaine. At first, he believed that the drug would fuel his creative vision, but, ultimately, it destroyed him. Poole did make one film during this time, based on the sexual fantasies of a group of gay San Francisco men, which opened to rave reviews from the gay and mainstream press. He also created a multimedia experience of solo masturbation to run together with his film, which proved immensely popular and extended the film's run.

The opening of this film, *Take One*, coincided with Anita Bryant's homophobic campaign and the emergence of hate speech against the gay community. Poole wanted to help in the campaign to defeat Bryant's message but was shunned because of his connection with pornography. Some members of the gay community, expressing internalised anti-gay prejudice and fear of sexuality, believed that Poole's work portrayed the most sordid aspects of the gay lifeway (Hostetler & Herdt, 1998). Attempting to do something about his despair, which had most likely been enhanced by the death of his mother, Poole drifted back and forth over the next few years between San Francisco and New York. He returned to New York in the late 1970s and attempted to reenter the legitimate theatre world. At this time, arranging for a rerun of his earlier films in New York, the word 'gay' replaced 'all-male' for the first time on the movie theatre marquee. However, the days of gay "porno chic" were over. Revenue from his films plummeted and the home video revolution meant the end of the gay movie theatre.

Travelling back to San Francisco, Poole arrived just before the assassination of his friend Harvey Milk, which led Poole into a period of paranoid seclusion in which he was totally preoccupied with getting and using drugs. He views this period of his life in the late 1970s as the time when he hit bottom. It was at this time that the first of his friends succumbed to what soon would be called AIDS. Totally preoccupied with drugs, Poole had little energy or desire for sex, which he notes may explain how he escaped HIV infection. He muses, "Maybe I'm still alive because I was a drug addict at the right time. I took so many drugs that I got to the point where I didn't think about sex. I didn't care about it anymore and when I finally cleaned myself up, I was too fucking scared . . . but there is life after sex, and hope is better than despair" (Poole, 2000, p. 286).

Earlier in his career, Poole's primary concern was to make films reflecting his own vision of gay desire. Feeling personally depleted and struggling with his expensive drug habit, Poole began making exploitation films such as *Boys in the Sand II*, which he knew possessed little artistic merit. Once again, the prints to the film were copied and released as *Men in the Sand II*. Poole, afraid of threats on his life from criminal groups involved in the pornography industry, decided not to fight the theft of these prints. He also witnessed the first deaths from AIDS of gay actors in his and other films, including his star and friend Casey Donovan, and 1960s generation actor and director Scott O'Hara. Unaware of the means for transmission of the epidemic, and involved in unprotected sex, many of these actors succumbed in the first years following the 1981 outbreak of the AIDS epidemic. As Poole observes, "One by one, news of infection and death invaded my life . . . it seemed as though death was using my address book to make his house calls. Over the next few years, most of the people I loved . . . would leave this world" (Poole, 2000, p. 283).

Among those Poole lost were his former partner Peter, who took his own life lest he become a burden to others during his last illness, and his partner Paul, who died from the consequences of heavy drug use. Significant in the account of Paul's final illness was the hospital's decision to accede to Poole's request that he be regarded as next of kin and be with Paul at his death. At the age of 50, suffering from many losses, Poole finally "kicked" his drug habit, went to culinary school and became a chef in a well-known New York restaurant. Poole's account of his life breaks off as he enters midlife, no longer a drug addict and no longer involved in gay pornographic films, but optimistic about his future.

SCOTT O'HARA: PORNOGRAPHY AND THE PURSUIT OF PLEASURE

People are born with the inherent desire for porn. This is a basic element of my philosophy: the idea that watching other people have sex, watching people enjoy themselves, is an essential human pleasure. Translating that to a video screen, or the four-colour page, or to a written or spoken fantasy does nothing to change the basic characteristic of porn . . . the vicarious joy of being a participant in an act that is giving the participants pleasure. (O'Hara, 1997, p. 83)

My goal is quite simple: To make people think about sex. Not just look for it, though I've no objection to that, but think about it. Because it's a subject that deserves thought, and yet we're all brought up to believe that it just "comes naturally," and doesn't need any thought. (O'Hara, 1999, p. 181)

While Wakefield Poole was able to rescue himself from his plunge into addiction, it was at the cost of his prominence in gay films and the loss of virtually everyone important to him. His life-story ends in midstream. Scott O'Hara, born in 1961, more than two decades after Poole, was able to take advantage of the genre in which Poole was a pioneer, and himself became an icon as an actor in the world of gay pornographic film. Although diminutive in stature, O'Hara had an erection that was legendary in size and he gained fame in the gay pornography world for his ability to perform auto-fellatio. O'Hara believed that humans possess an inborn propensity to voyeurism, which is reflected in watching pornography. Complaining that many gay pornographic films were laboured and grim portrayals of men having sex with other men, he portrayed himself clearly enjoying his filmed encounters. He reported that his pleasure was enhanced both by focusing on the act of pleasing another man, even in anonymous sexual encounters such as in a bathhouse, and also by the knowledge that he could enhance the pleasure of those viewing his films by performing sexually.

Tragically, one of O'Hara's many roles may have led him to become HIV positive (although he also attributed his infection to his experiences in San Francisco during the summer of 1981, just at the cusp of the epidemic, when he spent virtually the entire summer in a continual sexual tryst). Scott O'Hara was born just at the end of the conservative epoch in American society. A member of the second post-war cohort, he was only ten at the time of the Stonewall Inn riots and the birth of gay liberation, and was just reaching adulthood as the AIDS epidemic struck. O'Hara died at the age of 36 in 1998 after struggling with the ravages of AIDS for more than a decade. Throughout his illness, O'Hara maintained a positive perspective on his life, a sense of humour, and a determined effort to move gay sexuality from shame, which he presumed was enhanced by the AIDS epidemic, into pleasure. Steven Zeeland, editor of his posthumous collection of essays, reports receiving a postcard shortly after O'Hara's death featuring O'Hara fellating himself. The card read simply: "Scott 'Spunk' O'Hara wishes to announce his final relocation. If you ever find yourself in the vicinity, do drop in for a visit" (O'Hara, 1999, p. xiii).

This same sense of humour is pervasive in O'Hara's life-story, which is narrated in his memoir, *Autopornography: A Memoir of Life in the Lust Lane* (1997), and a book of posthumous essays, *Rarely Pure and*

Never Simple (1999). In the same manner, O'Hara's account highlights not only his sexual appetite but also his enjoyment of even the most controversial aspects of gay sexuality, including leather and "water sports" (i.e., having his partner urinate on him). It is not always clear that he enjoyed these activities; it is evident, however, that he realised some satisfaction from being "shocking" to his viewers. O'Hara (1997) writes, "I've tried to let people know that it's okay to laugh during sex. Orgasm is really not the serious business that some people would like to make it" (pp. ix-x). Indeed, he states that his goal in writing his memoir was to "open up all my closets, let you in on all the dark corners of my life, and give you a better picture of what goes into the making of a porn star" (p. x). He also observes that

> Trying to make sense of a life that seems, from all perspectives, perfectly improbable . . . is simple. You just live. It's the interpretation of it, the making sense of it, the conscious effort to force yourself to tell the truth, that's complicated. (O'Hara, 1999, p. 149)

O'Hara's (1997) memoir, *Autopornography*, includes two initial chapters narrating, in some detail, his early adolescent sexual fantasies and later sexual experiences; two chapters on his early experiences with his family, preceded by a warning to the reader that the "good parts" begin two chapters later, and then a description of his adult years, beginning with a chapter entitled "The good parts."[6] The sexually explicit portrayal of his life as an out, proud, and later HIV positive gay man follows from his goal of making people think about sex, particularly gay sex, as something which ought to come naturally but which society has made the source of opprobrium.

O'Hara's approach to his homoerotic desire is in sharp contrast with that of Wakefield Poole who expressed marked shame and, later, determined abstinence from his gay sexual desire, which he viewed as abnormal. O'Hara (1997) observes, "The development of my libido is a subject to which I devote a lot of time and energy . . . I find it fascinating to watch the way in which my turn-ons have changed over the years" (pp. 131-132). In part, the differences between Poole and O'Hara reflect wider-scale change in American society including a new discourse regarding gay sexuality that emerged during the 1970s and 1980s. Fisting, which played an important role in O'Hara's sexual experiences, was itself a gay sexual activity that gained prominence in the 1980s. The gay rights movement had been accompanied by increasing sexual experimentation and ever more novel use of the body for the purposes of making a counter-hegemonic statement of sexuality and sexual pleasure. O'Hara (1997) describes the extraordinary pleasure of feeling a fist up his butt, or, as he says:

> ... sticking my fist up someone's butt and then putting my dick inside also, and jacking off inside of him. Oh, it's awkward, I admit; mostly, it's a psychological thrill. But then what part of sex isn't? Fisting itself is mostly psychological overload. (p. 140)

O'Hara's own response to the social change that accompanied the gay rights movement and which fostered experimentation with new forms of sexual pleasure enacted on film were important in fostering a new discourse stressing the importance of pleasure in gay sexuality. As he observed, "with a couple of notable exceptions, I had fun making porn" (1999, p. 157). He was critical of the current crop of actors in pornographic videos who appear to be bored and unable to feel pleasure from their body or from engaging in sex with their partner in the scene. O'Hara believed these actors were sometimes less interested in what they were doing and more interested in the money they could earn from their performance.

The youngest of eight children, O'Hara had a brother twelve years older than he, three older sisters, the eldest of whom was lesbian, and twin brothers born on his own birthday but four years older. He was strongly attracted to the twins as they became adolescent and fantasised about them having sex together. His sister Nancy, eight years his senior, was his closest friend in the family and had a collection of books on dating, love, and sex, which he found very informative. For a time, Nancy had a boyfriend, Steve, to whom the ten-year-old O'Hara was wildly attracted. Steve wrestled with him and hugged and kissed him, giving him the affection O'Hara says was missing in his family.

O'Hara grew up reading books and was an honour student, much admired by his teachers for his keen intellect. He remembers that at the age of ten, he was already aware of his attraction to other boys at school and in boy scouts and was on the prowl for any book or magazine that explored sex. Although O'Hara's eccentric parents shielded him from popular culture, he reports having blissful masturbation fantasies during the fourth grade, courtesy of watching Batman and Robin struggle in restraints on a friend's television set. He acknowledged the rumour spread by a classmate with whom he had fooled around that he was gay and, subsequently, was ostracised by his friends. Even in his narration of his first sexual experience, O'Hara emphasises both how natural it was for him to be highly erotic and also how he had little shame regarding his same gender sexual desire. By sixth grade, this sex-starved preadolescent boy was already able to masturbate to ejaculation, particularly when reading any literature that was even faintly erotic or remembering his school locker room and the naked boys running around in and out of the showers. He narrates acquaintance with a number of mentors, teachers, and relatives who implicitly seemed to understand his same gender desire.

At the age of fourteen, O'Hara began to rebel against his puritanical family and its morality. His oldest sister, Claudia, was thirteen years his senior and lived in Chicago with Stephanie, her lesbian lover. At age fifteen, while visiting Claudia and Stephanie, O'Hara had his first sexual experience. He reports seducing one of Claudia's gay friends, a man in his late twenties who had stopped by for a visit. The experience was everything that young O'Hara had imagined, and was followed by several other adolescent sexual experiences while visiting Claudia in Chicago. Recalling his adolescent search for sex with other men, O'Hara reports being sceptical of the argument that older men intimidate adolescent boys into gay sex. Claudia and Stephanie introduced O'Hara to Chicago's gay culture: provided with suitable sexy attire, and introduced by leather-dyke Stephanie to the Chicago leather scene, O'Hara ventured into a month of wild sexual abandon. These early sexual experiences reinforced his belief that sex was the most important thing in the universe.

Shortly after this visit, Claudia committed suicide. O'Hara then recollects journeying back and forth across the country on a motorcycle before returning to Chicago and sharing an apartment with Stephanie, who by now had taken male lovers. Even though he enjoyed the gay leather scene, O'Hara asked Stephanie to marry him, a decision he does not explain but which is consistent with his passionate and somewhat impulsive personality. It seemingly just happened to occur to him one day, and Stephanie responded with enthusiasm. O'Hara (1997) observes, "Imagine: me, a thoroughly out and proud gay male, well-documented on video having sex with lots of other men . . . Ironic, ain't it?" (p. 48). The couple lived together for a time. However, O'Hara's "head over heels" brief love affair with one man led Stephanie to fits of jealous rage and then to divorce.

It is at this point in the text that O'Hara (1997) reveals he is HIV positive and may already have been so in 1981 at the time of his travel to Hawaii. Living in San Francisco, he had enjoyed threesomes with couples where he could see romance even as he shunned relationships and the burden of having a lover. Earlier in adulthood, O'Hara wondered how men could find the same person a source of pleasure for years on end and viewed his own efforts at creating satisfying relationships as disastrous. He doubted that it was possible to be faithful and to remain romantic with one man over a period of many years. He also doubted that being with a lover could cure loneliness and observed that he had never been so lonely as he was whilst in a relationship that had soured. Rather, he desired a life punctuated by periods of passionate sex with a variety of partners and professed to enjoy the pleasures of solitude.

O'Hara recounted his experiences during young adulthood with a number of sometime lovers. He met Marc, three years his senior, while fleeing from a dismal first year attempt at college on a cross-country motorcycle ride. The couple settled in San Francisco, but O'Hara soon found the sex boring and became irritated that Marc depended upon him for financial support. His second relationship was with Jay, only seventeen and three years his junior at the time they met and with whom he had ecstatic sex. Perhaps inspired by the ravages of the AIDS epidemic, O'Hara reports that having a relationship had become increasingly important for him at this time; yet, it remained a goal which he could not realise. His third relationship, with Michael, continued periodically from 1985 to 1990 in the midst of the AIDS epidemic and reflected some change in his belief that he was not capable of having long-term intimate relationships.

Although aware of the means of transmission of AIDS and the importance of safer sex, O'Hara found it impossible to use condoms in his relationship with Michael and did not focus on the ethical implications of this decision. This relationship soon ended with Michael moving to San Diego and working in a serious gay theatre piece written by gay author Doug Sadownick. Although Michael had found a new boyfriend and had moved in with him, O'Hara and Michael continued to have highly satisfying sex for some time after that, as well as a three-way sexual relationship with Michael and his partner. This relationship repeated his earlier, almost voyeuristic interest in observing a gay couple being intimate with each other, a goal he seemed unable to realise for himself. Michael became symptomatic and died a few years later.

Another sometime boyfriend from about this time also contracted AIDS. There were other brief relationships before two that were more lasting, one with Stephen, also HIV positive, who shared O'Hara's passion for acting, literature, and decorating, and rapid boredom within committed relationships. As O'Hara (1997) observed about his life at this time: ". . . I would be hard-pressed to name anyone in my life at this period with whom I *didn't* have sex. Sex was my social currency" (p. 162). Having been hurt by previous love affairs, O'Hara believed that even anonymous sex was better than having to put up with a regular lover, and maintained that the best he could hope for was "Love with a wide variety of partners . . . a vital, busy, love-filled *single* life . . ." (p. 175). While he admired friends who remained in committed relationships, he did not believe he possessed the capacity for long-term fidelity. He realised that he valued his own solitude but could easily find companionship when he wanted company.

O'Hara discusses his lifelong search for both printed and visual presentations of gay sex, noting the intense pleasure he experienced as a college student watching gay pornography while having sex with an older man and later watching pornographic films in gay bathhouses. He recalls with relish his discovery of the bathhouse in 1980; of being penetrated by ten men who had waited in line to fuck him; of the friendship and camaraderie among those enjoying the bathhouse, a space where he could let down his guard and talk and have sex with anyone; and the three succeeding years when he visited more than forty such bathhouses across North America.

It was at about this time that O'Hara decided to become a pornography star, although he says he had no definitive plans for realising that goal. Arriving in San Francisco with a friend after a cross-country tour, O'Hara frequented a gay pornography theatre featuring live jack-off shows. Soon he was invited by management to become a performer. From the outset, his primary concern was to show that gay sex was immensely pleasurable and certainly nothing to be ashamed of; he tried to let his audience know of his pleasure and hoped they would feel the same way. He was particularly proud of the possibility that at least some younger gay men watching his performance would feel better about themselves seeing his ease and pleasure as he came to orgasm. In this way, he hoped to help the next generation of gay men enjoy the pleasure of sex without the shame and guilt so often experienced by previous generations. He saw himself as a mentor for these younger gay men through his demonstration of the pleasure that could be realised from sex with other men.

O'Hara devotes a chapter to reviewing the numerous gay videos he made over the years from 1983 to 1988. He reports that he had purchased a video camera and filmed himself performing auto-fellatio and having sex with other men. He states that, for the most part, he really was turned on by the experience of knowing others would see him having sex. He enjoyed having sex with other men and was delighted to receive money to engage in activities he would willingly perform for free.

His experiences on film included every imaginable sexual experience, such as fisting, having toes up his butt, and water sports. He reported that, despite often being cast as a top (no doubt he was given this role because of his large penis), he most enjoyed being a bottom. Over the years, he remained in touch with many of his fellow actors, although, as he observed in both his memoir and essays, many of his co-stars died as a result of AIDS. O'Hara began working in this genre at a time in which the means of transmission for AIDS was not understood. When it was widely known that unprotected anal sex was a major vehicle for HIV infection, it was already too late for many gay performers. While he became aware of the importance of condoms in preventing HIV infection later in his acting career, by then it was too late for him as well. In 1987, while travelling in Australia, he noted a purple spot on his calf; it was only two years later that he was able to admit to himself that the increasing number of such purple spots were Kaposi's Sarcoma, evidence that his immune system had been compromised by HIV.

Recognising that his pornography career was over, and believing that his sex life was about to end as well, O'Hara retreated to gardening and writing. In keeping with the times, he tried a number of experimental and alternative purported cures for AIDS. Monette's (1988) memoir detailing his care for his partner Roger, who was suffering from the ravages of AIDS, and his own infection, captures this time of hopes raised and dashed, of purported cures which led only to other symptoms, and of the relentless dying of friends and former lovers.

With his characteristic charisma and honesty, O'Hara elected to become a "poster boy" for AIDS. He sported a large HIV+ tattoo on his arm, visible to all, as the ultimate "out of the closet" gesture. As with so many gay men, it had been difficult for O'Hara to discuss his HIV status with possible sexual partners, but he noted that the tattoo would solve this problem. As he observes about his experience living with AIDS:

> I've become somewhat notorious, over the past year, for my positions on HIV . . . I can't quite believe it's a curse . . . in my life, AIDS has been an undeniable blessing. It woke me up to what was important [and] gives me the freedom to behave 'irresponsibly.' I look at the HIV negative people around me, and I pity them. They must live their lives in constant fear of infection. (1997, p. 129)

Countering the stigmatising effects of HIV/AIDS by being infected and proud, O'Hara settled into a career of writing his memoir and producing *Steam*, an occasional journal of opinion and information regarding gay sex. Following the emergence of AIDS-related symptoms, O'Hara spent much of his time on a farm in Wisconsin where he took up his writing in earnest. He reports always having kept a diary, which served as the basis for his memoir. (O'Hara's papers have been deposited in the library at Brown University.)

Much of what we know of O'Hara's life during these last years when he suffered from the effects of his illness is reflected in his columns for *Steam*, which had a large "underground" following. He reported that because he did not have to worry about becoming infected, he was able to enjoy sex with other HIV positive men without using condoms. O'Hara ends his memoir in 1996; by then, many of his fellow gay pornography actors had died. He commented on the little things that continued to give him pleasure and which permitted him to remain optimistic. He realised comfort from reminiscing about his sexual past, together with less explicitly sexual pleasures such as a hot bath, the sound of waves crashing against the shore, watching the leaves change colour in the autumn, or enjoying fresh roasted corn-on-the-cob.

AARON LAWRENCE:
GAY PORNOGRAPHY FOR PLEASURE AND FOR PROFIT

I'm a well-adjusted, entrepreneurial, sexual liberal. (Lawrence, 1999, p. 155)

By the mid-1990s, the two post-war cohort defining events for the gay community were well understood: the Gay Rights revolution had taken hold, and, while the epidemic of AIDS continued to ravage the gay community, the primary means of HIV transmission was common knowledge. Gay men were cautioned to practice safer sex and to "wear their rubbers." Then, in 1996, reports of a new treatment for AIDS, this time promising significant symptom relief and life extension, based on well supervised clinical trials, further changed the experience of sexuality within the gay community (Sullivan, 1998). While safer sex was still important in order to curtail the spread of AIDS, the antiviral "cocktail" provided a new lease on life for many gay men.

Together with increasing acceptance of gay sexuality, "coming out" in the 1990s was a very different experience from that of previous decades. The emergence of the Internet and the development of gay Websites facilitated discussion of the gay experience, provided a means for meeting other gay men, and offered a seemingly endless supply of gay pornography. First-person accounts, videos, and downloadable pictures provided a new opportunity for younger gay men to learn about their sexuality. The embodiment of this new experience of gay sexuality is life-writer Aaron Lawrence, sometime nationally syndicated gay columnist, escort, and gay pornography video actor and producer.

Lawrence has done it all. The cover of the first volume of his memoirs, which features a color photograph of a grinning, naked Lawrence, dollar bills covering his genitals, illustrates the economic success realised by this young gay entrepreneur. Bright, cute, articulate, and well read, Lawrence is the icon of the new gay sexuality.[7] A self-professed geek, Lawrence has designed and manages a well organised and entertaining Website which includes his online store (www.aaronlawrence.com) and a paid membership area featuring sexually explicit photos of young men he has recruited for his videos and chapters of his memoirs. His online store sells all his videos and books, together with an increasing number of videos by other amateur gay pornography actor/directors. His e-mails to his subscribers are often folksy, complete with requests for a housekeeper or the celebration of the anniversary of his 1999 "marriage" to his longtime boyfriend, Jeff. His Website features detailed descriptions and pictures of his sexual experiences around the world, all designed to market his books, videos, and even a dildo based on a mould of his 8-inch erection. Lawrence has also starred in a few commercial gay pornographic videos and has provided a detailed narrative of his experience in the world of gay pornography.

Laptop at the ready, Lawrence communicates by modem with an appreciative viewership intrigued by his narratives while on location filming himself having sex with other gay men. Most recently, he has held back publication of these daily accounts of his travels until he is ready to release the three or four videos of himself having sex with young men in another culture together with the inevitable orgy video which follows these filmed accounts. In his letters, he reports wanting viewers to appreciate not only the sex he has with these young men from other countries, but also the culture in which he is filming. However, at least in his reports of his experience with Thai young men, he shows little sensitivity to cultural differences in terms of privacy or body display. For example, he reports being perplexed when Thai men, whose very formal culture emphasises complex ritual (Geertz, 1966), refuse his offer to appear in videos with him, and express discomfort having sex which is recorded on film and witnessed by other young men serving as translators.

Through his writings and involvement in gay pornography, O'Hara attempted to show that the gay body could be (and should be) a source of pleasure rather than embarrassment and stigma. His outrageous memoir emphasises this point. Lawrence's memoir takes it to the next level. The gay body is not only pleasurable, but profitable. Particularly in the second volume of his self life-writing, Lawrence (2000) sets out to tell other men how they can realise similar profit from escorting.

Lawrence says that he likes to tell stories about his work, and his enthusiasm and compassion for his clients is apparent in his writings. He notes that he uses his education in psychology in an effort to be supportive of his clients and to help them feel comfortable having sex with him. However, unlike O'Hara, who paid little attention to financial success, Lawrence uses sex primarily for commercial purposes. He is an entrepreneur and his product is the gay body featured in his videos, his books, and his Website, including his "members only" section which requires a monthly fee for entrance.

Lawrence began his career as an escort and later branched out into "amateur" videos featuring him having sex with other young men both in the United States and, later, in Europe and East Asia. Like O'Hara, Lawrence is diminutive in stature, and noted for his large penis. Lawrence is a vegetarian, drives a Honda Civic, reads *Doonesbury*, does not smoke or drink, has a life partner, a BA in psychology, and an MA in higher education administration. His body is perfectly sculpted, as a result of many hours spent working out; he has an easy time getting and maintaining an erection, and he reports being able to have multiple orgasms each day, as he services affluent clients who pay very large fees for the pleasure of his company. He notes that both his education and sophisticated cultural interests have been important since many of his middle-aged and prosperous clients prefer an articulate, interesting dinner partner and escort.

Moving into his late twenties, and anticipating a time when his age may be a detriment to escorting, Lawrence has begun producing videos featuring him and other actors and also recruiting other young men to join his escort business. His videos do not have dubbed music or dubbed sounds of sexual pleasure: the soundtrack is that of the encounter itself. He introduces each partner before filming, and often talks to his partner and his cameraman during the sexual encounter. His favourite cameraman, also a gay actor and producer whose videos Lawrence sells on his Website, sometimes trades places with Lawrence during the filming of a sexual scene (most recently, Lawrence's partner also has agreed to assist in filming these gay videos). Lawrence enjoys being filmed having sex with attractive young men across the world. Arriving in some foreign city, he contacts a local escort agency, finds boys interested in appearing in a video, for which they receive payment, and then invites these boys to be filmed with him. On occasion, he is able to convince these boys to have sex on video with their boyfriend, in which case the couple may choose not to use condoms.

Lawrence presumes that gay sexuality is pleasurable; he also assumes that it is so normal that it does not have to be presented as other than sexually explicit and arousing. While, as Burger (1995) notes, actors in gay pornographic films often are instructed by directors in how to show their pleasure, Lawrence's expressions of delight with the sensations of sexuality are evident on tape. Just as for O'Hara, Lawrence's primary focus is on insuring that his partner has a pleasurable sexual experience.

This gifted pornographic film actor and producer and life-writer was born in New Jersey to an affluent suburban family. He reports that his family was unable to make sense of his "strange desire" and feelings of being different from other boys his age, and failed to offer much support during the painful childhood years when he began to realise his gay sexual identity. Similar to both Poole and O'Hara, Lawrence enjoyed his first gay experience during adolescence. At that time, he was somewhat overweight and suffered from acne. He felt his body was unattractive and reports being unable to believe that others would find him sexually desirable. He does, however, note the satisfaction he realised from being wanted by other men. Lawrence suffered few of the problems purported to be characteristic of the hustler (i.e., he did not come from a 'broken' home; he was not abandoned by his family on account of his sexual orientation, etc.). Lawrence does report that he is perennially in search of admiration, perhaps the consequence of growing up within an emotionally distant affluent suburban family (Kohut, 1977).

Much of Lawrence's life-story emerges in the first of his two books as a refutation following a strange encounter he had serving as an escort to a middle-aged man who enjoyed verbally torturing him but expressed little desire for sexual activity. In response to this man's taunting, he recounts that his childhood was difficult:

> My entire childhood is filled with memories of never fitting in. In elementary school, I was picked on mercilessly. By fifth grade, I was a thief. By seventh grade, I was a social outcast. By tenth grade, I was considering suicide, and by twelfth grade, I was sleep-

ing with every guy I could get my hands on. My parents were always there, but they never wanted to listen, never wanted to understand. (1999, p. 163)

Lawrence's account is fairly typical of boys with acknowledged gay desire growing up in the 1980s and 1990s; boys aware they are somehow different from their peers (Herdt & Boxer, 1996; Savin-Williams, 1997). In fact, Lawrence reports (1999) that, as an adolescent, he contemplated suicide because he felt "strange," believed he was not appreciated by his parents, and struggled with feelings of social isolation.

Lawrence met Jeff, his life partner, while in college. Following graduation, the couple maintained their relationship, mostly at a distance, while Lawrence completed his MA degree. The couple was "married" a few years ago (wedding pictures were posted on his Website), even as Lawrence continued with his escorting business. Lawrence comments that continued escorting was necessary since Jeff had difficulty finding a job in the highly competitive New York metropolitan area.

Entry into the escort business was accidental. Lawrence had intended to become an administrator of a college residential life program following his MA degree in higher education administration. Though invited for numerous interviews, he was not offered a job and became depressed about his future. For a time, following graduate school, Lawrence worked as a supervisor in a group home for developmentally delayed adults, but found the work frustrating because of the lack of resources and a poorly educated and indifferent staff. Faced with large credit card debt and no way to pay it off, depressed by his lack of job prospects, with his boyfriend a continent away, Lawrence began spending his free hours in adult bookstores and bathhouses. He explains that hustling and the pornography business were the only things at which he was able to succeed.

One bookstore partner, particularly appreciative of Lawrence's skilful blow job, suggested that he could make a living from his sexual artistry. Recalling that twice he had received money from men with whom he had sex, and recognising that the Internet made possible easy contact with clients, Lawrence began his life as an escort. The apparent ease with which Lawrence entered the escort business may have reflected, in part, an attempt to quell the lowered self-regard that he felt earlier in life and his disappointment in not being able to find a job in his chosen profession (Kohut, 1977; Shelby, 2002).

With the AOL™ screen name of "NJescort," his online mailbox was soon filled with requests from prospective clients. AOL™ somehow learned of his service and closed his account. Lawrence then created his own Website. He continued to live at home, and with Jeff still on the West Coast, Lawrence's parents invited Jeff to move in with them.

Despite initial objections to Lawrence's new career, Jeff finally agreed to let him continue with his escort business, provided he obeyed a number of stipulations. These were: (1) since he was attracted to younger men, he would not accept clients under the age of twenty-five; (2) he would come home each evening, no matter how late it might be; (3) he would not engage in any free sex merely for pleasure; (4) he would not become emotionally involved with clients; and (5) he would be discreet about his employment around their families (Lawrence, 1999, p. 56). Lawrence acknowledges that since the couple moved in together, his escorting has sometimes been a source of tension between them. He often comes home in the evening exhausted from servicing many clients in a single day and evening. At such times, it has been difficult for him to have sex with Jeff. Lawrence does note in his e-mails that he resists occasional temptation to spend a night with a man he has met on his travels because of Jeff's possible reaction.

Lawrence markets his videos on his Website and also has arranged for nationwide distribution through adult bookstores. He fosters interest in his videos through e-mails reporting on his travels and sexual exploits, which he sends to a mailing list of nearly three thousand viewer-subscribers. In his e-mails describing his videos, Lawrence notes the difficulty attendant in making them. For example, performers recruited on site may be unable to achieve orgasm and may have to return for the "money shot"; some young men may be too nervous to participate; and others may turn out to be straight and unwilling to kiss or engage in other aspects of sexual intimacy. Lawrence's pornographic business reflects the broader trend towards globalisation in the new millennium and, perhaps, personifies the commodification of gay sex.

Anticipating a time when his age will make it more difficult for him to profit from his body, Lawrence is making a transition from escort and actor to producer of gay videos. Back home, Jeff works for one of New York's museums and the couple enjoys a quiet life together in suburban New Jersey. His goals are that he and Jeff might adopt children; he will earn sufficient income to support the family in the posh New York area suburbs; and Jeff will continue his work in the much less lucrative world of public art museums. Reflecting this desire to make a transition in his life, Lawrence reported in a recent e-mail to his subscriber list that, as he began the present year, "I realised I wasn't happy with my life. I was being stretched in too many directions, and wasn't able to give enough attention to any of them. As a result, I realised that it was time for a change." The change that he contemplates is to concentrate on his gay pornography, no longer filming "just for the hell of it" but rather for the sake of his financial survival.

Coming of age in the wake of the gay rights movement and the AIDS epidemic, with gay identity viewed as "virtually normal" (Sullivan, 1995), Lawrence may be the ideal example of postmodern gay sexuality. Sharing Scott O'Hara's (1997) view that gay sexuality is both pleasurable and devoid of shame or guilt, Lawrence conveys his message through performance in life-writing and filming, both of which have been personally and financially rewarding. The phenomenon of Aaron Lawrence could not have happened at any other time. History, social change, and technology all enter into this contemporary representation of gay desire as pleasurable, relaxed, and thoroughly enjoyable.

CONCLUSION

Bruner (2002) has observed that there is no biography apart from our present telling and writing about ourselves; Mills (1959/2000) has shown that telling or writing the life-story takes place in the context of distinctive social and historical changes experienced at particular points across the life span. Sexual identity is one of the central elements comprising the contemporary life-story. Stories of the realisation of a particular sexual identity, including the very terms used to portray this sexual identity for oneself and others, reflect the interplay both of a shared understanding of sexuality within a particular generation, and social and historical changes across generations (Mills, 1959/2000). This interplay in conjunction with particular life circumstances determines the manner in which we understand and enact sexual desire (Boxer, Cohler, Herdt, & Irvin, 1993; Elder, 1995; Plummer, 1995; Sadownick, 1997). Further, those events taking place in late adolescence and early adulthood have particular salience, influencing the manner in which subsequent life events are understood by the members of a generation-cohort (Schuman & Scott, 1989).

Since the Second World War, and particularly over the past three decades, there have been dramatic changes in this shared understanding of the meaning and realisation of gay sexual desire. Two historical events, the gay rights revolution beginning in 1969 and the emergence of the AIDS epidemic in 1981, have profoundly affected the manner in which men desiring sex with other men have understood and expressed this desire. However, gay men of varying generations have experienced these two events in somewhat different ways. Men born *before* the Second World War, such as life-writer and pioneer gay film director Wakefield Poole, were already approaching midlife at the time of the Stonewall Inn riots of June 1969. Growing up in the post-war era, which was marked by concern with a traditional and conservative lifestyle, men like Poole often felt ashamed of their sexual desire for other men and recognised that this desire was heavily stigmatised by a society demanding adherence to the "normal" (D'Emilio, 1998; Loughery, 1998).

Similar to many other men of his generation (Duberman, 1991), Poole sought help from psychiatrists who expected that he marry and suppress his sexual desire for other men. Poole's decision to make the first commercially successful film portraying men having sex with other men was shaped by his understanding of his attraction to men from childhood onward, and by social changes following the emergence of gay rights. His films portrayed a highly stylised and staged gay sexuality, perhaps reflecting both his own discomfort with his gay identity and that of the larger community which was not yet able to accept the idea of gay sexuality devoid of shame and guilt.

Two later actors/producers of sexual pornography, Scott O'Hara and Aaron Lawrence, evidence little of this sense of shame regarding their desire for sex with other men. At the time of Poole's pioneering efforts in gay pornography, O'Hara was still a child living in rural Oregon. Like so many other gay men born in the 1960s and coming to adulthood just on the cusp of the AIDS epidemic, O'Hara could not have known that his sexual adventures would eventually lead to his infection. While there is some reference to the AIDS epidemic in Poole's (2000) life-story, the death of lovers and fellow gay pornography actors from AIDS frames both O'Hara's (1997, 1999) memoir and his essays written in the years after he began to develop the symptoms characteristic of HIV infection. His own death is a tragic reminder of the devastation wrought by those early years of the epidemic when gay newspapers were filled with obituaries of men, particularly those born in the 1950s and 1960s, who had succumbed to the disease (Cohler, 2002).

Aaron Lawrence, born a decade after Scott O'Hara, came to adulthood well informed about the AIDS epidemic and the necessity for practising "safer sex." His memoirs include little mention of the HIV virus and its consequences, as he enjoyed "safer" gay sex in the "post-AIDS" era when antiviral medication appeared to have transformed AIDS from a fatal to a chronic illness. O'Hara's (1997) account reflects psychological resilience, personal energy and charm, and determination to pursue a gay lifeway (Hostetler & Herdt, 1998) in spite of what others might think. On the other hand, Lawrence (1999) recalls having poor self-esteem and disdain for his body, and feeling left out at school, perhaps because of his awareness of his gay sexual desire. The experience of having sex with other men, where he was admired and encouraged by his partners, appears to have been important in helping Lawrence overcome feelings of low self-regard and a sense of personal depletion. However, being gay in itself poses little psychological conflict for either O'Hara or Lawrence, and neither of these men retreated to substance abuse nor sought psychiatric treatment.

Both O'Hara and Lawrence self-identified without conflict as "gay," and show, through filmed sexual activity, the experience of sexual pleasure with other men. O'Hara, working from 1983, still believed that it was necessary to show the pleasures of gay sex on film in order to help men feel less guilty and anxious about expressing their gay desire. Stressing the significance of smiling and showing delight while making love with other men on video, O'Hara's pornographic work both reflected changing attitudes toward, and promoted new acceptance of, gay sexuality. By the time Lawrence began acting in and making gay pornographic films a decade later, gay sexuality was sufficiently accepted that he could appear relaxed and even be able to make jokes during sex with the men he recruited to join him. There is little editing of these videos which portray ordinary (albeit good-looking) young gay men, from introduction to postcoital embrace, thoroughly enjoying the sexual responses they induce in each other. Both the life-story accounts and the pornographic films of these three men as actors or producers, members of different generation-cohorts, reflect the significant cultural changes across the post-war period in the meaning and expression of gay sexual desire.

NOTES

1. It is common in the world of pornography for actors to use assumed names. While Wakefield Poole uses his own name, Scott O'Hara and Aaron Lawrence, two later actor/producers, write under their assumed names.

2. The term pornographic is used here strictly as description for the genre of films and videos portraying men having sex with other men. The use of the term, pornographic or gay porn should not be regarded as a moral or critical statement of this genre.

3. Earlier discussion of self life-writing emphasised a distinction between autobiography as a narrative covering life as a whole and memoir as narrative covering a less extended period of life. This distinction between autobiography and memoir fails to characterise much of recent self life-writing which recounts a presently remembered past, experienced present, and anticipated future within an account designed to convince self and others of the meaning of both idiosyncratic life circumstances and shared experiences of a generation. Indeed, identity is fashioned through the story as told or written

(Eakin, 1999). Writing a life story remakes identity in the context of the personal and social moment.

4. As contrasted with straight counterparts, gay teens have little opportunity for learning how to be sexual as a gay person. Straight adolescents talk about their "exploits" with girls. They hold hands and embrace in public settings in ways less possible for their gay counterparts. Although Aaron Fricke (1981) won a Federal Court case permitting him to take his boyfriend to his senior prom, in many high schools, it is still difficult for gay youth to take their boyfriends to the prom. (See, for example, the case of Marc Hall on EGALE and other Internet sites.) Explicit gay videos provide an education otherwise lacking in their socialisation to being gay.

5. Little has been written regarding the significance of semen for gay men in our culture. In fellatio, swallowing the semen enhances the physical pleasure of the act. In some instances, swallowing semen represents incorporation or identification with the admired attributes of the person fellated, such as presumed virility or strength. In other instances such as anal intercourse, it is sometimes regarded as the supreme form of intimacy in which a part of the partner becomes a part of one's self. Most recently, with the AIDS epidemic, semen has been regarded as dangerous and denotative of pollution. The statement, "on me, but not in me," reflects fear of infection, a cultural expression founded in medicine but made in cultural practice.

6. O'Hara (1997) does not present his life-story in a linear manner, starting with childhood and moving on through adolescence and the adult years. I have reorganised his narrative into a linear story for the purposes of the present paper in order to highlight the significance of social and historical change as factors related to writing and performing gay sexual desire.

7. In May 2002, Lawrence announced in an e-mail to his subscriber list that he was taking an "extended" leave from the escort business and also his personal advice column. He reported needing to devote time to his other projects and also to issues in his personal life.

REFERENCES

Barkin, K.D. (1976). Autobiography and history, *Societas, 6,* 83-108.
Boxer, A., Cohler, B., Herdt, G., & Irvin, F. (1993). The study of gay and lesbian teenagers: Life-course, "coming out" and well being. In P. Tolan & B. Cohler (Eds.), *Handbook of clinical research and practice with adolescents* (pp. 249-280). New York, NY: Wiley-Interscience.
Brown, R.J. (2001). *The evening crowd at Kirmser's.* Minneapolis, MN: University of Minnesota Press.
Bruner, J. (1987). Life as narrative. *Social Research, 54,* 11-32.
Bruner, J. (2002). *Making stories: Law, literature, and life.* New York, NY: Farrar, Straus, and Giroux.
Burger, J.R. (1995). *One-handed histories: The eroto-politics of gay male video pornography.* New York, NY: Harrington Park Press.
Clendinen, D., & Nagourney, A. (1999). *Out for good: The struggle to build a gay rights movement in America.* New York, NY: Simon and Schuster.
Cohler, B. (2002). Writing and reading desire: Generation and life writing by men having sex with other men. Manuscript submitted for publication.
Conway, M.A., & Pleydell-Pearce, C.W. (2000). The construction of autobiographical memories in the self-memory system. *Psychological Review, 107,* 261-288.

Delany, S.R. (1988). *The motion of light in water: Sex and science fiction writing in the East Village, 1957-1965.* New York, NY: William Marrow-Arbor House.
Delany, S.R. (1999). *Times Square red, Times Square blue.* New York, NY: New York University Press.
Delph, E.W. (1978). *The silent community: Public homosexual encounters.* Thousand Oaks, CA: Sage.
D'Emilio, J. (1998). *Sexual politics, sexual communities: The making of a homosexual minority in the United States, 1940-1970* (2nd edition). Chicago, IL: University of Chicago Press.
Duberman, M. (1986). Coda (Part Three). In M. Duberman (Ed.), *About time: Exploring the gay past* (pp. 343-377). New York, NY: Gay Presses of New York.
Duberman, M. (1991). *Cures: A gay man's odyssey.* New York, NY: Plume/Penguin Books.
Eakin, P.J. (1999). *How our lives become stories: Making selves.* Ithaca, NY: Cornell University Press.
Elder, G.H., Jr. (1974/1998). *Children of the Great Depression: Social change in life experience.* Boulder, CO: Westview Press/HarperCollins.
Elder, G. H., Jr. (1995). The life-course paradigm: Social change and individual development. In P. Moen, G.H. Elder, Jr., & Kurt Lüscher (Eds.), *Examining lives in context: Perspectives on the ecology of human development* (pp. 101-139). Washington, DC: American Psychological Association.
Elder, G.H., Jr. (2002). Historical times and lives: A journey through time and space. In E. Phelps, F.F. Furstenberg, Jr., & A. Colby (Eds.), *Looking at lives: American longitudinal studies of the Twentieth century* (pp. 194-218). New York, NY: Russell Sage Foundation.
Erikson, E. (1968). *Identity, youth and crisis.* New York, NY: Norton.
Fricke, A. (1981). *Reflections of a rock lobster.* Boston, MA: Alyson Publications.
Frontain, R-W. (2000). A professional queer remembers: Bibliography, narrative, and the saving power of memory. In S.L. Jones (Ed.), *A sea of stories: The shaping power of narrative in gay and lesbian cultures* (pp. 217-238). New York, NY: Harrington Park Press.
Geertz, C. (1966). Person, time and conduct in Bali. In C. Geertz (Ed.), *The interpretation of cultures* (pp. 360-412). New York, NY: Basic Books.
Goffman, E. (1963). *Stigma: Notes on the management of spoiled identity.* New York, NY: Simon and Schuster.
Harris, D. (1997). *The rise and fall of gay culture.* New York, NY: Hyperion Books.
Herdt, G., & Boxer, A. (1996). *Children of horizons* (2nd edition). Boston, MA: Beacon Press.
Holland, W. (2000). In the body's ghetto. In S.L. Jones (Ed.), *A sea of stories: The shaping power of narrative in gay and lesbian cultures* (pp. 109-138). New York, NY: Harrington Park Press.
Holland, D., Lachicotte, W., Jr., Skinner, D., & Cain, C. (1998). *Identity and agency in cultural worlds.* Cambridge, MA: Harvard University Press.
Hostetler, A., & Herdt, G. (1998). Culture, sexual lifeways, and developmental subjectivities: Rethinking sexual taxonomies. *Social Research, 65,* 249-290.

Humphreys, L. (1970). *Tearoom trade: Impersonal sex in public places*. Chicago, IL: Aldine.
Iser, W. (1978). *The act of reading: A theory of aesthetic response*. Baltimore, MD: Johns Hopkins University Press.
Jolly, M. (2001). Lesbian and gay life writing. In M. Jolly (Ed.), *Encyclopedia of life-writing: Autobiographical and biographical forms* (vol. 2, pp. 547-549). London, UK: Fitzroy Dearborn Publishers.
Kohut, H. (1977). *The restoration of the self*. New York, NY: International Universities Press.
Lawrence, A. (1999). *Suburban hustler: Stories of a hi-tech callboy*. Warren, NJ: Late Night Press.
Lawrence, A. (2000). *The male escort's handbook: Your guide to getting rich the hard way*. Warren, NJ: Late Night Press.
Loughery, J. (1998). *The other side of silence: Men's lives and gay identities: A twentieth century history*. New York, NY: Henry Holt/Owl Books.
Mannheim, K. (1928/1993). The problem of generations. In K.H. Wolff (Ed.), *From Karl Mannheim* (2nd edition, pp. 351-398). New Brunswick, NJ: Transactions Books.
McAdams, D. P., & Bowman, P.J. (2001). Narrating life's turning points: Redemption and contamination. In D.P. McAdams, R. Josselson, & A. Lieblich (Eds.), *Turns in the road: Narrative studies of lives in transition* (pp. 3-34). Washington, DC: American Psychological Association.
Miller, T. (1997). *Shirts and skins*. Los Angeles, CA: Alyson Books.
Miller, T. (2002). *Body blows: Six performances*. Madison, WI: University of Wisconsin Press.
Mills, C.W. (1959/2000). *The sociological imagination* (40th Anniversary Edition). New York, NY: Oxford University Press.
Mishler, E. (1999). *Storylines: Craft artists' narratives of identity*. Cambridge, MA: Harvard University Press.
Monette, P. (1988). *Borrowed time: An AIDS memoir*. New York, NY: Harvest Books/Harcourt Brace.
Monette, P. (1994). *Last watch of the night: Essays too personal and otherwise*. New York, NY: Harcourt, Brace and Company.
O'Hara, S. (1997). *Autopornography: A memoir of life in the lust lane*. New York, NY: Harrington Park Press.
O'Hara, S. (1999). *Rarely pure and never simple: Selected essays of Scott O'Hara*. New York, NY: Harrington Park Press.
Parks, C. (1999). Lesbian identity development: An examination of differences across generations. *American Journal of Orthopsychiatry, 69*, 347-361.
Plummer, K. (1995). *Telling sexual stories: Power, change, and social worlds*. New York, NY: Routledge.
Poole, W. (2000). *Dirty Poole: The autobiography of a gay porn pioneer*. Los Angeles, CA: Alyson Books.
Propp, V. (1928/1968). *The morphology of the folktale* (2nd edition). Austin, TX: The University of Texas Press.

Read, K.E. (1973/1980). *Other voices: The style of a male homosexual tavern.* Novato, CA: Chandler and Sharp.
Ricoeur, P. (1977). The question of proof in Freud's psychoanalytic writings. *Journal of the American Psychoanalytic Association, 25,* 835-872.
Robinson, P. (1999). *Gay lives: Homosexual autobiography from John Addington Symonds to Paul Monette.* Chicago, IL: The University of Chicago Press.
Sadownick, D. (1997). *Sex between men: An intimate history of the sex lives of gay men postwar to the present.* San Francisco, CA: Harper.
Savin-Williams, R.J. (1997). *. . . And then I became gay: Young men's stories.* New York, NY: Routledge.
Schuman, H., Belli, R.F., & Bischoping, K. (1997). The generational basis of historical knowledge. In J. W. Pennebaker, D. Paez, & B. Rimé (Eds.), *Collective memory of political events: Social psychological perspectives* (pp. 47-78). Mahweh, NJ: Lawrence Erlbaum Associates.
Schuman, H., & Scott, J. (1989). Generations and collective memories. *American Sociological Review, 54,* 359-381.
Sears, J.T. (1997). *Growing up gay in the South: An oral history of lesbian and gay Southern life, 1948-1968.* Boulder, CO: Westview Press.
Settersten, R.A., Jr. (1999). *Lives in time and place: The problems and promises of developmental science.* Amityville, NY: Baywood Publishing Company.
Settersten, R.A., Jr. (2003). Propositions and controversies in life-course scholarship. In R.A. Settersten, Jr. (Ed.), *Invitation to the life-course: Toward new understandings of later life* (pp. 15-48). Amityville, NY: Baywood Publishing Company.
Shelby, D. (2002). About cruising and being cruised. *The Annual for Psychoanalysis, 30,* 191- 210.
Stein, A. (1997). *Sex and sensibility: Stories of a lesbian generation.* Berkeley, CA: The University of California Press.
Sullivan, A. (1995). *Virtually normal: An argument about homosexuality.* New York, NY: Knopf.
Sullivan, A. (1998). *Love undetectable: Notes on friendship, sex, and survival.* New York, NY: Knopf.
Tierney, W.G. (2000). Undaunted courage: Life history and the postmodern challenge. In N.K. Denzin & Y. S. Lincoln (Eds.), *Handbook of qualitative research* (2nd edition, pp. 537-554). Thousand Oaks, CA: Sage
Tobias, A. (1973/1993). *The best little boy in the world* (Revised edition). New York, NY: Ballantine Books.
Tobias, A. (1998). *The best little boy in the world grows up.* New York, NY: Random House.
Turan, K., & Zito, S.E. (1974). *Sinema: American pornographic films and the people who make them.* New York, NY: Praeger Publishers.
Waugh, T. (1995). Men's pornography: Gay vs. straight. In C.K. Creekmur & A. Doty (Eds.), *Out in culture: Gay, lesbian and queer essays on popular culture* (pp. 307-327). Durham, NC: Duke University Press.
Waugh, T. (1996). *Hard to imagine: Gay male eroticism in photography and film from their beginnings to Stonewall.* New York, NY: Columbia University Press.
www.oasismag.com (Website run by and for queer youth, 2002).

Body Image, Eating Disorders, and the Drive for Muscularity in Gay and Heterosexual Men: The Influence of Media Images

Scott J. Duggan, PhD (cand.)

OISE/University of Toronto

Donald R. McCreary, PhD

Defence R&D, Toronto

SUMMARY. This Internet research project examined the relationship between consumption of muscle and fitness magazines and/or various

---

Scott J. Duggan is a graduate student at the Ontario Institute for Studies in Education of the University of Toronto, where he is working toward his PhD in counselling psychology. He received his Master of Arts degree from York University in social psychology. His main areas of research include self-esteem and body image of gay and lesbian individuals. He is also interested in gay individuals' perceptions of the public's attitude towards them. Dr. Donald R. McCreary is a Defence Scientist with the Stress and Coping Group at Defence R&D Canada–Toronto. His research interests include men's health, male body image, and the stress-health relationship. Dr. McCreary is Associate Editor of two journals: *The International Journal of Men's Health* and *Psychology of Men and Masculinity*. Correspondence may be addressed: Scott J. Duggan, OISE, University of Toronto, Toronto, ON, M5S 1V6, Canada (E-mail: scott. duggan@utoronto.ca).

[Haworth co-indexing entry note]: "Body Image, Eating Disorders, and the Drive for Muscularity in Gay and Heterosexual Men: The Influence of Media Images." Duggan, Scott J., and Donald R. McCreary. Co-published simultaneously in *Journal of Homosexuality* (Harrington Park Press, an imprint of The Haworth Press, Inc.) Vol. 47, No. 3/4, 2004, pp. 45-58; and: *Eclectic Views on Gay Male Pornography: Pornucopia* (ed: Todd G. Morrison) Harrington Park Press, an imprint of The Haworth Press, Inc., 2004, pp. 45-58. Single or multiple copies of this article are available for a fee from The Haworth Document Delivery Service [1-800- HAWORTH, 9:00 a.m. - 5:00 p.m. (EST). E-mail address: docdelivery@haworthpress.com].

http://www.haworthpress.com/web/JH
© 2004 by The Haworth Press, Inc. All rights reserved.
Digital Object Identifier: 10.1300/J082v47n03_03

indices of pornography and body satisfaction in gay and heterosexual men. Participants (N = 101) were asked to complete body satisfaction questionnaires that addressed maladaptive eating attitudes, the drive for muscularity, and social physique anxiety. Participants also completed scales measuring self-esteem, depression, and socially desirable responding. Finally, respondents were asked about their consumption of muscle and fitness magazines and pornography. Results indicated that viewing and purchasing of muscle and fitness magazines correlated positively with levels of body dissatisfaction for both gay and heterosexual men. Pornography exposure was positively correlated with social physique anxiety for gay men. The limitations of this study and directions for future research are outlined. *[Article copies available for a fee from The Haworth Document Delivery Service: 1-800-HAWORTH. E-mail address: <docdelivery@haworthpress.com> Website: <http://www.HaworthPress.com> © 2004 by The Haworth Press, Inc. All rights reserved.]*

KEYWORDS. Body image, gay men, eating disorders, sexual orientation, pornography, social comparison, sociocultural theory

The effect of media images on how women perceive themselves and their bodies, as well as how these images influence their self-esteem and attitudes towards eating and food, are well documented (e.g., Lin & Kulik, 2002; Stice, Schupak-Neuberg, Shaw, & Stein, 1994). Likewise, the trend towards a preference for thin-figured women also has been examined (e.g., Davis & Oswalt, 1992; Garner, Garfinkel, Schwartz, & Thompson, 1980; Silverstein & Perdue, 1988). These studies have shown how pervasive images such as those found in fashion magazines, *Playboy*, and even beauty pageant winners may contribute to women's body dissatisfaction, which in turn has been implicated in various eating disorders such as anorexia and bulimia.

In the past, few studies investigated men's body image concerns and pathogenic eating practices (Pope, Phillips, & Olivardia, 2000). *The Adonis Complex* (Pope et al., 2000) addresses these issues and discusses the emerging preoccupation men are having with body image. Specifically, the authors state, "For years we had studied eating disorders–but this work initially focused on women . . . gradually, in our research work and our clinical practices at Harvard and Brown Medical Schools, we began to recognise how much these problems affected not only women, but also men" (Pope et al., 2000, p. xiv). The authors provide numerous examples of men obsessed with their bodies who share feelings of "inadequacy, unattractiveness, and even failure" (p. 4), and who attempt to compensate for these feelings through physical exercise. Unlike their female counterparts who are motivated to be thin, men are more likely to associate attractiveness with increased muscle definition and leanness (Salusso-Deonier, Markee, & Pedersen, 1993) and, thus, may possess what McCreary and Sasse (2000) refer to as the *drive for muscularity*.

In contemporary Western society, men are being told that their bodies define them, and they are bombarded by advertisements that capitalise on their physical insecurities. These ads include diets and diet supplements, fitness programs, hair-growth remedies, and products designed to enhance sexual performance. A quick look at any one of a variety of men's magazines (e.g., *Men's Health*) will demonstrate this point. Irrespective of the product being sold, these advertisements disseminate the message that men constantly need to improve themselves.

Since men are conditioned not to care or at least not to "whine" about how they look, they often suffer in silence or address the "problem" by buying a product designed to enhance their physical appearance (Pope et al., 2000). Pope et al. also suggest that the self-ideal discrepancy is worse for men than for women. They believe that women have learned, from decades of appearance-related advertisements, to ignore or confront the impossible ideals of beauty promoted by mass media. Men, on the other hand, are socially prohibited from discussing such issues, and may not be comfortable acknowledging concerns over physical appearance.

According to Pope et al. (2000), gay men may have even greater problems with body image because they likely suffered more teasing about their purported lack of masculinity during childhood and adolescence. Therefore, homosexual males are desirous of a muscular body because it "proves" to themselves and to others that they are, indeed, real men.

Pope et al. (2000), however, were not the first to suggest that there may be differences between gay and heterosexual individuals with regard to body image. For example, Siever (1994) found that the gay men and heterosexual women in his sample were dissatisfied with their bodies, and that this dissatisfaction was due to an overemphasis on the importance of physical appearance in terms of attracting and pleasing men. Heterosexual men and lesbian women were less concerned about their own physical attractiveness and, therefore, less dissatisfied with their bodies. From this perspective, gay men's body dissatisfaction reflects anxiety that their physical appearance may be unappealing to prospective partners.

Another explanation for potential differences in body image between gay and heterosexual men forms the basis for this study. Specifically, it is proposed that these differences may reflect variations in media use, especially pornography exposure. Pornography is prolific in the gay community, and high consumption appears to be normative. This does not seem to be the case for heterosexual men. Further, "mainstream" gay male pornography (i.e., imagery produced by companies such as Bel Ami, Falcon, and Studio 2000) is rife with muscular, attractive men. According to the Cultivation Hypothesis (e.g., McCreary, 1997), viewers may internalise the messages contained in mass media, even when those messages are implicit. Thus, gay men may look at pornographic imagery and embrace the belief that they need to possess a similar physique in order to obtain sexual gratification.

The current study looks at pornography exposure from various sources as well as exposure to muscle and fitness magazines, and how these forms of media may be associated with the body images of heterosexual and gay men. Three hypotheses were tested:

> H1: Gay men will report greater exposure to pornography and muscle and fitness magazines than will heterosexual men.

> H2: Gay men will report higher overall levels of body dissatisfaction than will heterosexual men. Specifically, they will evidence more maladaptive eating attitudes, a greater drive for muscularity, and greater social physique anxiety.

> H3: Exposure to muscle and fitness magazines and pornography will correlate positively with level of body dissatisfaction for heterosexual and gay men.

METHOD

Participants

Participants were 101 males, of whom 67 (66%) self-identified as gay, 5 (5%) as bisexual, and 29 (29%) as heterosexual. Due to the small number of bisexuals, they were excluded from all analyses. Thus, the final sample consisted of 96 participants.

Measures

Balanced Inventory of Desirable Responding (BIDR; Paulhus, 1991). The BIDR is used to determine whether a participant is responding in a socially (or personally) desirable way. The scale measures two basic constructs: (1) the tendency to present honest but positively biased responses; and (2) deliberate self-presentation. On a 7-point scale that ranges from *not true* to *very true*, participants rate 40 statements (e.g., "I never swear"). Higher scores represent more desirable response tendencies. In this study, Cronbach's alpha was .82.

Centre for Epidemiological Studies Depression Scale (CES-D; Radloff, 1977). To assess the extent to which participants exhibited depression, the CES-D was used. This scale consists of 20 items (e.g., "I was bothered by things that usually don't bother me"), and respondents are asked to rate the extent to which each item applies to them. The CES-D uses a 4-point scale that ranges from *rarely or none of the time* to *most or all of the time*. Higher scores represent a greater degree of depression. In the current study, the alpha coefficient for the CES-D was .93.

Drive for Muscularity Scale (DMS; McCreary & Sasse, 2000). The DMS was used to assess participants' perception of the need to have larger muscles. The DMS is a 15-item, self-report questionnaire. Respondents are asked to rate the extent to which each item applies to them, using a 6-point scale from *always* to *never*. A sample item is "I think that I would look better if I gained 10 pounds in bulk." Higher scores on the DMS represent a greater drive for muscularity. A Cronbach's alpha of .91 was obtained for this study.

Eating Attitudes Test (EAT; Garner, Olmstead, Bohr, & Garfinkel, 1982). The EAT was used to assess participants' desire to be thin. The scale consists of 26 items that assess maladaptive eating attitudes and behaviours. These behaviours are closely related to anorexia and bulimia. Using a 6-point scale that ranges from *always* to *never*, respondents are asked to rate their agreement with items such as "I am terrified about being overweight." Higher scores on the EAT represent a greater drive for thinness. In the present study, Cronbach's alpha was .87.

Exercise and Health. Participants were asked to respond to questions examining the amount of time, per week, they spend weight training and engaging in cardiovascular exercise. They also were asked if they were currently dieting to lose or gain weight.

Media Image Exposure. To determine consumption rates for pornography and muscle and fitness magazines, individual questions were used. Two of the questions referred to the viewing or purchasing of muscle and fitness magazines. The remaining five questions asked about viewing or purchasing various types of pornography. Such questions are often used in lieu of a psychometric measure of consumption. At the beginning of this section, participants were asked, "During the past month, how often did you . . . ?" Each item had a 5-point scale, which ranged from *none* to *more than ten times*. Due to the vast amount of free pornography available on the Internet, it did not seem relevant to ask about the purchasing of Internet pornography (e.g., access fees to Websites). Individual questions for media usage can be found in Table 1.

Rosenberg Self-Esteem Scale (RSES; Rosenberg, 1965). To assess participants' self-esteem at the time of the study, the RSES was administered. This scale consists of 10 items, and is a well-known and often used measure of individual (as opposed to social or group) self-esteem. Respondents are asked to rate the extent to which they agree with each item using a 4-point scale that ranges from *strongly agree* to *strongly disagree*. Higher scores represent lower self-esteem. Items in the RSES include statements such as "I feel that I am person of worth, at least on an equal basis with others." In the current study, Cronbach's alpha was .86.

Social Physique Anxiety Scale (SPAS; Martin, Rejeski, Leary, McAuley, & Bane, 1997). The SPAS was used to assess the extent to which people become anxious when showing their body in public. This scale contains 9 items, and respondents are asked to rate the extent to which each item applies to them. Items include statements such as "I wish I wasn't so uptight about my physique/figure." The SPAS uses a 5-point scale that ranges from *not at all like me* to *like me a lot*. Higher scores represent a greater degree of social physique anxiety. For the SPAS, Cronbach's alpha was .91.

Procedure

Participants were recruited from the following sources: Internet sites such as <Gay.com>, <GayCanada.com>, and <GayToronto.com>; listservs (e.g., York University graduate lists, APA Division 44, and a friendship list), and through word of mouth. The recruitment e-mail described the purpose of the study as looking at the relationship between body image and media exposure and included a direct link to the survey, which was posted on an isolated Web page (i.e., a Web page to which there are no links from other pages). Once the participant arrived at the survey Web page, a user-prompted computer program administered the survey instruments. Participants were asked to read information about the study, were informed that they could quit at any time, and were provided with information on how to contact the researchers. To encourage participants to be as truthful as possible, assurances of confidentiality and anonymity were given. Informed consent was obtained by asking participants to read a short disclaimer that indicated consent was implied once they began the survey. Each participant was then instructed to enter the first two letters of his or her last name plus the last two digits of his or her telephone number. This became the code for that individual, which was used in combination with other variables as a check to determine that participants did not complete the survey multiple times.

RESULTS

Hypothesis 1: Volume of Pornography Consumed

It was hypothesised that gay men will report consuming more pornography than will heterosexual men. It also was hypothesised that gay men will consume more muscle and fitness magazines. To test these hypotheses, a series of independent samples *t*-tests were used (a Bonferroni correction procedure was used to control for the increased probability of making a Type I error as a result of multiple *t*-tests; to this end, *p*-values less than .01 were viewed as significant). As Table 1 shows, for each of the five categories that asked about pornography exposure (viewed or purchased pornographic magazines, viewed or purchased pornographic videos, and viewed Internet pornography), gay men reported significantly more consumption than heterosexual men. There were no significant differences, however, between gay and heterosexual respondents in the consumption of muscle and fitness magazines.

Hypothesis 2: Reported Levels of Body Dissatisfaction

It was hypothesised that gay men will report higher overall levels of body dissatisfaction as measured by scores on the EAT, the DMS, and the SPAS. This hypothesis was only partially supported. A series of independent samples *t*-tests revealed that there were no significant differences between gay and heterosexual men on the DMS or the SPAS (see Table 2). However, there was a significant difference in EAT scores between gay and heterosexual men. Gay men reported more negative, thinness-oriented eating attitudes and behaviours than did heterosexual men.

TABLE 1. Mean Frequency of Pornography and Muscle and Fitness Magazine Consumption (Standard Deviations in Parentheses)

During the past month, how often did you . . . ?	GM	HM	t	d
View Muscle/Fitness Magazines	1.03 (1.01)	0.79 (1.15)	1.01	
Purchase Muscle/Fitness Magazines	0.33 (0.73)	0.14 (0.58)	−1.27	
View Pornographic Magazines	1.64 (1.46)	0.93 (1.41)	−2.21*	0.495
Purchase Pornographic Magazines	0.23 (0.52)	0 0	−2.35*	0.626
View Pornographic Videos	1.33 (1.21)	0.59 (1.27)	−2.72*	0.597
Purchase Pornographic Videos	0.24 (0.43)	0 0	−2.96*	0.789
View Internet Pornography	2.48 (1.54)	1.62 (1.59)	−2.48*	0.549

Note: GM = gay men; HM = heterosexual men; 0 = none; 1 = once or twice; 2 = three or four times; 3 = five to ten times; 4 = more than ten times; *$p < .01$; d = Cohen's d (.2 = small effect; .5 = moderate effect; .8 = large effect).

Hypothesis 3: Muscle and Fitness Magazines, Pornography Consumption, and Body Dissatisfaction

It was hypothesised that increased consumption of muscle and fitness magazines and pornography will correlate positively with scores on the EAT, DMS, and SPAS. For this analysis, overall measures of both muscle and fitness magazine and pornography exposure were created. The muscle and fitness measure calculated mean usage, as defined by the two questions related to viewing and purchasing of muscle and fitness magazines. The pornography measure calculated mean usage, as defined by the five questions related to consumption of various types of pornography. Cronbach's alphas for the overall measure of muscle and fitness usage was .72 and for overall pornography consumption, .67.

TABLE 2. Body Image Scale Comparisons (Standard Deviations in Parentheses)

Source	Consumption GM	HM	t
Eating Attitude Test	2.59 (0.57)	2.17 (0.42)	−3.57*
Drive for Muscularity Scale	2.93 (0.97)	2.81 (0.89)	−0.57
Social Physique Anxiety Scale	2.93 (0.99)	2.57 (0.79)	−1.75

Note: GM = gay men, HM = heterosexual men; *$p < .01$; Cohen's d for the significant t-test is .839.

While these alphas are not excellent, there are adequate for the exploratory nature of the current analysis.

For the gay men in this study, hypothesis 3 was supported in that those who read/purchased more muscle and fitness magazines reported higher levels of social physique anxiety, a greater drive for muscularity, and a greater desire for thinness (see Table 3). Similar results were found for heterosexual men, except for the correlation between muscle and fitness magazine consumption and social physique anxiety, which failed to reach significance. With regards to pornography, a positive correlation was obtained between social physique anxiety and pornography exposure for gay men. There were no other significant correlations between pornography consumption and the body image measures for either gay or heterosexual men.

Exploratory Analysis

Several scales were utilised in this study that were not directly related to the hypotheses regarding media usage and body image. These include a measure of self-esteem, a depression inventory, and a measure of social desirability. If relationships were found between these measures and muscle and fitness magazine or pornography exposure in either gay or heterosexual men, such data would prove important. The

TABLE 3. Body Dissatisfaction and Media Usage Correlations

	1.	2.	3.	4.	5.
1. Social Physique Anxiety	-	0.32**	0.58**	0.27*	0.28*
2. Drive for Muscularity	0.42*	-	0.31*	0.05	0.42**
3. Eating Attitudes Test	0.27	−0.04	-	0.04	0.30*
4. Pornography Usage	−0.16	0.08	0.16	-	0.27*
5. Muscle and Fitness Usage	0.22	0.44*	0.54**	0.28	-

Note: Correlations for gay men above the diagonal and correlations for heterosexual men below the diagonal; * $p < .05$ (2-tailed); ** $p < .01$ (2-tailed).

only statistically significant finding that emerged was a negative correlation between self-esteem and pornography exposure in heterosexual men, $r = -.40$ $p < .05$, $n = 29$.

DISCUSSION

This study indicates that gay men consume larger amounts of pornography than do heterosexual men. Taken at face value, this result might indicate that the consumption of pornography is more accepted in the gay community or that it is more acceptable to admit to its consumption, which in some ways might represent perceived acceptance. It also is possible that gay men believe their lifestyle is not accepted by society in general and that, consequently, there is no need to accept the status quo that pornography is taboo. Conversely, heterosexual men may have been socialised to believe that pornography is "dirty" and that they should deny using it.

Regardless of who uses more, pornography exposure is prolific. In the current study, over 72% of heterosexual participants and over 98% of non-heterosexual participants reported consuming some type of pornographic material during the past month. As far as the medium of choice for this consumption, participants overwhelmingly favoured the Internet by a margin of nearly 2 to 1. Viewing magazines was the next most popular pornographic outlet, followed by viewing movies. Purchasing either magazines or movies was least popular.

These results indicate that there is no shortage of images to which a man may compare himself. Even if the participant did not consume pornography in the last month, there are plenty of other venues in which body comparisons can be made. In fact, one-third of those in the "no-pornography" category reported either viewing or subscribing to muscle and fitness magazines or male fashion magazines within the last month. The results of this study indicate that increased exposure to such magazines is related to decreased body satisfaction regardless of sexual orientation.

As well, the results indicate that gay men are more concerned with thinness than are heterosexual men, as reported by scores on the EAT. On average, non-heterosexuals scored much higher than heterosexuals, which indicated poorer eating attitudes and a greater desire to be thin. Also, when asked about dieting habits, over 26% of the gay men sampled reported being on a diet to lose weight. None of the heterosexual men sampled reported being on any kind of weight loss program. Eight percent of participants sampled reported being on a diet to gain weight, but there was no relationship between this factor and either muscle/fitness magazine or pornography exposure.

Limitations

There are several limitations to this study that need to be addressed. First, the sample size is relatively small and the participants were self-selected. A larger sample size, taken from a more diverse population, would have allowed us to conduct multivariate data analyses that permit testing the proposed interaction between sexual orientation, body image, and pornography exposure. Second, since this study was Internet based, the geographic location of participants is unknown. Caution, therefore, should be used when generalising the results to specific geographic areas. It also should be noted that because this was an Internet study, participants were required to have access to, and knowledge of, computers.

Another limitation was that ethnic identity was not measured. The rationale behind this decision was that it is necessary to identify that a robust phenomenon exists before narrowing it down to specific ethnic or other cultural identities. Therefore, it was important to see *if* there was a significant relationship between body image and other variables such as pornography usage. If no relationship existed, there would be little reason for further study. Also, there was an attempt to keep the survey manageable in size. That being said, however, ethnic minority status could potentially play a major role in one's body image.

Finally, the current study operated from the assumption that gay and heterosexual pornography are similar. It is plausible that the two forms of media are distinct and, thus, possess different implications vis-à-vis body image. For example, in gay pornography, the male body likely receives more attention in terms of close-ups than in heterosexual pornography. Also, gay pornography may place greater emphasis on the attractiveness of the male body.

Future Directions

One of the limitations of a purely quantitative study is that questions are limited to Likert-type or numerical response items. While necessary for statistical analysis, quantitative data often lack the depth needed to truly understand an issue. Therefore, qualitative research may serve to expand researchers' understanding of the relationship between media imagery and male body image. The current study found that gay men are more concerned than heterosexual men with being thin, but failed to provide any insight as to why this is the case. A qualitative study may be able to tease out this information by supplying open-ended questions to participants that ask about this relationship in greater detail. Also, while the current study found no differences in the drive for muscularity between heterosexuals and non-heterosexuals, the latter spent more time weight training than the former (although this finding fell just short of statistical significance). These results indicate a need for further investigation.

CONCLUSION

Qualitative research, as outlined above, may provide insight as to how a small group of men feel about their bodies by looking at unconstrained responses to questions and scenarios about these issues. A more thorough understanding of the experiences of men with respect to body image may be required to advance inquiry in this area. Intriguing questions remain when one considers what has been observed. For example, according to current research, similarities and differences exist between gay and heterosexual men in terms of body image. Although gay men demonstrate poorer eating attitudes and spend more time weight lifting than do heterosexual men, both groups evidence a considerable amount of anxiety about showing their physiques in public. This is an interesting phenomenon. One explanation that reconciles these findings might hinge on the proliferation of media images in today's society that denote trim and healthy idealized males. These images deliberately create expectations of what men are supposed to look like and may be more damaging than commonly supposed. Women may have been confronting these issues for quite some time, but considering the issues with respect to men is a relatively new line of inquiry. Maybe it is time to take a page out of the feminist handbook in learning how to deal with such negative messages and expectations. We spend a great deal of time with others. How we feel about ourselves in relation to those around us is very important to our quality of our life. Increasing this quality makes research of this kind vital.

REFERENCES

Davis, J., & Oswalt, R. (1992). Societal influences on a thinner body size in children. *Perceptual and Motor Skills, 74*, 697-698.

Garner, D. M., Garfinkel, P.E., Schwartz, D., & Thompson, M. (1980). Cultural expectations of thinness in women. *Psychological Reports, 47*, 483-491.

Garner, D. M., Olmstead, M. P., Bohr, Y., & Garfinkel, P. (1982). The Eating Attitudes Test: Psychometric features and clinical correlates. *Psychological Medicine, 12*, 871-878.

Lin, L. F., & Kulik, J. A. (2002). Social comparison and women's body satisfaction. *Basic and Applied Social Psychology, 24*, 115-123.

Martin, K. A., Rejeski, W. J., Leary, M. R., McAuley, E., & Bane, S. (1997). Is the Social Physique Anxiety Scale really multidimensional? Conceptual and statistical arguments for a unidimensional model. *Journal of Sport & Exercise Psychology, 19*, 359-367.

McCreary, D. R. (1997). Media influences. In S. W. Sadava & D. R. McCreary (Eds.), *Applied social psychology* (pp. 209-227). Upper Saddle River, NJ: Prentice-Hall.

McCreary, D. R., & Sasse, D. K. (2000). An exploration of the drive for muscularity in adolescent boys and girls. *Journal of American College Health, 48*, 297-304.

Paulhus, D. L. (1991). Measurement and control of response bias. In J. P. Robinson, P. R. Shaver & L. S. Wrightsman (Eds.), *Measures of personality and social psychological attitudes* (pp. 17-59). New York: Academic Press.

Pope, H. G., Phillips, K. A., & Olivardia, R. (2000). *The Adonis complex: The secret crisis of male body obsession.* New York: The Free Press.

Radloff, L. S. (1977). The CES-D Scale: A self-report depression scale for research in the general population. *Applied Psychological Measurement, 1*, 385-401.

Rosenberg, M. (1965). *Society and the adolescent self-image.* Princeton, NJ: Princeton University Press.

Salusso-Deonier, C. J., Markee, N. L., & Pedersen, E. L. (1993). Gender differences in the evaluation of physical attractiveness ideals for male and female body builds. *Perceptual and Motor Skills, 76*, 1155-1167.

Siever, M. D. (1994). Sexual orientation and gender as factors in socioculturally acquired vulnerability to body dissatisfaction and eating disorders. *Journal of Consulting and Clinical Psychology, 62*, 252-260.

Silverstein, B., & Perdue, L. (1988). The relationship between role concerns, preferences for slimness, and symptoms of eating problems among college women. *Sex Roles, 18,* 101-106.

Stice, E., Schupak-Neuberg, E., Shaw, H. E., & Stein, R. (1994). Relation of media exposure to eating disorder symptomatology: An examination of mediating mechanisms. *Journal of Abnormal Psychology, 103,* 836-840.

If You Look at It Long Enough . . .

Paul Hallam

Kingston University

SUMMARY. "If You Look at It Long Enough . . ." is a user's account–40 years of looking at pornography. It attempts to raise issues around gay studies and academic "detachment." It is, to a great extent, autobiographical. But it also is the voice of a character speaking. A persona. It is a tribute to pornography and pornographers. *[Article copies available for a fee from The Haworth Document Delivery Service: 1-800-HAWORTH. E-mail address: <docdelivery@haworthpress.com> Website: <http://www.HaworthPress.com> © 2004 by The Haworth Press, Inc. All rights reserved.]*

KEYWORDS. Gay pornography, pornography, sexual fantasy, masturbation, gay men, gay culture, ageing, autobiography

---

Paul Hallam has written or co-written numerous screenplays including *A Kind of English*, *Caught Looking*, *Nighthawks*, *Strip Jack Naked* and *Young Soul Rebels*. He has written a play, *The Dish*, performed in London, New York, and Toronto. A BBC Radio 4 adaptation of *The Dish* was broadcast in August 1998. His first book, *The Book of Sodom*, was published by Verso. He is currently working on a second, *For the Asking: The Promise of Prostitution*. He also is writing *Raw Material*, a book on diaries. His current *Briefplay* series on prostitute/client relations is appearing in various forms–performance, video and publication–and he is working on *Bookmobile*, an equally multifaceted art/design research project. He was Writer in Residence at Central Saint Martins College of Arts and Design (1996-1997) and continues to teach there, at Kingston University and at the Canterbury School of Architecture. Correspondence may be addressed: 21 Hurst House, Penton Rise, London, WC1X 9ED, United Kingdom (E-mail: paul@paulhallam.worldonline.co.uk).

[Haworth co-indexing entry note]: "If You Look at It Long Enough . . ." Hallam, Paul. Co-published simultaneously in *Journal of Homosexuality* (Harrington Park Press, an imprint of The Haworth Press, Inc.) Vol. 47, No. 3/4, 2004, pp. 59-74; and: *Eclectic Views on Gay Male Pornography: Pornucopia* (ed: Todd G. Morrison) Harrington Park Press, an imprint of The Haworth Press, Inc., 2004, pp. 59-74. Single or multiple copies of this article are available for a fee from The Haworth Document Delivery Service [1-800-HAWORTH, 9:00 a.m. - 5:00 p.m. (EST). E-mail address: docdelivery@haworthpress.com].

http://www.haworthpress.com/web/JH
© 2004 by The Haworth Press, Inc. All rights reserved.
Digital Object Identifier: 10.1300/J082v47n03_04

And how might I discuss my near daily dose of pornography, since pornography links my past to the present, the present of the watching of the porn, and links that present to future desires? Links pleasure to regret, memory to fantasy. It also is intensely personal, almost comically so. I found myself, on the rough draft, censoring myself. As if I didn't want anyone to know; porn as the last vestige of privacy. I've enjoyed porn since I was ten; few days have passed without a glance, or a more sustained, and often stained, look at it. Why then do I find it so difficult to give it proper consideration? Why do I hesitate slightly over the word "enjoyed"?

I wonder about the reader, the one who buys or borrows this publication. And I'm curious about the contributors. Who might use the frowned on "I" in their essay, declare an interest? Who will remain detached? Who will celebrate "self-abuse," my favourite term for wanking? I will be looking through this seminal publication in search of the "I" (the abused selves amongst you making notes). "Wank," that most common of the British terms for the act that usually, but not always, accompanies the viewing of porn, is useful and direct–yet it displeases me. Sometimes we watch, buttoned up, with friends. Sometimes we laugh, and sometimes porn is just a backdrop, pleasingly repetitive wallpaper. I find watching porn enjoyable whilst ironing, for example, but I wouldn't risk a combination of the two activities. "Jerk-off," too, displeases me; it sounds too hurried and erratic. The one hundred other terms– slang dictionaries have pages of them–also are dissatisfying. Mostly embarrassed words, comic-edged. I will stick to the condemnatory and curious "self-abuse." If the academic abused selves don't appear in this volume, this record, I will be disappointed. I hope that some of you, at least, will admit to porn's fascination and submit to its seduction.

Do words in an academic journal or in a book categorised "Gay Studies" have the same seductive power for you as, say, the videos you might hold in your collection? I trust that you have read or watched gay porn. That you have enjoyed it, and I wonder about your experience of it? I can only tell you about my own search for porn, from soft to hard, from porn disguised in academic tomes to the dirty bits of great literature. Even in charts, statistics and sociological surveys. A relentless search over decades, though I've cut down now. There is so much of it, too much of it on the Internet (too much for me I mean, I'm glad it's there). Not unlike many a newcomer to the Internet, a few years ago, my days were devoted to joining "Groups." I received hundreds of photos; some were sought out or requested, others just turned up as if by magic.

I was caught up in the semi-fictional games of the chat rooms and found myself awake, far too often, at 4 a.m. The addiction soon wore off.

Though porn is clearly marketed, targeted to appeal to a wide or a more selective but still substantial market, what I see in my videos, and look at in my porn collection, is not, of course, what you would see. I collect dirty videos. I have magazines and porn stories, photo porn kept for thirty years now, sometimes older porn found in junk shops. I wonder about the provenance of my junk shop porn. Was the viewer just bored? Relieved to be rid of it? Or did a lover or close friend of someone who had died recently take the material there? Whatever the reason, I thank those who kept the material in circulation; I thank as well all manner of sociologists, ethnologists, academics, book cover designers, collectors and curators for this wealth of material. I thank them for all the dirty bits found, rescued and brought to my attention. I thank all those who have celebrated porn, and even those who have condemned it. All who have led me to seek it out, the dubious and sometimes ruthless industry included. A "special thanks" to the actors. I watch you but you can't see me. I can be, and look, a total mess whilst watching you; I can relax in your company. You won't know what I'm thinking. Nor will anyone else. I can switch off the phone, and ignore the e-mails; mostly, I will have locked the door, making certain that no one is around. Gentlemen, I address you privately; gentlemen, I watch you privately. Gentlemen, I thank you publicly.

But I'm never precisely sure who or what you are, and what pornography is. A few porn pics from my own life might shed some light, but then again, they might entirely confuse the issue.

To watch pornography is to disrupt time, to play with memory and to look forward to scenarios unlikely to happen. It rarely just simply takes me back, as does, say, a photo album. My relationship with porn favourites has lasted as long as, if not longer than, love and as long as my most valued friendships. A lover wanted me to get rid of my sizeable collection. Instead, I hid it. He perceived my looking at a magazine or a porn video as betrayal, unfaithfulness, a lack of attention to our relationship, to him. When the relationship broke up (or rather changed to a different relation) the porn was awaiting my return. It came out of the cupboard, back in the open. I was, once again, on my own. Living on your own, you can leave the magazines around, return to them. There might be the dilemma–hide or show–when family or friends visit, or when the repairman calls. A classic role, the repairman, in many a porn scene. Perhaps then the porn should come out of hiding in a kind of hope/fantasy that it might trigger action. If you live alone, porn can be there for more relaxed viewing, not just looked at in the time it takes to wank (followed by its swift return to the hiding place). You can develop a friendlier relation with the porn images; an altogether more drawn out, day-to-day affair. An affair that allows for accident/incident with whomever might (but probably won't) enter your flat. And if he does, it's unlikely that he will fulfil the fantasy repairman role. Repair or reparation. The fantasy figure, at least, provides some small compensation for all the things that went wrong with the more "ordinary" relations–family, best friends and lovers included.

Self-abuse is an extraordinary mix of fictional plays. The fantasies, triggered by porn, so often included the lover both before and after the breakup. In looking at porn, I'm looking for reminders/remainders of sexual encounters; there's nostalgia to the looking. I'm astonished how, even in mass-produced porn, I find a trace of someone met, a one-night stand, a childhood sexual experience, a longer-term lover. Older porn takes me back to haircuts and pullovers and wallpapers past. And, always, it reminds me of age and death. Boys from the seventies; some will be dead now, of course. The haircuts, oddly, the most off-putting feature, but given the right face and body, I can mentally crop the hair, cut it short back and sides. I can play with the image like a doll I might dress. It's as hard to describe the porn experience as it is to describe a dream. Collectors are notorious for their obsessive focus on particular acts, particular moments, repetitions and variations on them. For me, the relation with porn is more like an exploration of the "what if?" The possible but unlikely relations, playful in a way that reality seldom is. I can watch almost anything "adult." "Scat," perhaps, excepted. But "scat," too, I've watched with a kind of fascination, even a kind of concern. Misplaced concern, maybe; the "scat" boys certainly appeared to be enjoying themselves.

* * *

First there was Pete, aged nine, a rapidly maturing friend. Pete's brother had a drawer full of the stuff. Roneo machine porn, stories in lilac ink. I remember a rape in a railway carriage. A woman alone–alone that is until three men joined her. There was no corridor permitting her escape. We would take the story, should Pete's parents be out at the pub, to Pete's bedroom to read it. "What do men do to women?" Pete would ask. I had no clue. We improvised on the theme, the mimicry of adult behaviour based on porn. It led to my first oral sex. (I didn't think much of it at the time.) It introduced me to the importance of nipples. To this day, if we play, I want your exposed chest as much as your cock. Well, with Pete I got to play "the woman," and fiction turned into a different kind of fact/act. I've never understood the argument that pornography doesn't trigger action. It might not be a predictable or an immediate action. I have never been involved in a rape scene or rather I have never tried to rape. I did watch a girl once, Avril, have her small breasts exposed by Pete. I remember the unbuttoning of her blouse. It went no further. I was part of our small street gang (boys only) watching. I wanted it to go further, but only so that I could see more of Pete. I remember endlessly rereading bits of the Bond novels around that time. Bond's shirt seemed forever to be unbuttoned by the girls. Pete was my Bond. Or perhaps I've confused him with Sean Connery, that handsome face and hairy chest in the films. Pete was "mature" for his age, but not that mature. I wasn't entirely happy with my casting in Pete's porn-based scenarios, but it seemed, at the time, worth the compromise. Pete needed the excuse of porn and a sex education/teaching role. I knew what I wanted: Pete. He is now part of my porn collection, though I have no photograph. And, if truth be told, so is Avril. Her firm breasts, small and sweet. It's only memory, imprecise memory, yet with many a detail. It's strange that I remember him, and remember her so often whilst watching porn tapes, forty years on.

He isn't a 9-year-old boy. I'm not having sex with a 9-year-old. He has grown. Perhaps his shape relates to the "adult material" I'm watching now in some strange way. He is a "type" that is endlessly reproduced. The "boy next door" category in porn catalogue promotions. Though the boy next door is probably married and in a room where the fittings and furnishings, the textiles and the bed, are chosen by his wife. Much sexier for me than the jock/locker room scenarios. I've yet to see this porn film, men against a backdrop of flounce, chosen by women. A chest against a purple or a pink sheet, floral wallpaper. If you have come across this sort of tape, let me know . . .

Rewriting Pete, re-envisaging him. Adding porn memories to "real" ones. I've met the odd boy next door in my time. The porn based relation leading to a kind of imagined relation. What would it be like to be with the boy next door? Or to be with the girl next door, or to be, perhaps, a part of their relationship? To play "Uncle Paul"? I await the porn script.

* * *

I was once locked in a classically dank basement, I thought I might never get out, not unless I submitted. We met in an ornate Victorian-style, mirrored pub. I had a ticket to the opera and was determined not to miss it. We agreed to meet later, near his home, by a tube station in a smart part of London. To my surprise, he turned up. He took me to a flat with metal bars on the windows. He locked the door. I had no choice really, and this, I quickly realised, was a major mistake. I hope you are imagining the scene, and enjoying it; adding your own memories and fantasies. I didn't enjoy it at the time. Revised recollections have failed to transfigure it. I could give you more detail, the room, dark and fetid, with hideous wallpaper. You might like that. Or I could transform it into a glossy and glamorous scenario. I could let you pick and choose from the available options you have seen and read so many times before. Add or subtract details that make it work for you. Delete all reference to "opera," for example. Closer? Was he wearing the cleanest of briefs, or baggy boxers, stained? If I add that he was handsome and smooth, would it ruin the fantasy or make it more appealing? Would you prefer ugly and rough? Can you avoid certain words and add your own memories to the scene? Does cock size matter? I have no memory of his cock, only that I had to take it, as quickly as possible, in order, I hoped, to be allowed out.

I could tell you about a different lover, an earlier one who loved porn. That was a more "open" relationship; I wasn't jealous of his affairs and adventures, I was envious. I wanted to be a part of them. He went out one evening. Just cruising. The man who picked him up took him back to a flat. Others lay in wait. They tied him up. A gang-bang. I did manage to transform that scenario, in spite of the damage that was done to him. The porn fantasy seemed to make the reality of a messy, painful and hideous experience easier for both of us. He admitted that, in retrospect, once he was over the shock and the pain, it seemed like a sexy thing to have happened. I could read from the book or show you the film version of Hubert Selby's *Last Exit to Brooklyn,* complete with searing music, and remind you of the rag-doll character, Tralala, gang-banged, a bottle pushed inside her. Tralala abandoned and finally done with. To have done with. To be done with. I could transform *Last Exit* into a gay scenario, though I suspect the scene was sexy enough for gay men, with the rapists, in turn, unbuttoning. Guilt, perhaps, at reading/seeing the rape, but a sexiness tinged with sorrow. Another function of porn. To get rid of the painful memory, play with it, transfigure it.

Porn is part of the history of every room I've ever lived in, and I've lived in many. Every window that I've regularly and repeatedly looked out from. Often transfixed and reluctant to move from the desk, always placed with an eye to the view. Every room with a stash of porn under the bed. The fantasies so often combine the view with the hidden material, the private collection. The self-abuse draws them inexorably into one dreamlike picture, a picture I need to possess only for the time it takes to cum. Porn: your very own picture gallery, one that permits you to slip and slide between images. It needs no museum, no home, no walls, and little money. Not even a picture hook, nails and a hammer. Cheap pictures easily acquired. Landscapes/ladscapes. The images you create watching porn would be almost impossible to reproduce. You can't sell them, share them, make a print of them or pass them on. The images you create might be blurred, awkward and imperfect, but they are, perhaps, beyond value. It is astonishing how fantasies, unless interrupted by the day-to-day ("Did I switch that iron off?") forever give satisfaction; how they seem for that moment, just right. And no one is around to bother you, as they are in a gallery. No irritating voices, no security guard, no gift shop seller. All of them miraculously disappear from the scene. You don't need to buy a catalogue, though you might have created a rough and ready one, a cheap one of your own. Even that is a catalogue you are unlikely to cling to. You will let it fall from your hands as the perfect relation with the image, the perfect moment, arrives. And you can replace and replenish your handmade catalogue, create your own "private view," complete with drinks and whatever else might assist the pleasure. You need no fully annotated and referenced guide. You have picked and mixed a hundred images, and there is no academic requirement to cite your sources. No need for a list of illustrations starting with Fig. 1.

Is pornography any different from voyeurism? Revisiting the walks, often carefully taken. Always passing that window, on that side of the road, at that time of day when the time is right, when that building site is, weather depending, in full and shirtless progress. Or that chanced on, once only moment, forever remembered. I get to edit, of course, and I'm not trying to attract another viewer. I'm not trying to make money out of the man, or out of the home movie running in my head. But the repeat, that man with the child on his shoulders, seen from the back, close, tight hair. Tattoos, but small, discreet almost. Walking in front of him, pretending to be watching the Red Devil Air Display, red, blue and white spray in the sky, a striped smoke. He keeps coming back to me. He entered my diary and my private porn collection. Remembering him, regretting now that brief and silent pleasure on an otherwise dull day. Few published diary entries record so many acutely important, at that time, on that day, men. The men the writer deliberately watched for hours or quickly walked past, day after day. Walks and windows, forever staring, hoping that if I look at it long enough . . .

Is pornography just a fixation, wank fodder? Is it trying to tease out something more, something new? Is it adding to experience or erasing it? It is certainly irresponsible, or perhaps an avoidance of responsibility, an avoidance of intimacy, a sin in so many eyes. Call me irresponsible, call me unreliable. Call me a wanker.

> Another explanation for the artist's fragility is, paradoxically, the resoluteness and the insistence of his gaze. Power, of whatever form, because it is violence, never gazes; if I were to gaze a minute more (a minute too long), it would lose its essence as power. He, the artist, pauses and gazes closely, and I can imagine that you became a filmmaker because the camera is an eye, that is, constrained by its technical nature to gaze. What you add, as do all great filmmakers, is to gaze at things radically, to the point of exhausting them. . . . This is dangerous, because gazing at something far longer than you were asked to (I insist on this supplement of intensity) upsets the established order in whatever form, since the extent or the very duration of the gaze is normally controlled by society. Whence–if the work escapes this control–the scandalous nature of certain photographs and certain films, not the most indecent or the most aggressive ones, but merely the ones that are the most "posed." (Barthes, 1989)

Perhaps it is too grand a claim for pornography, but then again, surely the authorities are worried about something else in pornography, something other than the preservation of family values, the protection of women, the exploitation of children? Trotted out equally often, another complaint. Porn is a rip-off industry. Often, the makers want you to look at the tape again, to trust their product whilst also persuading you with teasers/trailers to purchase another. The next tape in the series or all of the tapes featuring one of their models. Of course, much the same goes for many a consumer product. It can't be the commercial exploitation that so offends the detractors of porn. Note their silence and indifference when the customers/clients/"punters," should they pluck up the courage, report porn and peep show rip-offs; worse when punters die in porn cinema blazes. What is it about this sort of material that so bothers the authorities? Could it be that the porn viewer squanders time? That pornographer plays with time courtesy of edits and repetitions of the notorious "cum shot" in particular? The pornographer hooks the viewer, plays with him, and makes him play with himself. The sheer sterile waste of it all. Perhaps to squander time is a kind of resistance.

To look forward to scenarios which are unlikely to happen. And to look back on and revise your relations; even relations with old porn favourites. So many tapes I've watched repeatedly have finally jammed in the video player or, if bought cheaply, their colours have slowly dissolved. Then the frustration. Can you find another copy of that particular "Russian Soldier" tape when you need it? New titles only in stock. Just as with favourite books, favourite films, you revise your relations with old porn, the porn you keep, the porn that survives. You might find that certain images no longer work; yet, you hang on to them. Much as you might keep a photo of an ex-lover. The look of the lover changes, of course, if you keep in touch, if you see him over the years. The porn image remains the same. New models arrive, new tapes. The contemporary "ideal" changes: new styles, new haircuts and clothes, new markets, new openings for boys from new countries. Fresh to-be-desired images. The old ones, though you might retain affection for them, seem seriously past their sell-by or their imaginary shag-by date. To be stashed away, perhaps to make a rare reappearance, an eventual comeback. If you calculate the age and condition of the old model now, it could be off-putting.

As I get older, I find that I want increasingly to detach myself from the business of "present" sex. I don't go out with the intention of finding it, or even a lover, anywhere near as often as I used to. In some ways, I prefer my adventures secondhand, pornographic ones created for myself and thousands of others. Or I might prefer an Internet connection. Tell me your story; show me your image. Send it, addressed to me, electronically or privately in the post and under "plain cover." I don't really want to join my dated German video suburban bisexual orgy, but I might enjoy observing it. On tape, on the Net, or in the flesh. Any which way really. To observe action, to not be a part of it. To delete myself, even from the fantasy scenarios. I never felt totally outside of porn before. I was always looking for that be-shorted boy in the tree, a picture kept for years. I was the one that converted the soft-core porn (stipulated by UK law) into something altogether more hard and harsh. I have abused myself with so many boys, times, places, texts and images, all to the accompaniment of a vast range of music (from the tape or, volume turned down low, from my own music collection). I've been aided and abetted by all manner of toys, ointments and apparatus. I've found comfort and consolation in courtroom dramas, old documents. The clinically reported sodomitical acts, from the eighteenth century to the present. Imagined the circumstances and acts that led to the imprisonment, and even to the death, of the participants. The changing shape of my desires, from the rare and snatched images found in the 1960s, mostly American physique magazines, to the occasional English boy next door. Now it tends to be the boy next country or next continent. The Web assists the search. (Thank you, Google.) Porn from the Arab world, from North Africa, often produced in France. Marseille now my fantasy city. A porn World Cup. The cup filleth and the cup runneth over. Is that the phrase?

Pictures of miners, pictures of sailors, pictures of footballers, they're still in my collection, mixed with memories of those older fantasies, the boy next door, even a football player brother-in-law. I can create interracial scenarios, mix images of people met; the cute but scarred, the damaged, and the "drugfuct" (recent slang–almost affectionate) boys in clubs included. Added to that, my witnessing of many a prostitute/client exchange, the show courtesy of a male prostitute friend. The watching was always with the client's consent, and seeming pleasure. I looked on, sometimes for hours. A privilege, a pleasure that returns, often as I'm watching an unrelated porn tape. A mad, shifting and joyous porn theatre in my head.

Nowadays when I watch porn, I'm not exactly detached, but, like many of the performers, I'm not that engaged either. I look for a degree of realism in the facial expression, the moments when the guard drops, when the pleasure seems genuine. I'm fascinated by the clothes (and hate it when the film starts with the actors already near naked). I'm caught by the backdrops, the detail, the bedding, the landscape. Backdrops that I suspect often belong to the filmmaker. A curious relation of the actors to the set to the maker, rare in mainstream film. Rough boys in smart apartments. I enjoy the often clumsy relation of performer to the unfamiliar surroundings, unlikely objects. I love tapes with words, the awkward dialogue. Sometimes the performer will introduce himself to another performer, or directly to the camera (and, thus, to you the viewer). Often, the dialogue is in a language I don't understand, or it's simply a verbally embarrassed performance, or the shoddy sound quality makes it impossible to hear. People complain about the lack of narrative in porn; I welcome the "trite" stories and scenarios, I can add subplots of my own. I realise that often, though I'm enjoying the view, the acts themselves no longer necessarily fascinate or even appeal to me.

From John S. Barrington's 1950s and 1960s collections, under such titles as *The Male Nude in Fine Art* through to the much later and little known *Barbican Tapes*, I retain a fondness for the amateur, especially when the "straight" man is "caught" by the gay camera. For the *Barbican Tapes*, an antique collector handed out cards to boys in and around this exclusive City of London estate. They might model sportswear, swimwear, skateboard clothes. Paid modelling possibilities on offer. He caught a number of skateboarding boys on the expensive city estate; others were city boys. They came round. They might have been shown his razor collection. An alarming collection, to say the least; blades from across the world. Don't ask me how I know. The boys posed, as if for a collection of catalogue/mail-order clothes. If they were interested, they could view a sample portfolio of men undressing. Catalogues with varying degrees of the explicit. They might, if interested, care to look at the orgies. The videos were recorded for his own purposes, he assured them, unless they were interested in sales to magazines. The tapes were circulated around London, an underground network of tape deliveries. Specialist, seemingly "straight" male pose stuff. Some stayed in swimwear, some wanked, and some joined the circle jerks. Tapes passed on and sold for gay consumption. Real boys in real clothes undressing and then trying on his handy and cherished collection of menswear. My memory is hazy, as I had to return the borrowed tapes. I was sad to lose sight of them. A friend who suddenly wanted to rid himself of his addiction sold them on. I do have fragments of my notes on the tapes; a few words that bring back to life the not entirely handsome and elderly man who kept leaving his camera on the tripod to give the boys a hand. I remember his posh and squeaky voice. And the Irish, I think, soft-spoken voice of the awkward model. Sadly, the Irishman's words have long gone.

> Can you stand with your back to the light? . . . black pants on . . . do some muscle poses? . . . fantastic . . . yes . . . slightly to the left . . . Smile . . . do a back view . . .

Dozens did this, thousands do it. It seems that thousands of boys enjoy being photographed the world over. Thousands, I think, want a record of their bodies. Prime-time flesh on tape. I don't believe that the majority were either conned or desperate for the cash. I've seen the desperate ones–they're not hard to spot. Often, there are marks on their arms, or in their eyes. From 1962 to 2002, from ages 10 to 50, I have looked, starting with stories, through to downloaded video clips from the Net. I've only ever (thanks to new technology) made one porn appearance myself. A man I was having sex with, unusually for me, in an alley, after meeting in a pub (turned out he had been at the funeral wake for a friend), asked if he could use his digital camera. I was startled and flattered and I hope, a few years on, that he still enjoys the show.

Many a tape has broken, but I've kept most of my porn collection. Even when the bulk and burden seems heavy, even when, on rare occasions, I resolved to cut down or give up. Only one or two videos have been altered, a careful taping over any hint of child-sex. Usually just carefully shot swimming pool images in ads for other tapes available from commercial gay porn companies of the 1970s and '80s. However, they had to go. Abusive adult stuff, in all its theatricality, I've held on to. The supplement to the collection: clips taped from TV (neatly labelled "News Clips"). Highlights from dramas, but also from the news, documentary transformed. ("News Clips" not an entirely euphemistic device for keeping the tapes from prying flatmate eyes.) I'm not alone in finding Israeli soldiers and their Palestinian prisoners sexy. News pictures find their way onto many a porn site. Then there is the notebook I kept; the record of the male prostitute's activities, a list of codes and words to describe every act, and every price. Words enough to trigger the memories. Walls of academic books, many of them "Gay Studies." Diaries of my window watching days . . .

Of late I've taken to "solo" acts, to the solitaries. I've abandoned the couples and the group sex tapes, or put them in cold storage. The current favourite is my collection of solo "beurs," the North African boys of Marseilles. The boys undress, sometimes looking to the camera as if to ask if they are doing what is required, doing what they're being paid for. Some look entirely off-screen, perhaps at a silent straight porn tape to keep the interest up? Most seem distant from the task, though some clearly enjoy their own bodies, and enjoy the display. A few of the boys, while cumming, even hold back on the final sigh. They won't allow you to think they're enjoying it. Why do I want to cum at the moment they do, especially the reluctant ones? Why do I enjoy their distance? I certainly relish their awkwardness in the striptease. And then the occasional spots, the "flaws" on their bodies, the scars and the cheap tattoos. The underwear selection that is clearly their own, not an item supplied on a glossy US porn production budget. It feels quite intimate, watching the solo boys, timing myself to their timing, though I can't do the repeat shots (that final moment shown over and over, shot from a range of angles). One of them reminds me of a man I once fell for and remain fond of. A bittersweet viewing.

* * *

My home is a book-lined flat. In the living room, the books are arranged, wall to wall, in blocks of colour. There is space on the shelving for a television screen, under a row of huge eighteenth century books. It's where I might watch the videos. It's the room that my flatmates have often brought friends back to, handsome friends. Sometimes they've had sex in the room. Just the sight of a handsome man in this room is far more exciting to me than a man in my bedroom. When the boys, or their guests, pass through the living room to the kitchen, they're often shirtless. Mostly unaware of the contents of the books lining the walls. Books with the footnotes I've found fascinating, books and their omissions, where asterisks mark the spot. Bowdlerised books. All my older books, alongside the more recent hardbacks. Hardbacks–their dust jackets taken off, naked, to let the sun or the lamp light catch their gold and silver stamped spines. My more academic collection is relegated to the hall; there's a section reserved for official "Gay Studies."

* * *

I've watched bodies in clubs for decades, but I mostly prefer to stay home now. A certain weariness has set in. For all the adventures, the gay scene–once my obsession–has grown tiresome. From gay liberation to government sanctioned forms of gay marriage. A withdrawal. I'm no longer anxious to pick up the weekly free gay papers, no longer keen to read the latest in gay studies, to see the newly opened gay film. I've stopped counting the gay men on TV. I try to keep in touch with news from more dangerous states. I know that the work isn't over. I know I'm unlikely to stop writing, at least part of the time, on gay themes. I'm weary.

But the porn boys still arouse me.

Porn plays its part in facing many things and in the avoidance of others. I'm never worried whilst watching it. When I'm with it, no mobile is allowed to ring, no e-mail can reach me. Nothing rushes through my mind; I forget the neverending "to be done" list. Porn is curiously moving in relation to thoughts of age and death. The photo, the video, a record of something already over; though you watch it as if it is taking place, right now, just in front of and for you. Old porn might remind you of how the models must have aged, new porn reminds you of those who will. Memories of old lovers (or hoped for ones) are part of my porn viewing. Memories of some that are dead now. But these memories are different from more ordinary ones. They ease and simplify past relations. They make me more benevolent, relieve me of responsibility, sometimes of guilt.

Boys in video boxes, by the books, including shelves of rare and old erotica. All the reading, all the searching, all the looking, all the memories contained in the room. The library would feel incomplete without that screen. Of late, I've been looking for porn featuring books. Well, for naked boys in rooms of books, naked boys occasionally reading them. I've found a few images. Should you happen to have any, in your private collection, let me know. Porn scenarios played out against a backdrop of words. Flesh and text. It's what I enjoyed with Pete and his brother's drawer of porn. It's what I enjoy now, forty years on. Porn tapes and photos in the library. Live flesh in the room is a bonus. (It does happen from time to time, but it's not essential or, at least, at this moment, it seems less essential than it did. If that makes me a sad, old pervert tucked away with my porn, so be it.)

Home Movie: My ideal would be a cum shot, the cum spilling onto the printed words, down the spines of the books. The spines naked with gold and silver lettering, the stains would remain and wouldn't wash out. My own private pornography. A remnant, a reminder, like the cum-stained underwear on sale in many a gay magazine. A desire for flesh against a backdrop of books, with minimal words, preferably foreign words, or broken English. Something not quite comprehended, certainly not there to be corrected. Simple, limited, and to me, at the time, oddly and pleasurably obscure. Men undressing and dressing in the living-room library. A couple of weeks ago there were two men in the living-room library. Guests of a flatmate, straight boys, one Greek, one French. They loved the room, they slept there on the pull-out couch. They were relaxed, comfortable, often shirtless. Sometimes just lounging, boxer shorts only. They flicked through the old volumes, noticed my bibliographies of banned books, the Victorian erotica, straight and gay. Picked up slang dictionaries, laughed at the language. The guests asked about the English for various words, for various acts. Neither appeared to have any problem with me, my age, my sexuality. I think I detected a mild flirtation. Intensely erotic for me, the memory might become part of my porn repertoire. I lie, it already is. It is a memory now. I never take photographs. But for a diary note, I have no record; I don't keep a spycam, though it has crossed my mind. I enjoyed talking to them about London, showed them guidebooks to the city, old and new. Red-light districts included. I wouldn't have wanted to try anything; the moment was too perfect as it was. Besides, it would never have worked. Face it, sometimes straight means straight. Close . . . so close to my fantasy scenario.

The video surrounded by so many autobiographies, biographies, books of diaries; few of them even mention porn. There are diary-based details of every love affair, occasionally of every one-night stand. But few diarists consider a wank to a porn image worthy of attention or mention. Samuel Pepys hinted at it once or twice, Gide too. Other diarists supply asterisks and codes. The great "Walter" of *My Secret Life* confessed all. Most of us take our memories of self-abuse with us to the grave. Many must be anxious to be rid of the source material before death. How many libraries, passed on, retain the owner's porn? I suspect my collection–fire or raid notwithstanding–will be with me till the end. I couldn't bear to see it go before I do.

Yes, porn is banal, repetitive, exploitative sometimes, but it isn't domestic; it is intense, but without the repercussions of desire. It's cleaner and less awkward than most encounters. It provokes a restless and insatiable need. Sometimes it substitutes for going out, for making an effort. It is a waste of time, but surely it's a glorious one? Surely it makes us think in different ways about our past, our hopes? It allows an escape from the flesh and its imperfections; takes away some of the pain of ordinary relations. Removes the aggravations and irritations of the day to day (unless, that is, the tape jams and, to your fury, unfurls in the machine). It's a well-known aid for insomniacs. I'd fallen asleep watching a porn tape on the night Diana died. I woke to the news on TV. (One of the first to know–such useless knowledge.) The tape had automatically switched off, and the BBC had returned. Some must have been watching old porn movies when Kennedy died or when Lennon was shot. No one seems to give that answer to the "What were you doing on the day . . . ?" question. Tasteless or not, it's also true I'd been watching a porn tape minutes before the live footage of 9/11 broke. I had just switched from video to the TV. I was the first to ring my friends, to tell them to turn on the television.

Do I make too large a claim for porn, too many claims? Perhaps. I can tell only my own experience, and at some of the bleakest moments in my life, when all else seemed to fail, it obliterated, if only for half an hour, all thoughts of the deaths of family, the deaths of friends. More respected forms of culture, working hard, and all those other tried and tested methods simply failed. They drew attention to the deaths, and perhaps brought useful tears. Porn is an anodyne. I feel a kinship with the millions of others who wallow in porn, find consolation in its confines. Porn admits an absolute focus. But if it can obliterate the thought of death, it also has the sneaky habit of reminding you, perhaps after the viewing, of the very thought it seemed to shut out. Orgasm has so often been described as "a little death," a poetic cliché. There are millions and millions of orgasms, forever spurting from the porn factories.

My porn fantasy home, featuring Paul Hallam (fully dressed) would be of a book-lined hotel room. People passing through the hotel. Always changing, always fresh faces, with a few older, retained favourites remaining. From the window, passing bathers, palm trees and a view of the sea. The room supplied with all the latest in cable, satellite, digital. All the right switches. Waiters and repairmen would drop by. Boys might visit, spit and spoil, spunk all over my books, my room, my fantasy. Spurt all over my much abused self.

REFERENCE

Barthes, R. (1989) "Dear Antonioni." In S. Chatman & G. Fink (Eds.), *L'avventura: Michelangelo Antonioni, director* (p. 212). New Brunswick, NJ: Rutgers University Press.

Homecoming:
The Relevance of Radical Feminism for Gay Men

Robert Jensen, PhD

University of Texas

SUMMARY. Sexual politics in the gay male world would be enhanced by a serious engagement with radical feminist politics, particularly critiques of pornography and the sex industry. As the domination/subordination dynamic at the heart of patriarchy damages homosexual men, such engagement is crucial to the future of a gay movement. *[Article copies available for a fee from The Haworth Document Delivery Service: 1-800-HAWORTH. E-mail address: <docdelivery@haworthpress.com> Website: <http://www.HaworthPress.com> © 2004 by The Haworth Press, Inc. All rights reserved.]*

KEYWORDS. Gay pornography, feminism, sex industry, gay men, gay culture, homosexuality, sexual politics, objectification

---

Robert Jensen is an associate professor in the School of Journalism at the University of Texas at Austin, where he teaches courses in media ethics, law, and politics. He is the co-author of *Pornography: The Production and Consumption of Inequality* and author of *Writing Dissent: Taking Radical Ideas from the Margins to the Mainstream*. Correspondence may be addressed: School of Journalism, University of Texas, Austin, TX 78712 (E-mail: rjensen@uts.cc.utexas.edu).

[Haworth co-indexing entry note]: "Homecoming: The Relevance of Radical Feminism for Gay Men." Jensen, Robert. Co-published simultaneously in *Journal of Homosexuality* (Harrington Park Press, an imprint of The Haworth Press, Inc.) Vol. 47, No. 3/4, 2004, pp. 75-81; and: *Eclectic Views on Gay Male Pornography: Pornucopia* (ed: Todd G. Morrison) Harrington Park Press, an imprint of The Haworth Press, Inc., 2004, pp. 75-81. Single or multiple copies of this article are available for a fee from The Haworth Document Delivery Service [1-800- HAWORTH, 9:00 a.m. - 5:00 p.m. (EST). E-mail address: docdelivery@haworthpress.com].

http://www.haworthpress.com/web/JH
© 2004 by The Haworth Press, Inc. All rights reserved.
Digital Object Identifier: 10.1300/J082v47n03_05

I am sexually homeless.

By that I do not mean I am confused about my sexuality, though my sexual desire has meandered all over the map and at various times I have wondered (as, I suspect, most people do at some point in their lives), "Just what the hell am I?" But, at 44 years of age, I have a reasonably clear sense of that map and the terrain I cover: I sometimes find myself attracted to men, other times to women. I am gay, except when I am straight. Call me bisexual if you like, though it is not how I identify myself. My sexual self-description is: I feel straight when I am with a woman and I feel gay when I am with a man. And during periods of celibacy, I bounce between the two.

Instead, my sense of homelessness grows out of the intersection of my sexuality and my politics. I came to understand my gayness through radical feminism (e.g., Frye, 1983) and, more specifically, through the radical feminist critique of pornography (Dworkin, 1988; MacKinnon & Dworkin, 1997). At the same time I was engaging those political philosophies and issues, I was working through personal questions about my sexuality. The political analysis, which highlighted the construction of sexuality and the power dynamics behind it, helped me to understand the personal in a new way, allowing me to move from being trapped in a conventional heterosexual life to a place where I could acknowledge and begin to express my desire for men. Once those things became clear to me, I felt an understandable sense of liberation, of hope for charting a new path that could combine my sexuality, sexual politics, and radical politics more generally. Nearly a decade later, my short-term optimism (though not necessarily my long-term hope) has mostly evaporated, primarily because I have found no community in which my sexuality and politics easily fit, except perhaps for the radical lesbian feminist community. That is the irony of it all–the source of the ideas that have helped me understand myself is unavailable to me in life. I have learned from radical lesbian feminism and have worked on intellectual and political projects with lesbian feminists, all to my benefit. But men simply cannot be part of some aspects of that community's social and sexual life.

The claim that I am sexually homeless does not mean that I cannot find anyone with whom I can share intimate, philosophical, or political connections. I am fortunate to have close friends with whom I have had a variety of relationships. I am not complaining that "nobody likes me" or that "I cannot find a date." I am surrounded by a number of people–gay and straight, men and women–whom I consider to be quite remarkable. I often meet individuals to whom I feel attracted and with whom I can imagine being intimate. I am fortunate to have an active professional and political life that provides satisfaction and a sense of accomplishment. If I were to continue in my current partner-less state indefinitely, I would not consider it a tragedy.

What concerns me most is not my own particular state of being at the moment but, rather, the state of the world. The fact that I can find no community in which I feel at home, in which I can integrate my sexuality, sense of self and political orientation, should be of no interest to others except for what it says about the wider culture. If I were to meet the man and/or woman of my dreams tomorrow, this question of community remains. Consequently, the objective for me–indeed, for all of us–should not simply be finding that "special someone" but, rather, helping to build such a community based (for me) on principles of justice and equality as understood within a radical framework.

Let me expand on my conception of sexuality and sexual politics. The radical feminist analysis in which my ideas are rooted identifies sexual activity as one of the key sites of the oppression of women by men. In patriarchy, sex is based on a dynamic of domination and subordination. Men, generally, are trained through a variety of cultural institutions to view sex as the acquisition of pleasure through adversarial relations with women. Sex is a sphere in which men are trained to see themselves as naturally dominant and women as naturally passive. Women are objectified and their sexuality commodified. Sex is sexy because men are dominant and women are subordinate; power is conceptualized as erotic. The predictable result is a world in which violence, sexual violence, sexualized violence, and violence-by-sex are so common that they must be considered normal; expressions of the sexual norms of the culture, rather than violations of those norms.

The foundation of this routine fusing of sexuality and various levels of violence is men's power over women, but in patriarchy other disparities of power such as race and ethnicity can be, and routinely are, sexualized. Power dynamics can be created–tops and bottoms, masculine and feminine–within same-sex relationships, even when the participants are of relatively equal status. The fact that people may move between those roles (that is, a man can be both a top and a bottom in a sexual relationship) does nothing to undermine the existence of those roles and the power dynamic of which they are an integral part. Instead of eroticising power, the radical feminist critique challenges us to eroticise equality. While we should work to eliminate the differences in power that stem from illegitimate authority such as sexism and racism, there is no way to equalize all differences in power that emerge because of people's differing talents and temperaments in specific situations (and, in fact, attempting to eliminate those differences would be disastrous). So, there will always be complex questions about power, even when people consciously work at establishing egalitarian relationships. The goal is not some totalitarian imposition of rules, but a constant awareness of how power differences are routinely sexualized and how that affects relationships. The task is to engage in critical self-reflection about the way those power relations affect the most intimate aspects of our lives and ask if there are not other ways to structure our lives that will be more satisfying.

Understanding the role power plays in sexuality is a complex endeavour; however, some integral components of that understanding are fairly straightforward. I believe that a fundamental tenet of a progressive sexual ethic is that people and their sexuality should not be bought and sold, that intimacy is not a commodity for the market. This assertion is based on a principle of justice and a sense of empathy, growing out of a conception of what I believe human beings are for, and a concern for those who are routinely and predictably hurt in such a system. That same sense of justice and empathy leads me to oppose capitalism more generally, again for that simple reason: People are people, not things to be used by others. But to remain focused on sexuality: If intimacy is an arena in which people have maximal freedom to explore themselves and others in relatively egalitarian relationships, sexuality can be a source of liberation. If intimacy is an arena in which people's erotic experiences are structured by dynamics of domination and subordination, sexuality can be a tool of control. Buying a person for sex is domination; in a world based on equality, sex would not be a commodity.

I am aware that some individuals clearly state they want to offer themselves and their sexuality for sale, whether it is in prostitution, pornography, strip bars, or other aspects of the sex industry (Delacoste & Alexander, 1998). I am not contesting their capacity to make such a decision. Instead, I am arguing for a different sexual ethic; my goal is not to harangue those who make that choice but instead to be part of a movement that tries to change the society so that the sex industry becomes obsolete. My goal is not to impose my sexual ethic on others, but to explain why I think a radical feminist critique is compelling and why the norms of the society should change.

I am aware that gay pornography has been one of the few sites where gay youth have been able to see representations of same-sex love and gay men have been able to see their desire for men validated. But these putative advantages do not mean that we must continue to accept this medium; rather, new, and perhaps better, ways to achieve self-affirmation should be pursued. I am not against the exploration of sexuality through art and literature but, instead, am arguing against the pornography industry's use of people to create profit, and not a deeper understanding of sexuality.

Pornography, straight or gay, often is defended on the grounds that it frees up people's sexual imaginations. I argue the opposite; pornography tends to limit our imaginations, forcing sexuality into channels that typically reproduce a domination/subordination dynamic. I am suggesting we should reject the commercialization and objectification inherent in the sex industry and look for new ways to validate gay sexuality.

This argument brings me back to my homelessness. I have met some men who are interested in these kinds of questions and this kind of analysis, and are willing to talk about it. But I have found very few gay men who are interested in this as a *political project*. That is, I have not met many gay men who are willing to publicly identify with (or sometimes even engage in) the radical feminist critique, and use that framework to analyze gay culture.

Let me be clear: By arguing this position I am not accepting the hackneyed stereotype that all gay men are promiscuous, bar hopping, bathhouse dwellers. Certainly that stereotype describes some percentage of the gay male world, and I think the radical feminist critique offers a way for gay men to critique those practices. But just as certainly there are many gay men involved in what the straight world would consider (if not for the same-sex partner) conventional relationships, and that same critique offers a way for us to examine aspects of those relationships as well. Unfortunately, there has not emerged in contemporary gay male culture significant space for a political and cultural project rooted in radical feminism or a radical politics more generally. In my experience, there is virtually no public critique of pornography and, more generally, the sex industry in the gay male world. To the degree there is critical discussion about promiscuity and the practice of anonymous sex, it is rooted mostly in conservative reaction against the "homosexual lifestyle." In my experience, most gay men consider these issues to be matters of personal preference, and not politics. Again, I am not arguing that gay men refrain from thinking or talking about such things, but that those discussions are conducted largely in private and rarely as part of a coherent political project rooted in an egalitarian ethic. The discussion among gay men that goes on in public is largely a contest between a sex liberal/libertarian position and those who want to see gay men fit into the existing heterosexual system. There are some notable exceptions to this, such as the work of Christopher Kendall (1995) and John Stoltenberg (2000), but I think this quick sketch is a reasonable account of the main currents in the culture.

Why is it the case that gay male culture seems to be invested in sexual objectification and commodification to a degree at least as intense as its heterosexual counterpart? The simple answer is that being gay does not automatically mean a rejection of patriarchy, its sexual ethic, or its values. The struggle against patriarchy is a political struggle, one in which people must make a choice to resist. For men, gay or straight, that means a choice to resist a system that in various ways gives us privilege. To recognise that gay men are discriminated against in society, in some ways, should not keep us from seeing the ways that they retain privileges as men.

Of course, the feminist analysis in which I am rooted is but one approach to gender and sexuality. Other men, gay and straight, may endorse other feminist analyses (including some that celebrate pornography and the sex industry) and may contend that they are just as committed to the end of patriarchy. I am not suggesting all other political positions are illegitimate but instead am making a case for the one I find most compelling. I believe a radical feminist analysis accounts for the evidence in an intellectually and morally honest fashion. It confronts difficult truths and offers a politics with integrity.

Given the brevity of this essay, I am not attempting a thorough defence of the radical feminist analysis or its relevance to gay life and politics. Instead, I am sketching my own alienation from gay politics and culture, perhaps with the hope that others, who see some aspect of their own experience reflected in these comments, will be motivated to look further into the work of these feminists.

After completing a book on heterosexual pornography a few years ago, I gave some thought to undertaking a similar project on gay pornography. I did not pursue it. One reason was because my intellectual and political interests were increasingly centred on understanding and resisting the threat to the people of the developing world that is posed by the militarism and greed of the United States government and the corporations that set its agenda. What time I allocate to other projects tends to focus on sexism and racism, places where–as a white man–I think I have compelling moral obligations. I return regularly to the feminist critique, issues of the sex industry, and the project of resisting patriarchy because I still believe the issues are important and because I think resistance is integral to my other political interests. Eroding the power of patriarchy will help in the struggle against militarism, capitalism, and racism.

But the decision to focus on other work also had to do with an assessment of what seemed possible at that moment in gay culture. I wish I saw more signs that these interests could find a home there, but for now I do not. However, I believe that over time, the value of radical feminism's resistance to patriarchy will become clearer to gay men. While it often seems more "realistic" politically for marginalized groups to work to carve out a space in the dominant society rather than challenge the fundamental patriarchal norms of that society, I think such an approach is dangerous. There are many compromises one makes in political struggles, and dogmatic assertions of political purity are mostly self-indulgent. But there is a great difference between making judgments about short-term compromises with an unjust system to advance a political project and accepting without question the unjust norms and principles on which the system is based. I believe that in the long run, a gay-rights movement that accepts the norms of commodification and objectification in capitalism and patriarchy will flounder. The future–if it is to be a decent one–lies in a consistent rejection of a world structured on domination, from the most intimate parts of our lives to the largest questions of global justice.

REFERENCES

Delacoste, F., & Alexander, P. (1998). *Sex work (2nd ed.)*. San Francisco, CA: Cleis Press.
Dworkin, A. (1988). *Letters from a war zone*. New York, NY: Dutton.
Frye, M. (1983). *The politics of reality: Essays in feminist theory*. Freedom, CA: Crossing Press.
Kendall, C. (1995). Gay male pornography and the sexualization of masculine identity. In L. Lederer & R. Delgado (Eds), *The price we pay: The case against racist speech, hate propaganda and pornography* (pp. 102-122). New York, NY: Farrar, Strauss & Giroux.
MacKinnon, C., & Dworkin, A. (1997). *In harm's way: The pornography civil rights hearings*. Cambridge, MA: Harvard University Press.
Stoltenberg, J. (2000). *Refusing to be a man: Essays on sex and justice*. New York, NY: Routledge.

Educating Gay Male Youth: Since When Is Pornography a Path Towards Self-Respect?

Christopher N. Kendall, SJD

Murdoch University

SUMMARY. In 2000, in the case of *Little Sisters Book and Art Emporium*, the Canadian Supreme Court was asked to determine whether gay male pornography violated the sex equality protections guaranteed by the *Canadian Charter of Rights and Freedoms*. Throughout this case, gay male activists and academics emphasised the risk posed by antipornography legal strategies to the dissemination of materials intended to promote safer sexual behaviour. Other arguments were advanced that gay male pornography should not be restricted because it serves as a learning tool for young men and, in so doing, does much to re-

Dr. Christopher N. Kendall is Dean of Law at Murdoch University in Perth, Western Australia, where he teaches and writes on law and sexuality, feminist jurisprudence, and equal opportunity law. He holds degrees from Queen's University, Canada, and the University of Michigan Law School and has published extensively in Canada, Australia, and the United States on the sex-based harms of gay male pornography. In 2000, Dr. Kendall was part of the litigation team acting for "Equality Now," in proceedings before the Supreme Court of Canada in the case of *Little Sisters Book and Art Emporium*. The author would like to thank Professor Catherine MacKinnon for her guidance and support throughout the writing of this work. Correspondence may be addressed: School of Law, Murdoch University Perth, Western Australia, 6150 (E-mail: kendall@central.murdoch.edu.au).

[Haworth co-indexing entry note]: "Educating Gay Male Youth: Since When Is Pornography a Path Towards Self-Respect?" Kendall, Christopher N. Co-published simultaneously in *Journal of Homosexuality* (Harrington Park Press, an imprint of The Haworth Press, Inc.) Vol. 47, No. 3/4, 2004, pp. 83-128; and: *Eclectic Views on Gay Male Pornography: Pornucopia* (ed: Todd G. Morrison) Harrington Park Press, an imprint of The Haworth Press, Inc., 2004, pp. 83-128. Single or multiple copies of this article are available for a fee from The Haworth Document Delivery Service [1-800-HAWORTH, 9:00 a.m. - 5:00 p.m. (EST). E-mail address: docdelivery@haworthpress.com].

http://www.haworthpress.com/web/JH
© 2004 by The Haworth Press, Inc. All rights reserved.
Digital Object Identifier: 10.1300/J082v47n03_06

duce the alarming incidence of gay youth suicide. The author examines these assumptions within the context of the gay male pornography defended in *Little Sisters*. His conclusion is that the present gay male obsession with hyper-masculinity, best evidenced in the pornography now widely touted by some gay men as a source of gay male identity and freedom, undermines safer sexual practices and the self-respect needed to combat youth suicide. The author concludes that gay men must commit to a sexuality built on mutuality, respect and caring (i.e., an identity politic built around sex equality). *[Article copies available for a fee from The Haworth Document Delivery Service: 1-800-HAWORTH. E-mail address: <docdelivery@haworthpress.com> Website: <http://www.HaworthPress.com> © 2004 by The Haworth Press, Inc. All rights reserved.]*

KEYWORDS. Gay pornography, pornography, feminism, sexual equality, gay culture, gay men, internalised homonegativity

Research on gay male youth highlights two issues that need immediate action from educators and social activists. The first is an alarming suicide rate among gay adolescents (Bagely, 1997; Jennings, 1994; MacDonald & Cooper, 1998; Martin, 1992; Urbine, 1992). The second is an apparent increase in HIV/AIDS transmission amongst young gay men between the ages of 17 and 22 (Bull, 1994).[1] These issues, and others, point to a generation of young gay men very much in need of self-acceptance.

In addressing these issues, many educators have, understandably, turned to the gay community in an attempt to develop strategies that counter the stereotypes and prejudices that cause both homophobia and self-harm amongst young gay men. While this is a necessary alliance, it is one that will prove inadequate unless gay men confront the types of messages their community sends out to young men about gay male sexuality and identity.

In Canada, the need for such an analysis has become particularly evident in light of a recent Supreme Court of Canada ruling on Canada's obscenity laws. The case, *Little Sisters Book and Art Emporium* (2000), dealt primarily with the legal regulation by Canada Customs of lesbian and gay male pornography. This paper will not analyse the facts of the *Little Sisters* case in detail, as this has been done elsewhere (Kendall, 1997). Of importance, however, insofar as the issue of educating gay male youth is concerned, are the arguments raised by the plaintiff, Little

Sisters, a lesbian and gay bookstore located in Vancouver, British Columbia, and a number of lesbian and gay groups that intervened on behalf of Little Sisters in an attempt to exclude same-sex pornography from legal regulation. The arguments advanced by these groups about the role pornography plays in educating gay youth, and the specific materials defended by them, say much about the types of sex-based messages the gay community now deems necessary for the development of gay male identity and sexual freedom.

My comments will be directed specifically at gay men and their defence of gay male pornography. This is for a number of reasons. To begin with, as a gay male, I have a vested interest in the outcome of those litigation and social reform strategies allegedly undertaken on my behalf. Also, despite the claims of those who would argue that the feminist movement has abandoned its fight against pornography (Strossen, 1995), much has been written in recent years by lesbian feminists in particular, detailing the harms that result from the production and distribution of lesbian pornography (Jeffreys, 1993; Linden, 1982; Reti, 1993). Such analyses do not, however, squarely address the topic of gay male pornography. Thus, there is a need for work devoted to this issue.

Throughout this paper, I will argue that, in attempting to educate young gay men about sex, educators will need to work together with the gay community to help gay youth come to terms with the reality of homophobia and the self-hate it causes. This cannot occur, however, until all of us, gay and non-gay, confront the types of messages that many gay men now hold out as indicative of gay male identity and sexual freedom. This paper will conclude that, far from liberating, these messages, best personified by the pornography now defended by many gay men as life affirming, increase the types of sex-based inequalities that are central to homophobia and prevent young gay men from developing the self-confidence and self-esteem needed to maximise their psychological and physical well-being.

GAY MALE YOUTH AND THE NEED
FOR SEXUALITY EDUCATION

Cranston (1992) contends that self-esteem is the linchpin of self-preservation. Hence, if we do not offer young gay men positive role models and a sense of self-worth, we do little to encourage them to protect themselves, for we merely reinforce the belief that they are devalued socially, and unworthy of the protection offered by safer sexual practices.

In addition to the self-esteem needs of gay male youth, safer-sex education programs must deal with the realities of same-sex sexual activity such that young gay men are made aware of what is and is not "safe." At times, this requires a blunt and explicit description of what gay sex is and how best to ensure that any sexual activity engaged in is, in fact, safe. Given that most high schools have adopted sex education curricula, the responsibility to do so should and must rest upon those charged with developing and implementing these programs. Safer-sex education is not just about wearing condoms, however. Young gay men also must be taught that self-loathing and shame are neither normal nor permissible. Teaching self-acceptance will assist in saving lives by indicating to gay youth, and students in general, that homosexuality is not a taboo subject; that homosexuals are not socially deviant (hence worthy of abuse and ridicule); and that heterosexuality is not the only sexual orientation worthy of respect, support and basic human rights protections. Until this occurs, young gay men (indeed all gay men) will not be in a position to make the types of choices needed to ensure personal safety (de Bruyn, 1998; Pereira, 1999; Sanatioso, 1999).

Cranston (1992) argues that this process must begin within schools and cannot be left entirely to the gay community. This is not to say, however, that the gay community does not have a role to play. Nor does it deny the fact that many schools fail to do that which they *should* do. The goal, Cranston argues, must be personal and collective empowerment, a supportive environment in which young gay people can enter into a critical dialogue about their lives in the presence of both HIV and homonegativity.

THE GAY COMMUNITY'S RESPONSE– THE LITTLE SISTERS *LITIGATION*

On December 20, 2000, the Supreme Court of Canada ruled unanimously in the case of *Little Sisters Book and Art Emporium*, a case concerning the right of Canada customs to detain lesbian and gay male pornography, that same-sex pornography violates the sex equality test for pornographic harm first set down by the Court in its 1992 decision in *R. v. Butler* (1992).[2] In *R. v. Butler*, the Court ruled that legal efforts aimed at prohibiting the distribution of pornography were constitutionally sound because pornography undermines the rights of all Canadians to be treated equally on the basis of sex. In *Little Sisters*, the Court ruled that lesbian and gay male pornography should not be excluded from this approach.

In *R. v. Butler*, the Supreme Court of Canada offered a radical redefinition of the harms of pornography. Rejecting the argument that pornography should be illegal because of its effect on society's moral fibre (the position traditionally advocated by the courts), the Supreme Court chose instead to tackle the harms that result from the production and distribution of those materials that undermine society's interest in equality. The legal briefs submitted in *R. v. Butler* provided overwhelming evidence on the harmful effects of pornography on women and men, and thus on society as a whole–research from which the Court found there is sufficient reason for Parliament to conclude that pornography amounts to a practice of sex discrimination (MacKinnon, 2001).

The scientific and testimonial evidence accumulated for over 30 years proves that pornography, as a discriminatory practice based on sex, denies women the right to participate equally in society. It maintains sex as a basis for subordination, fosters bigotry and sexual contempt along gender lines and, in so doing, ensures that inequality remains society's central dynamic (Cole, 1989; Dines, Jensen, & Russo, 1998; Itzin, 1992; MacKinnon, 2001; MacKinnon & Dworkin, 1997; Russell, 1993). In *R. v. Butler*, the Supreme Court of Canada ruled that:

> [t]he effect of [pornographic] material is to reinforce male-female stereotypes to the detriment of both sexes. It attempts to make degradation, humiliation, victimisation, and violence in human relationships appear normal and acceptable. A society which holds that *egalitarianism and non-violence are basic to any human interaction*, is clearly justified in controlling any medium which violates these principles. (1992, p. 493)

In *Little Sisters*, the Appellant and a number of Interveners argued in favour of exempting same-sex pornography from this analysis. Specifically, these groups attempted to persuade the Court that sexism and inequality were not the result of the lesbian and gay male pornographic magazines and videos before the Court in that case. One of the pro-pornography Interveners in the case, Equality for Gays and Lesbians Everywhere (EGALE), argued, for example, that in addition to helping gay men discover and feel empowered about their sexuality, same-sex pornography can be seen to be beneficial to society generally because "sexually explicit homoerotic materials have liberating effects that benefit women as a whole, as well as lesbians and gay men. By subverting dominant constructs of masculinity and femininity, homoerotic imagery and text challenge the sexism believed to be endorsed and reinforced by mainstream heterosexual pornography" (Factum of the Intervener EGALE, 1999, paragraph 17).[3] Attempting to distinguish gay male pornography from heterosexual pornography, EGALE continued:

> The specific materials at issue in *R. v. Butler* consisted of mainstream pornographic videos produced for a heterosexual, predominantly male audience. In contrast, this case involves the systematic detention and seizure of sexually explicit homoerotic imagery and text, produced by and for lesbians, gays and bisexuals. The expressions conveyed by the *R. v. Butler* videos echoed the dominant refrain on sexuality, while the expressions conveyed in the materials at issue in this case are those of dissenting minority voices. The evidence establishes that the Customs Legislation silences a form of expression that challenges conventional notions of sexuality, undermines the cultural hegemony of heterosexuality, and thereby contributes significantly to the social and political vitality of our marginalised communities. (Factum of the Intervener EGALE, 1999, paragraph 14)[4]

This view was shared by the Women's Legal Education and Action Fund (LEAF) who argued, "the equality rights of heterosexual women are also affected by the targeting of non-heterosexual materials. These materials benefit heterosexual women because they may challenge sexism, compulsory heterosexuality and the dominant, heterosexist sexual representations which often portray 'normal' heterosexuality as men dominating women and women enjoying pain and degradation" (Factum of the Intervener LEAF, 1999, paragraph 7).

Little Sisters and many of the groups that intervened in support of the store before the Supreme Court of Canada argued that gay pornography, because it is used and interpreted by gay youth in a society where same-sex sexual activity remains taboo, offers positive affirmation of same-sex sexual desire. Thus, these materials go a long way towards saving gay youth from self-destruction. At trial, the Canadian AIDS Society (CAS), for example, noted the need for safer-sex educational materials aimed at promoting self-esteem and preservation. Arguing that a healthy sexual identity fosters responsible sexual behaviour and the practice of "safer sex," which is essential to curbing the transmission of

HIV/AIDS, CAS called for the distribution of materials that are sexually explicit, frank and direct:

> Altering human sexual behaviour, the object of AIDS education, is a daunting task. Simply put, safer sex education is impossible without talking about sex. Clinical depictions of safer sex are simply not as effective as materials with erotic content or with an erotic subtext. (Factum of the Intervener Canadian AIDS Society, 1999, paragraph 9)[5]

Similarly, EGALE argued:

> The unequivocal message conveyed by mainstream cultural representations is that heterosexuality is the (almost universal) norm, and our lesbian, gay, and bisexual sexualities are unnatural, deviant, and perverse. (Factum of the Intervener EGALE, 1999, paragraph 4)

In this regard, EGALE relied on the testimony of gay author Thomas Waugh, who in earlier testimony before the British Columbia Supreme Court (1996) stated that, "the gay community is a stigmatised and abused community," within which young gay people are taught to feel shame about their bodies and their sexuality (Factum of the Intervener EGALE, 1999, paragraph 4). According to EGALE, one solution to the isolation resulting from this stigma is "sexually explicit lesbian, gay, and bisexual materials," because they "challenge the dominant cultural discourse" and provide "affirmation and validation of our sexual identities by normalising and celebrating homosexual and bisexual practices, which mainstream culture either ignores or condemns" (Factum of the Intervener EGALE, 1999, paragraph 5).

In a similar vein, LEAF, relying on the fact that suicide attempts appear to be two to 14 times higher among lesbian, gay and bisexual youth than among heterosexual youth, argued that the suppression of lesbian and gay materials fosters the oppression of lesbian women and gay men through invisibility and denigration (Factum of the Intervener LEAF, 1999, paragraph 15). Arguing that these materials perform a critical role in developing and nurturing non-heterosexual communities and cultures, LEAF reported that, in order to overcome social isolation, lesbian women and gay men set out to learn about a new culture and to find more accepting communities (Factum of the Intervener LEAF, 1999, paragraph 19). Sexually explicit materials, according to LEAF, serve as a compass, pointing lost gay men in the right direction, particularly when it comes to learning about safer sex:

> Materials about safer sex practices, sexual health and HIV must present information in a format appropriate for the intended audience. The format must be sensitive, amongst other things to the literacy level, sexual orientation, occupation, language, abilities, and age of that audience. Prohibiting access to this information endangers health. (Factum of the Intervener LEAF, 1999, paragraph 18)

There is little reason to disagree with arguments concerning the need to educate gay youth about sexuality and identity. In isolation, the points raised about the need to teach young gay men about safer sex and positive sexual attitudes are supported by those working in the field of youth health education; it is hard to imagine anyone in this field of study taking issue with them. It is the context and purpose of these arguments that become problematic. Specifically, it is important to keep in mind that the defence of gay male pornography outlined in *Little Sisters* was made within the context of a court case aimed at ensuring the production and distribution of lesbian and gay male *pornography*. This point should not be overlooked, particularly once the content of the specific materials at issue in *Little Sisters* is examined.

This was not a point overlooked by the Supreme Court of Canada when responding to these arguments. In the final analysis, the Court dismissed the claims made by Little Sisters and others, holding that Parliament was justified in controlling distribution of materials, gay or non-gay, which threaten the sex equality interests of all Canadians. In other words, to the extent that same-sex sexual materials are pornographic–that is, to the extent that imported gay male materials reinforce male-female stereotypes to the detriment of both sexes, make degradation, humiliation, victimisation, and violence in human relationships appear normal and acceptable and undermine egalitarianism and non-violence (*R. v. Butler*, 1992), then these materials should, like heterosexual pornography, be subject to legal scrutiny. Rejecting the arguments made by LEAF, for example, the Court concluded:

> The intervener LEAF took the position that sado-masochism performs an emancipatory role in gay and lesbian culture and should therefore be judged from a different standard from that applicable to heterosexual culture . . . The portrayal of a dominatrix engaged in the non-violent degradation of an ostensibly willing sex slave is

no less dehumanising if the victim happens to be of the same sex, and no less (and no more) harmful in its reassurance to the viewer that the victim finds such conduct both normal and pleasurable. (*Little Sisters*, 2000, paragraph 63)

GAY MALE PORNOGRAPHY: IS THIS LIBERATION?

Unfortunately, although ruling that same-sex pornography violated the *R. v. Butler* sex equality standard, the Court did not offer a detailed analysis as to why and how this pornography undermines society's equality interest, focusing instead on the right of legislators to stop the importation of pornography generally. While I support the Court's findings insofar as it refused to distinguish gay male pornography from heterosexual pornography, the Court's failure to offer a more thorough analysis of what gay male pornography is and what it says risks leaving considerable room for pro-pornography advocates to argue that the Court simply failed to understand the meaning and significance of gay male pornography.

Thus, it is helpful to discuss and describe what gay male pornography *is*. Indeed, despite the written and oral evidence presented by pro-pornography advocates throughout *Little Sisters*, what is less well focussed, indeed often entirely unmentioned, is the specific content of the materials defended by proponents of gay male pornography.

I have reviewed the materials defended in *Little Sisters*,[6] as well as other materials that, while not specifically defended before the Supreme Court of Canada in that case, would nonetheless be legal in Canada had Little Sisters Bookstore convinced the Court to allow the unrestricted importation of pornography into Canada. These materials included gay male pornographic videotapes, magazines and books. What follows is only a brief overview of some of the materials defended in *Little Sisters* as harm free. An analysis of these materials, however, says much about those arguments which would have us defend gay male pornography as "different from" heterosexual pornography or "subversive of" the types of sexist, racist and homophobic power structures the Court sought to tackle in its 1991 *Butler* decision and which it reaffirmed in *Little Sisters*.

If the materials defended in *Little Sisters* represent gay male identity, as pro-pornography advocates say they do, and if these materials are as ideologically and socially significant as their proponents claim, what has the Supreme Court of Canada just been told about homosexual identities? In answering this question, it is worth noting the quotation below, found in an article in *Manscape Magazine* (1985), not at issue in *Little Sisters*, but available nonetheless from the Plaintiff's bookstore prior to the case being heard. It, like many of the materials defended in *Little Sisters*, reminds the reader that to be "male" is to be empowered, but that to be male requires conformity to a clearly defined gender role–a role according to which some are entitled to sexually abuse and control, while others, because they are descriptively less "male," are socially less relevant, less equal, denied the respect, compassion, and human dignity that true equality provides. In the *Manscape* article, one man is described as "straight-acting" and sexualised for his ability to be more "male" (i.e., less gay) than his partner, whom he uses to reaffirm the power this position promises:

> I pushed him lower so my big dick was against his chest; I pushed his meaty pecs together. They wrapped around my dick perfectly as I started tit-fucking him like a chick. His hard, humpy pecs gripped my meat like a vice. Of all the things I did to him that night I think he hated that the most. It made him feel like a girl. I sighed, "Oh, my bitch got such pretty titties! They was made for titty fucking, made to serve a man's dick." (Wilcox, 1995, p. 15-18)

As in a great deal of written or pictorial gay male pornography, the physically more powerful, ostensibly straight male is glorified. This linking of manliness with heterosexuality and overt masculinity is a common theme throughout these materials, with masculinity often gained at the expense of a woman or ostensibly gay male's safety and self-worth.

The omission of women in gay male pornography does not mean that such material is devoid of sexism and misogyny. Like its heterosexual counterpart, gay male pornography promotes violence and/or the sexual degradation of others along gendered lines. Many of the materials defended in *Little Sisters*, for example, sexualise large, hyper-masculine men, many of whom are described as "straight" and who are sexually aroused by inflicting pain on sexual subordinates (read: gay men) who, in turn, are described as enjoying the pain, humiliation and degradation to which they are subjected. *Advocate Men*, for example, modelled along the lines of *Playboy* and *Penthouse*, offers photo spreads of young, muscular men–the type of men frequently used in these magazines (Kendall & Funk, 2004)–and stories from readers allegedly detailing real life experiences. The article that accompanies one of the magazine's photo spreads reads:

> The first thing people notice about Glen Fargus, apart from his stern masculinity and animal sexuality, is those muscles of his. It is easy to resent him when he remarks that he has never lifted weights but all is forgiven when Glen gives the reason for his physique. "I like to fuck a lot," he says. He is described as working as a foreman and although this requires a lot of heavy lifting, this is nothing compared to "the work I put into pumping some young stud's butt." . . . "Sometimes my muscles get me in trouble. Some guys say I'm too rough during sex. I get into it and all the other guys end up all bruised. Like they say, no pain no gain." (Little Sisters Trial Exhibits, Exhibit 198)

An article in the same magazine, "Perfect Husband," tells the story of a young gay man's attraction to a married (not gay) male who is described as, "so hetero, it's unbelievable." Jack (the married, heterosexual man) is described in terms that make it clear that he is the "real" man in this sexual relationship. For example:

> Usually Jack brings over a porn flick to watch while I take my sweet time sucking him off. The tapes always star the same large breasted, incredibly pink females. I can't see the action very well but I don't mind at all. My taste in porn is quite different. Jack comes around for my services just often enough that neither of us becomes bored nor frustrated by lack of action. He does get awfully excited, even a bit brutal, when he shoots his wad. But I don't mind at all. Rather, the contrary. And he is considerate, always keeping the scotch well supplied, casually dropping a gift on me now and then. And sometimes stock market tips, all of which have proved to be good ones. He is always deliciously clean and good smelling. I am so lucky. He is a wonderful gentleman and a good provider. I couldn't ask for more. He is the perfect husband. (Little Sisters Trial Exhibits, Exhibit 198)

A similar theme is emphasised in the next story in the same magazine. Titled "The Plan," this story describes the sexual encounters of a young gay man in drag, and details the ways he is used sexually by an older man (who is described as not gay). At one stage, the younger man is forced to have sex in public. When he explains that he is worried about what people might see and say, the older man says, "Fuck'em. You're my cunt. Not theirs" (Little Sisters Trial Exhibits, Exhibit 198).

In many of the other materials defended in the *Little Sisters* case, sexual subordination is enforced through extreme forms of torture and violence, with masculinity epitomised and celebrated in men who ridicule and emasculate others in the name of sexual pleasure. Humour, we are told, is found in the sexual debasement of another, assertiveness tied to aggression, resulting in an identity politics that creates, packages and re-sells a sexuality that epitomises male supremacy. Femininity, in turn, is linked with emasculation, inferiority, and inequality. Indeed, in many of these materials, the men who are stripped of their masculinity through sex are often described as gay, while those who abuse them and who are iconised as sexual role models are described as heterosexual. Note, for example, *MAC II 19: A Drummer Super Publication, Volume 19* (Little Sisters Trial Exhibits, Exhibit 49). This magazine contains an article entitled "Prisoner" that details the torture and sexual mutilation of prisoners of war during a fictional military coup. Many of the prison officers are described as "straight" and "real men" whose masculinity is shown through the sexual abuse of their prisoners, most of whom are belittled as gays, queers, and sissies (Little Sisters Trial Exhibits, Exhibit 49).

A similar theme is found in *Bear: Masculinity Without the Trappings* (Little Sisters Trial Exhibits, Exhibit 197). The emphasis in this magazine is on overt hyper-masculinity. Like *MAC II 19*, many of the stories in this magazine mock gay men for their "femininity." One article, for example, quotes a trucker who, while bragging about the men who have "serviced" him at truck stops, says:

> ... truckers sure know about the clean finger nail faggots taking up stalls all day playing footsies, tossing toilet paper and love notes at any pair of boots along side. Most truckers ignore them. Some want to kill them and others figure a blowjob for free is one hell of a lot better than tossing dollars at a whore. (Little Sisters Trial Exhibits, Exhibit 197)

This publication, like many others, promotes violence and aggressive, non-egalitarian behaviour. The theme throughout is self-empowerment found at the expense of someone else's liberty and self-worth. Merit is found in degradation and equality in reciprocal abuse.

In many of the *Little Sisters* materials, rape is normalised. In the story, "Sucks Brother Off Before Wedding" from *Juice: True Homo-*

sexual Experiences (Little Sisters Trial Exhibits, Exhibit 213), for example, the writer describes being raped by his older brother and other men. Explaining that these experiences formed the basis of his preferred sexual experiences as an adult, the author then details another of his sexual encounters:

> Once, when I was about 25, I got raped by a powerful young guy that I had taken home to blow. I always say that was the best sex I ever had. Rape at that stage of the game was enjoyable. God, he was good. He knew just what to do to a willing asshole that kept saying no. He took me with force and I fought him right to the bitter end and–thank God–he won out. When he got through with [me] I knew I had had it. The bastard never came back though. (Little Sisters Trial Exhibits, Exhibit 213)

The identity sold in these materials is one in which violence by one man against another man is normalised for the consumer. This is a common theme. Note, for example, the magazine *Dungeon Master–The Male S/M Publication* (Little Sisters Trial Exhibits, Exhibit 48), which would now be freely imported into Canada had Little Sisters had its way. It presents men torturing other men with hot wax, heat and fire, while sexualising this abuse as sexually arousing for the abusers, the persons injured, and, again, for the consumer. The magazine *Mr. S/M 65* (Little Sisters Trial Exhibits, Exhibit 216) presents photographs of men being defecated on and who derive pleasure from eating faeces. The film *Headlights and Hard Bodies* (Little Sisters Trial Exhibits, Exhibit 192) includes footage of men sexually using other men who are being pulled by neck chains, hit and whipped while tied to poles, penetrated by large objects and/or subjected to clamping, biting and pulling of their nipples and genitals. Men, presented as "slaves," are shown in considerable pain but finding sexual enjoyment from the abuse inflicted on them. Those released from bondage kiss their "master," who has just beaten them, and thank him for putting them in their place. *MAC II* magazine, in turn, details the kidnapping, torture and sexual mutilation of prisoners of war (Little Sisters Trial Exhibits, Exhibit 49). In one photograph, two young men are shown confined in a cage. One, face down and bent over, is being slapped by an older man in a Nazi military uniform. Another is chained and hung in stirrups with a hand shoved down his throat.

What one sees in these materials, defended as harm-free by Little Sisters and others, is an almost pervasive glorification of the idealised masculine/male icon. Through them, inequality is sexualised; dominance, non-mutuality, and submission remain central to the sexual act. In those photos where men are alone, positioned, and posed, their humanity is removed. They are denied subjectivity, becoming little more than objects. As Men Against Rape and Pornography (1993), a US activist group, explain, the man exposed becomes a non-human, an object waiting for you to do something to him or waiting to do something to you because he has what it takes to do so. Either way, the result is a sexuality that is hierarchical and rarely compassionate, mutual or equal.

This was the conclusion first offered by LEAF in its submission to the Supreme Court of Canada in *R. v. Butler* in 1991. Specifically, in summarising the materials before the Court in that case, LEAF argued:

> Some of the subject materials present men engaging in sexual aggression against other men, analogous to the ways women are treated in the materials described above. Men are slapped with belts. A man is anally penetrated with a rifle. Men are presented as being raped. Men's genitals are bound. They are in dog collars and in chains. Men lick other men's anuses and are forced to lick urinals during anal intercourse. Men are presented as gagging on penises down their throats. Men urinate on men and ejaculate into their mouths. Boys are presented with genitals exposed, surrounded by toys. (Factum of the Intervener LEAF, 1991, paragraph 5)

These materials lead LEAF to conclude that:

> Individual men are also harmed by pornography. . . . LEAF submits that much of the subject of pornography of men for men, in addition to abusing some men in the ways that it is more common to abuse women through sex, arguably contributes to abuse and homophobia as it normalises male sexual aggression generally. (Factum of the Intervener LEAF, 1991, paragraph 48)

An overview of the materials available since *R. v. Butler* was heard reveals that little has changed–other than LEAF's rather unfortunate and inexplicable decision eight years after successfully litigating *R. v. Butler* to reject its own sex equality analysis by supporting similar materials in the *Little Sisters* case.

These materials characterise the type of gay sexuality pro-pornography litigants, academics and activists defend when they seek to exempt gay male pornography from the sex equality harms-based analysis long advocated by antipornography feminists, and now accepted by the Supreme Court of Canada. Their effect? What is being advocated in the name of liberation and equality creates, packages and re-sells a sexuality that epitomises inequality on the basis of sex. In sum, gay male pornography, typified in the materials just described and defended by others as "different" from heterosexual pornography, merges with an identity politics that exalts all that is masculine (i.e., "male") and rejects all that is feminine (i.e., "female"). What one gets is a sexual politic based on a male/female dichotomy, a user's guide on how best to get and hold onto heterosexual male privilege.

BUT ARE THEY HARMFUL? SOME THOUGHTS ON GENDER AND THOSE WHO PLAY WITH IT

In *Little Sisters*, those attempting to justify the production and distribution of gay male pornography offered a number of arguments to advance their case. Having responded to some of these arguments in earlier work (Kendall, 1993, 1997, 1999, 2001), I want here only to examine the claim, advanced in *Little Sisters*, that gay male pornography avoids the gender-based harms of heterosexual pornography. I will then turn to an examination of the effects these materials are likely to have on gay youth.

Some gay activists have argued that even if heterosexual pornography is harmful, any perceived inequality evident in gay male pornography is rendered non-harmful, indeed subversive, because in it, unlike in heterosexual pornography, women are not sexually exploited within a heterosexual context. This was a central argument throughout much of the *Little Sisters* proceedings and is best represented by the testimonies and evidence relied upon by Little Sisters Bookstore and EGALE. Little Sisters, for example, cited the work of gay male author Thomas Waugh who, acting as an expert witness for the store, restated his earlier writings in which he distinguished gay pornography from straight pornography on the basis that "gay men fuck and suck and are fucked and sucked, etc., in a wide range of combinations and roles not determined by gender" (Waugh, 1985, p. 33). Elsewhere, Waugh continues:

> To be sure, gender is the ultimate determining factor of power relations within and around heterosexual eroticism rigidly prescribing roles for men as producer, consumer and inserter, and for women as model, commodity and insertee. But the absence of gender as a

determining factor distinguishes gay eroticism from straight eroticism, and this is crucial, politically and morally as well as aesthetically. (Waugh, 1996, p. 48)

In a similar vein, Canadian sociologist Gary Kinsman, cited as a leading authority by EGALE during the *Little Sisters* trial, stated that with respect to the Court's concern about those materials which are "degrading" and "dehumanising" on the basis of sex:

> [These] terms . . . have been generated from an analysis of some of the problems that are presented within heterosexual pornography made for men and if we look at gay sexuality and gay sex representations, it's organised in quite a different way. So that those relationships of gender inequality, gender power relations, are not a central defining feature of gay male pornography. (Factum of the Intervener EGALE, 1999, paragraph 40)

Finally, it is again worth noting the testimony of Thomas Waugh who concluded:

> Unlike straight male porn, gay porn does not directly and systematically replicate the heterosexist patriarchal order in its relations of production, exhibition, consumption or representation. Kathleen Barry's assertion that "homosexual pornography acts out the same dominant and subordinate roles of heterosexual pornography" cannot be shown to be true of any of these terms. . . . The fantasy universe of gay porn resembles the gay ghetto in its hermeticism as well as in its contradictory mix of progressive and regressive values, in its occupancy of a defensible enclave within heterosexist society. It subverts the patriarchal order by challenging masculinist values, providing a protected space for non-conformist, non-reproductive and non-familial sexuality, encouraging many sex-positive values and declaring the dignity of gay people. (Factum of the Appellant Little Sisters Bookstore, 1999, paragraph 34)

The experiences of some of the men used to make gay pornography fail to support the claim that harm does not occur because gay men have more say in what gets produced and how (Edmonson, 1998; Isherwood, 1996; Kendall & Funk, 2004; Reynolds, 1995). Further, arguments like those above tend to imply that because, in gay male pornography, men can and do assume the submissive role normally afforded women, the whole idea of male dominance is undermined because it becomes evident that men, too, can be (and are) dominated within gay male sexual relationships. I have responded to this argument elsewhere (Kendall, 1993, 1997, 2001) but it is worth repeating here that this reasoning is not sustainable. Arguments that focus predominantly on the use of men in gay male pornography risk claiming that what makes heterosexual pornography harmful is the use of biological females by biological males and that it is this biological polarity that makes women unsafe and unequal. This is misleading, as well as sexist and homophobic. Sexist because it implies that harm to men is not harm and homophobic because it implies that harm is avoided if it is done to gay men. The mere absence of biological "opposites" does little to undermine the very real harms of rape, abuse, assault, harassment and discrimination resulting from materials in which "male" equals masculine, equals dominant, equals preferable. Indeed, the coupling of two biological males does nothing to destabilise sexual and social power inequalities divided along gender lines if those behaviours–central to the preservation of gender hierarchy (aggression, homophobia, sexism, and compulsory heterosexuality)–are not themselves removed from the presentation of sexuality as power-based.

Gay historian John Burger (1995) argues that the inequalities evident in straight pornography are undermined in gay male pornography because the men in gay pornography, and gay men generally, have the "option" of participating in a role reversal not normally afforded women–that is, they can "take turns" being top and bottom. Roles become fluid and the harms of gender hierarchy are subverted. As a result, they further challenge the idea that gender roles are fixed or immutable and thereby question the assumption that men must always be on top. According to Burger, because women are removed from the sexual dynamic, the notion that men are always on top, always dominant, is immediately undermined:

> [i]n male homosexual sex, gay men wield "power" over other men (instead of women) at the same time as they allow themselves to be rendered "powerless" by men (like women are supposed to be in the orthodox world of sexuality). The gender power system breaks down in homosexual sex. Gay men embody both masculine and feminine traits, thereby disproving the constructed quality of absolute gender and gender roles. Orthodox sexuality's untruths are made visible, and when this occurs, new truths can be constructed and substituted. (1995, p. 103)

This argument also was raised by EGALE, who, in their Factum in *Little Sisters*, claimed, "the presumption that homoerotic materials cause the type of social harm identified in *R. v. Butler* is contrary to logical reasoning. Indeed, the academic literature suggests that sexually explicit homoerotic materials have liberating effects that *benefit* women in general, as well as lesbians, gays and bisexuals. By subverting dominant constructs of masculinity and femininity, homoerotic imagery and text challenge the sexism that is believed to be endorsed and reinforced by mainstream heterosexual pornography" (Factum of the Intervener EGALE, 1999, paragraph 41). In making this point, EGALE rely on the work of British legal academic Carl Stychin, who argues that gay male pornography subverts the power and gender hierarchies present in heterosexual pornography because "the ability of gay men to assume both dominant and submissive roles establishes fantasy as open and boundaryless" (Stychin, 1992, p. 878). For Stychin, gay pornography has liberatory potential because it exposes the artificial nature of gender by challenging the notion that gendered hierarchies are fixed, immutable, "real." He writes:

> Because gay men exhibit behaviour that does not conform to the dominant culture's understanding of gender, the concepts of gender and subjectivity begin to unravel. This failure to conform to the cultural construction of gender fragments the coherence of the concepts of male and female. Once gender is deconstructed and reduced to performance, that performance is evaluated for its potential to interrupt and fragment the social construct of gender. If performance reveals the artificiality of gender, it also undermines hierarchical gendered arrangements. Gay male pornography then should not be understood to reinforce objectification. Rather, it redefines the sexual subject and reveals new possibilities. (1992, p. 883)

Stychin's work builds on the writings of lesbian writer Judith Butler (1990) who argues that gender is little more than "drag," something artificial, a "performance," a concept to play with, an idea that reveals that there is no "inner sex or essence or psychic gender core" (Fuss, 1991, p. 28). Stychin applies this concept to gay male pornography, arguing that because gay pornography shows the artificiality of gender, it undermines and destabilises heteropatriarchy.

At its most basic, the problem with this analysis is that it appears removed from the power relations under which gay men and women actually live. This is a point made by Jeffreys (1993), who, responding to Butler's claim that "gender is drag" asks, "if this is to be a revolutionary strategy then how would it effect change?" Jeffreys's response is that it cannot. Dismissing the argument that gender is mere performance, rather than something concrete and oppressive, she writes:

> Male supremacy does not carry on just because people don't realise gender is socially constructed, because of an unfortunate misapprehension that we must somehow learn how to shift. It carries on because men's interests are served thereby. There is no reason why men should give up all the real advantages–economic, sexual, and emotional–that male supremacy offers them because they see that men can wear skirts. Similarly the oppression of women does not just consist of having to wear makeup. Seeing a man in a skirt or a woman wearing a tie will not be sufficient to extricate a woman from a heterosexual relationship when she will suffer socially, financially and quite likely physically, in some cases with the loss of her life, if she decides to slough off her oppression. (1993, p. 84)

Applying Jeffreys's analysis, it is evident that Stychin's fascination with the subversive potential of gay pornography tends to ignore the *reality* of gay men's lives, their social marginalisation, and the desire, now sexually promoted and promised in pornography, to get and benefit from male dominance. If gay men and men generally were willing to give up male privilege, then *maybe* playing with gender would work. But many are not (Dotson, 1999; Frye, 1983). Accordingly, many gay men seem obsessed with getting and taking advantage of that which their straight counterparts have had all along, including pornography. For many, gender and male privilege promise a great deal in a world in which being a man still means something. As such, any medium that promises validation through gender conformity tends to lose its subversive potential and, on the contrary, ensures that those constructs that constitute and define male supremacy, that make it what it is, remain in place. For many gay men, pornography is not a game. It offers them something very real: namely, power over men, as men. And there is nothing particularly challenging about this bit of "theatre," regardless of the biological attributes of those who "perform" it.

Others argue that they find validation in the pornographic representation of dominance and submission because it reaffirms that they can be sexually penetrated and should not feel ashamed of the pleasure found in anal and oral intercourse. Sherman (1995), for example, notes that young gay men in particular need to see explicit, unashamed sexual imagery–one assumes he means anal and oral penetration, given his disapproval elsewhere in his work of gay male sexual imagery that only shows men embracing, kissing and holding hands[7]–to overcome the immense stigma and social disapproval attached to gay sex:

> [t]he struggling gay adolescent or young gay man requires sexual images, not images of locker room buddy-buddy bonding. Only sexual images possess the liberatory power to counteract society's heterocentrism and homophobia and offer young gay men models of affirming and unashamed sex between men. Without such models, a gay man may never take those crucial first steps towards self-acknowledgment and liberation. (1995, p. 685)

While I am not convinced that gay male sex is defined through the act of penetration, I might be less quick to reject the argument that gay men need to see it if the pleasure promised in being penetrated did not require that the person who is penetrated assume the status of someone being demeaned for his failure or inability to be a gendered equal; that is, the status of someone who socially is deemed worthy only of abuse and insult.[8]

Gay male pornography tells us that we should find validation in submission laced with humiliation. For example, it is not uncommon for gay male pornography magazines and other pornographic media to sexualise childhood abuse. In the January 1995 issue of *Manscape Magazine*, for instance, a gay man purports to recount his first sexual experience with his father. This is a lesson that, according to the writer, apparently served to teach him the importance of obedience and the pleasure to be found in pain and submission:

> [t]he first session I remember with Dad was wild. He told me to go down to the basement and wait for him. He came down in ten minutes and told me to strip totally naked. I cringed at the thought of this . . . I was a little slow for his tastes . . . and he slapped my face. I was stunned but quickly tore off the shirt and jeans and underwear as I was told. Dad started to lecture me about being obedient and that he was going to make a man out of me because I was nothing but a pussy . . . All of a sudden he started to slap my ass with the flat of his hand. I guess I whimpered because he called me a girl and a baby and I cried bitterly . . . Then it happened. I have no idea

why, but I got a hard-on which I could not hide . . . This made him hit me harder and I was getting a little high from it all. The shit hit the fan when Daddy's little faggot shot a massive load of cum all over the workbench. (Anon, 1995, p. 112)

In detailing this experience, the author queries why he got a "hard-on" from being abused. Given what gay men are told about sex and sexuality through pornography, the answer would seem self-evident. To those who find this sexually arousing and validating, I would ask what it says about being gay in our culture that our chosen identity must be determined by a hyper-masculine, ostensibly straight male? Through pornography, we are told that sexual pleasure (and the empowerment allegedly promised by it) can be found only in the form of abuse presented as compensation for some perceived gender inadequacy. Sexual pleasure is to be found in the form of a role play that does little more than mimic the punishment many of us experienced as children for not being "man enough." We are led to believe this abuse and pain can be forgotten simply by reliving it through sex.

Kleinberg (1987) writes, "the homosexual whose erotic feelings are enhanced by the illusion that his partner holds him in contempt, who is thrilled when told his ass or mouth is just like a cunt, is involved in a complicated self-deception" (p. 123). One might hope that gay men, living in a society in which anti-gay violence is rampant, have had quite enough abuse for one lifetime. Does gay male pornography lead us to believe that our sexual identities depend on and require it? And for those who choose to abuse, rather than be abused, I ask: What does it mean for gay male liberation that power is found only in the ability to emulate those sexual/social behaviours that, once accepted, ensure that sexual power is attained only by those who reject equality? And what does it mean for gay male liberation that those who do reject equality do little more than reinforce the very foundations of compulsory heterosexuality and the harm, including homophobic harm, that results from the conqueror-victim paradigm upon which it is built? Kleinberg (1980) explains that, "to play with powerlessness is to deny it, and worse, to immune oneself from sympathy for those who are truly helpless prisoners" (p. 196). Given what we know about male rape (Scarce, 1997), and the alarming reality of gay male domestic abuse (Island & Letellier, 1991), one might have hoped that gay men would now denounce, rather than promote, any expressive medium that ranks self-gratification ahead of mutual compassion, integrity and physical safety.

I also query whether the pleasure and affirmation allegedly found in being the bottom to a masculine top and the ability/willingness to take turns being that bottom is in fact as readily promoted in gay pornography as advocates would have us believe. Although one must acknowledge that there is always a bottom in gay pornography, the real power is found in the hands of those who are presented on top and who, as such, assume the status of "real" men. As Dyer (1985) explains:

> [a]lthough the pleasure of anal sex (that is, of being anally fucked) is represented, the narrative is never organised around the desire to be fucked, but around the desire to ejaculate (whether or not flowing from anal intercourse). Thus although at a level of public representation gay men may be thought of as deviant and disruptive of masculine norms because we assert the pleasure of being fucked and the eroticism of the anus, in our pornography, this takes a back seat. (p. 28)

Stoltenberg (1989), expanding on this analysis, notes that penetration is not only central, but aggression, control and dominance also are prominent. This is particularly troubling in that these traits, sexualised in pornography, signify male identity generally:

> all that is shown in gay male sex films is presented as conspicuously male, of course . . . [g]ay male sex films characteristically depict the male body as sex object, but insofar as they also display the male body functioning prominently as sexual subject, gay male sex films present a distillation of what nearly all men believe enviable sex in an anatomically male body might be like if they were ever to have endless quantities of it themselves. As artefacts of a heterosexist culture that is rigidly polarised by gender, gay male sex films exhibit the apotheosis of male sexual functioning as imagined by men, who, not unlike straight men, dread the taint of feminisation. (p. 110)

Stoltenberg's argument is best supported by the status of the gay male "folk hero": the gay pornography celebrity. Straight acting, muscular, well endowed and quick to note his preferred position (on "top"), he is the glorified norm. When the gay male superstud does assume "bottom status," hence assuming a role reversal, its significance is not lost on the viewer. While Jeff Stryker, for example, pornography's ultimate top, is (at least physically) capable of assuming the role of a submissive bottom, the fact remains that were he to do so, he would become descriptively less relevant, less powerful. He would be stripped of the male power derived from eroticised masculinity and instead would assume the role of someone whose manhood is weakened. Thus, while gay men have the option of being both top and bottom, the fact remains that the top represents the idealised masculine norm. As the top is overtly masculinised, he ensures that those beneath him are emasculated (read: "feminised"). As gay male pornography focuses on the party who ultimately penetrates, and because in gay pornography the characteristics of the more aggressive, more masculine, more male penetrator are always valorized, this offers much support to the argument that in order to "fuck" you need to be superior and that in order to be "fucked" you need to be sexually accessible, inferior and socially less relevant. The gay male pornography "star," typified by men like Stryker,[9] offers the viewer two choices: he can be like him or the one who replaces him (i.e., "masculine") and be empowered, or he can be the one who is taken by him (i.e., "feminine") and, as such, assume the status of those who, in gay male pornography, as in real life, *are* degraded and expendable. Either way, he is invited to participate in a sexual/social, always gendered, hierarchy–a hierarchy that is not undermined by simply taking turns being the "real" man.

The argument has been made that this analysis leaves no room for intercourse or penetrative sex in gay male relations. This is a misreading of the critique offered. Those who oppose pornography on the basis that it sexualises harm and normalises inequality are not, as many pro-pornography writers would have others believe, anti-sex. Rather, their analysis, insofar as penetrative sex is concerned, is directed at pornography's definition of sex, gender and sexuality, through which penetration is equated with dominance and inequality.

Gay male pornography sexualises this dynamic and asks that we accept it as definitive of what gay male sexuality means. While this is a hierarchy that gay men can (and should) reject, mere role reversal will not eradicate its harms so long as penetration remains defined and promoted sexually as an act of male dominance. What any focus on role play, as a means of undermining gender hierarchies, overlooks is the fact that the pleasure found remains pleasure derived from dominance and submission. Although roles can be reversed, there are still clearly defined roles. There is always a top and there is always a bottom, and these roles are gendered so as to differentiate between those with and without power. While there is mutuality, it is in the "pleasure" found in shared degradation–the excitement derived from controlling or being controlled by someone else. Mutual abuse does not eradicate abuse, however. Rather, it risks trivialising it through sex. While gay men can embrace violation (and some, unfortunately, do), the fact remains that in so doing, dominance and submission remain central to the sexual act. Thus, masculinity remains in place; the self still empowered through the hierarchical ridicule of another; gender anything but subverted.

An overview of the materials defended in *Little Sisters* as "safe," "harm free," and "liberating" indicates that what these materials really provide is a sexualised identity politic that relies on the inequality found between those with power and those without it; between those who are dominant and those who are submissive; between those who "top" and those who "bottom"; between straight men and gay men; between men and women. From these and other materials, we are told to glorify masculinity and men who meet a hyper-masculine, muscular ideal. The result is such that men who are more feminine are degraded as "queer" and "faggots" and are subjected to degrading and dehumanising epithets often used against women, such as "bitch," "cunt," and "whore." These men are, in turn, presented as enjoying this degradation. In sum, these materials reinforce a system in which, as MacKinnon (1989) explains, "a victim, usually female, always feminised" is actualised (p. 141). Hence, gay male pornography presents and, therefore, is a form of male sexuality and male power.

It is this sexuality of dominance, of hierarchy, through which women are sexually violated. It is this sexuality that leads to the oppression of gay men as well. To talk of sex discrimination is to talk of gender and the inequalities that arise within a society in which gender differences are polarised and hierarchical–a society in which those who are "male" get privilege and those who are not, do not. Under this system, "masculinity is seen as the authentic and natural exercise of male agency and femininity as the authentic and natural exercise of female agency" (Franke, 1995, p. 4). To subscribe to masculinity, and to benefit from the privilege afforded "real" men, however, one *also* must support compulsory heterosexuality–an ideology and political institution that embodies those socially defined sets of behaviours and characteristics that ensure heterosexual male dominance (Rich, 1980).

In this sense then, gender (a system of social hierarchy) and sexuality (through which the desire for gender is constantly reproduced) become inseparable. As MacKinnon (1989) notes, within a system of gender polarity in which male equals dominance, female submission, "the ruling norms of sexual attraction and expression are fused with gender identity and formation and affirmation, such that sexuality equals heterosexuality equals the sexuality of (male) dominance and (female) submission. . . . Sexuality becomes, in this view, social and relational, constructing and constructed of power" (pp. 131, 151). Heterosexuality must be made compulsory because it is deemed necessary to ensure the survival of masculinity and femininity, constructs that safeguard male dominance. Lesbian women and gay men deny the inevitability of heterosexuality and, thus, constitute a potential threat to male supremacy. Once we see the extent to which heterosexuality, made compulsory, ensures the maintenance of gender as a system of dominance and submission, of sexual hierarchy, we can begin to see the extent to which anti-gay stereotypes play into and underlie sex inequality (Sunstein, 1994, p. 21). Together, sexuality and gender form the basis of institutionalised sexism. Sexuality, as constructed, represents the normative ideology of male superiority over women and the hostility directed at homosexuals finds its source in this power structure, which is aimed at preserving compulsory heterosexuality. It is in this sense that the harm resulting from the production and distribution of gay male pornography becomes most apparent. Indeed, because it glorifies the masculine and denigrates the feminine, gay male pornography reinforces this male/female social dichotomy and hierarchy. It sexualises a male/female polarity and strengthens those stereotypes that allow society to view certain behaviours as either feminine, hence inferior, or masculine, hence superior.

IF I SAID YOU HAD A BEAUTIFUL BODY WOULD YOU HOLD IT AGAINST ME? SACRIFICING SAFETY FOR SEXUAL ACCEPTANCE

In this setting, the argument that gay male pornography may play an important role in sexuality education becomes less convincing. In *Little Sisters*, the Canadian AIDS Society (CAS), for example, pointed out that schools are not doing what they must do to promote positive and life affirming gay sexualities. Thus, according to CAS:

> homosexuals, especially young gay men, are more likely to turn to sexually stimulating material available at well known commercial outlets like Little Sisters to become informed about their sexuality and health. (Factum of the Intervener Canadian AIDS Society, 1999, paragraph 23)

Justifying pornography as a source of effective AIDS education, the group concluded, quoting from the Yale AIDS Law Project, that "when the only known means of curbing an epidemic is education, but effective educational materials offend some members of the public, how should the interests of the public's sensibility and the public's health be balanced? When the cost of not offending someone is someone else's death, the answer to the question should be clear" (Factum of the Intervener Canadian AIDS Society, 1999, paragraph 1).

Similarly, EGALE argued that, "explicit . . . gay . . . materials also serve as an important source of information used to promote healthy and safe sexual practices within our communities. In that respect, they perform a crucial educative function that is not fulfilled by mainstream pornographic materials, which are directed at heterosexual audiences and are therefore largely irrelevant to us" (Factum of the Intervener EGALE, 1999, paragraph 8). In this context, the group relied on the work of Chris Bearchall, who has written:

> . . . the health of individual lesbians and gay men and of our community itself–and the success of the overall battle against AIDS–are seriously threatened by efforts to restrict or eliminate those aspects of lesbian and gay culture and community which foster sexual knowledge, discussion, representation and safe sexual behaviour. (Factum of the Intervener EGALE, 1999, paragraph 8)

Doubtless some who advocate eliminating Canada's antipornography laws in *Little Sisters* did not specifically intend their call for safer sex materials to include all of the materials that would be permitted to circulate if their side won. But the fact remains that their arguments did *not*–and rarely do–draw distinctions between such materials and those they do defend. Nor do individuals who rely on their efforts and analysis when defending this same pornography. As Myrick (1993) explains, gay community-based safer sex education strategies show men engaged in various sexually explicit activities in which condoms are used. The men shown in these materials are supposed to be representative of the gay community, generally. As such, these materials frequently present men dressed in leather or cowboy attire, and show various sexual activities including sadomasochism, water sports, and phone sex. This, we are told, allows gay communities to "construct erotic messages that speak to their desires and correspond to their various relationships to the world" (Myrick, 1993, p. 52).

Given what is already known about the content of gay male pornography and the messages contained in that content, the question that needs to be asked is whether the mere act of showing a condom or discussing its use (and often this is not done) is sufficient to ensure that the sexual acts and relationships referred to by Myrick and defended throughout the *Little Sisters* trial are in fact "safe."

Chambers (1994) is not convinced that gay male pornography plays an important educative function vis-à-vis safer sex. In fact, he criticises the gay movement's safer-sex strategy in general, which he labels "the Code of the Condom." According to this Code, the dangers of unsafe sex lie only in unsafe anal intercourse. Hence, the core rule is that "anal sex is fine, but always use a condom." Chambers (1994) expresses concern with this strategy, noting the reliability problems associated with condoms generally and the dangers of unsafe oral sex (something not readily incorporated into the Code). Even more importantly, Chambers queries whether the Condom Code, as it now stands, can save lives if the messages conveyed *also* do not address the emotional baggage, shame, and self-loathing often carried by men who have sex with men. That is, is it enough to insist on the use of a condom during anal sex without addressing the social stigma under which these men live? Put more bluntly, can condoms work if some gay men do not feel they merit protection in the first place? Chambers (1994) writes:

> If research about stigma and self-labelling in other contexts applies here, some of these men, already struggling with heterosexual society's judgement that they are immoral because of who they are, may well redefine (or reconfirm) themselves as the sort of person who does bad or stupid things. These men become more likely to engage in unprotected sex in the future. Moreover, their feelings of shame may keep them silent about the risks they take, when they should talk to others for counselling and renewed resolve. (pp. 368-369)

Chambers offers a number of alternatives to the Code. One is to encourage gay men to avoid anal sex. The fortitude it takes to even suggest such a radical alternative should not be underestimated. Gay men have attached a great deal of significance to the act of fucking and are not likely to respond favourably to the suggestion that they abandon it.

Personally, I am not convinced that gay men will give up anal sex. Nor am I convinced that gay men are in any great rush to reduce their number of sexual partners. The questions that need to be asked then are: how do we encourage gay men to use a condom when they do have sex;

and, more importantly, is there a way to get them to think about what it means to have sex with each other that reduces participation in dangerous sexual activities? Chambers (1994) concludes by asking that we find new ways to deliver current messages more effectively and to think afresh about what these messages should be. I want to accept this challenge by suggesting that, rather than simply telling gay men not to have anal sex, we must reconstruct the ways in which male intimacy is conceptualised. In this regard, I want to build on the work of Rotello (1997) who argues that what we need now is a gay sexuality that is not premised on the idea of sexual conquest:

> . . . In many ways the prevailing gay urban ethos seems just as overwhelmingly sex-oriented in the 1990s as it was in the clone culture of the 1970s. Although there are now gay churches and community centres and sports clubs, the central gay institutions in large cities remain bars and discos, and much of the urban social scene continues to confer status and self-respect primarily on the basis of looks, muscles, and sexual conquest. This seems so deeply embedded at the heart of the gay male world that virtually all of the behaviours that need to be modified if we are to build a sustainable culture instead continue to be hailed by some leaders as the essence of gay life. (p. 204)

In the remainder of this paper, it will be argued that, to the extent that pornography is used to learn about sex and to the extent safer-sex and youth oriented campaigns rely on the sex pornography sells in order to educate about safety, one cannot expect condoms, seen as *the* means of protection, to work. Nor can one expect young gay men to take those steps necessary to even begin questioning the types of sexual and personal behaviours in which they presently engage; behaviours that are, quite literally, killing them.

SAFER SEX AS GAY SEX:
THE CONDOM AS STIGMA

Torres (1989) explains that, within the context of the heterosexual pornography industry, unsafe sexual practices are always a risk:

> . . . the nature of adult motion picture production encourages unusual and unsafe working conditions. Producers have been known

to force actors to do sexual acts that they would really rather not do. In most of the productions, producers do not test the performers for sexually transmitted diseases and do not require that performers practice safe sex. Additionally, some producers ignore the risks associated with allowing a performer, who may be infected with HIV, to perform in a film. In these situations, the performers are faced with the greatest risk of contracting AIDS. (p. 99)

Similar dangers exist in the gay pornography industry. In his work on 1990s gay porn icon, Joey Stefano (born "Iacona"), who died of a drug overdose soon after his audience lost interest in him (Kendall & Funk, 2004), Isherwood (1996) describes the industry's reluctance to reveal Stefano's HIV positive status to the public and to the men paired with Stefano in his films. Nor had the industry taken precautions to ensure that condoms were always used to protect Stefano and those paired with him in his early films.

It would appear that some in the industry have not learned much from the death of this young man and others. As noted in *Frontiers Magazine* (Anon, 1997), the gay adult video industry leapt to the forefront of safer-sex promotion early in the AIDS crisis by introducing condoms into their pornographic videos–and even incorporating their use into their storylines. It would appear, however, that the tide is turning and more unsafe sex is now creeping back into gay pornography videos.[10] Richard Douglas, a leading director in the industry, justifies this reemerging trend by arguing that:

> . . . being gay is about sex for gay men and it's about dick, and we've been denied that. While I may have some personal problems with it, pornography is only porn if it represents the culture it is a part of. Gay men want unsafe sex. I don't give a damn about responsibility. This is business, and someone is going to do a video without condoms and get rich doing it, so it may as well be me. (Anon, 1997, p. 53)

While it is not the case that all producers avoid the use of condoms in their films, there is clearly a move amongst some gay pornography producers to disguise the use of condoms, thus offering the viewer a sexual act in which the condom is barely visible. What these producers risk sexualizing in so doing is a practice now referred to as "barebacking" or unprotected anal sex. As Menadue (1999) explains, the term was initially referred to by pornography star Scott O'Hara who, in his magazine *Steam*, a journal about sex in public places, first wrote, "I'm tired of using a condom and I won't . . . and I don't feel the need to encourage negatives to stay negative" (p. 8).[11]

Although the practice of deliberately and knowingly having sex without a condom was initially engaged in only between HIV positive men, it is now apparent that it has taken on far greater significance, becoming instead something "subversive," "daring," and "sexually liberating." Inspection of a number of the newer barebacking Websites from the United States, for example, suggests that what appeals to some gay men is the element of danger involved in unsafe sex:

> I'm negative and I want to play Russian roulette with poz cum. The thought of getting infected has me rock hard. I like lots of danger sex, like letting strangers tie me up and blindfold me and fuck me bareback, so I don't know anything about the guys fucking me. Make arrangements to meet me on a street corner or a park where you'll find me blindfolded and lead me to your van to use me. Anyone want to give me a gift? (Menadue, 1999, p. 10)

Thus, dangerous sex is experienced as more sexy (i.e., when you risk death, you heighten arousal). Safer sex, under this model, does not eroticise danger and harm; hence, it is not sexy. As Menadue (1999) notes, while it is clear that some of these men are generally just opposed to the "AIDS establishment" in the United States, describing mandatory condom use as too limiting to the point of being oppressive, it is clear that others simply see safer sex as boring and not "really" gay sex. As one writer explains:

> I was so afraid of becoming positive for such a long time and once it happened I felt relief. I also decided I didn't want to spend my whole life going without the sex I love the most. (Menadue, 1999, p. 10)

These attitudes, now enforced in pornography, say much about what gay sex means today. What one sees in gay pornography, and in the statements of those who like what it says and does, is a sexual model that copies the power inequalities present in straight sex–sex through which (male) power is gained by controlling, dominating and feminizing those around you. The gay sex presented in gay pornography attempts to look (quite successfully) a lot like the sex that straight men have in straight pornography. Socially, the act of penetration determines who controls whom and who, as a result, gets male power. Given that all gay male pornography focuses on the right of the masculine top to penetrate the disempowered bottom, it is not surprising that some gay porn presents unprotected penetrative sex–i.e., penetration in which the condom either is not used or, for the purposes of pornography, is carefully concealed. Safer sex has come to be regarded as gay sex (hence less "male"). It is less male because it is less dominant; not as dangerous; not as life threatening; not as stimulating sexually. Thus, gay sex that rejects safer sexual presentations becomes descriptively less gay, socially more "male."

Given that the "sex (gay men) love the most" remains the sex seen in pornography, it is apparent that those of us who do care about protection and self-preservation have our work cut out for us. For safer sex to work, one needs to accept that both partners merit protection and, more importantly, both have the right to a recognised human existence. In a sense, safer sex represents a form of sexual negotiation that imposes limits on sexual conduct–negotiation that presupposes relatively equal parties. It also recognises there are limits on what you can do to someone else through sex and what he can do to you.

Michelangelo Signorile (1997) writes that AIDS exacerbated men's insecurities about masculinity and eventually cemented rigid gender roles defined though sex:

> Many straight men felt the need to distance themselves further from the homosexual, to prove their heterosexuality, their manhood. Gay men too experienced this and perhaps even more acutely. Now the sexual "bottom" was the focus of negative attention. In much of the public's eyes–and certainly in the eyes of many gay men–it was the submissive "feminine" role in homosexual sex that led to disease. Being healthy was now associated with taking the "manly" role in sex, the top–or at least pretending to. The term "straight-acting," a term to signify masculinity, became more popular than ever in the personals of gay publications and throughout gay cyberspace and was seemingly accepted–or at least reluctantly so–by much of the community. (p. 67)

Given that gay pornography presents a sexuality in which "real" men can do what they want sexually, when they want, and to whom, it is not surprising that the condom, an "appliance" that imposes a limit on this right, becomes gendered and, thus, is not promoted. Gay sex, as taught in gay male pornography, teaches gay men that "real" men do as they please, while fags, because they are feminised, simply hope for the best–an option that is particularly troubling given that the message conveyed in much of the pornography examined thus far sexualises a power dynamic in which some men are offered no voice with which to insist on safer sex and are instead told that they should simply find gratification underneath the weight of a real man who wants to use them–to death, in some instances.

Given the ubiquity of gay pornography in gay male subculture, it is not surprising that the messages gay men now use to educate each other about safer sex tend to mimic and rely on the body imagery and sexual identity sexualised in gay pornography. For example, HIV/AIDS education aimed at the gay male community almost invariably relies on the use of young, white men who are hyper-fit, hyper-masculine, hyper-male. A recent flier circulated by the West Australian AIDS Council, for example, features the muscled torso of a young man posing in a pair of tight fitting Calvin Klein underwear, the outline of his semi-erect penis clearly visible. The flier was intended to encourage gay men to attend a series of workshops on safer sexual practices. It is typical of the materials used today to teach gay men about safer sex. A similar flier can probably be found in most HIV/AIDS organisations throughout Canada, the United States and elsewhere in Australia.

The efficacy of this image, as a method for teaching gay men about AIDS and HIV transmission, needs to be questioned. Analysis of the messages it and others like it convey says a great deal about how gay men are supposed to look, act and feel about their sexual identity. This is particularly evident if we examine what safer sex is and what safer sex requires.

Safer sex is often referred to as a process of "negotiation." Building on this, I propose the following theory regarding safer sexual practices:

1. Safer sex requires negotiation between those having sex.
2. Such negotiation requires that the parties treat themselves and each other as valued human beings, deserving of equality, reciprocity and respect.
3. Self-esteem is required before we can respect both others and ourselves and ultimately engage as an equal with others.
4. Equality lies at the heart of self-esteem.
5. Individuals must want to be safe. Safer sexual practices thus have to be arousing sexually if they are to find acceptance.
6. Equality then must be made sexy.

The question that needs to be asked is whether the messages gay men are currently conveying to each other about same-sex sexual activity support the type of equality-based relationships needed to ensure safer sexual practices, self-preservation and the preservation of others. In other words, is the sexuality of pornography consistent with safer sex?

To return to the flier mentioned earlier, we cannot tell from the flier "who" this young man is (as we are presented only with a muscular, white torso). We are left only with the option of asking "what" he is. He–what we see of him–is only part of a person. He is incomplete and anonymous, without an identity other than his body. He is presented as an object, not as a whole person. In a world in which gay men are forced (sometimes violently) to hide their real identities, this image invites us to treat others as objectified parts of bodies, as "things" devoid of human identity.

This is problematic for a number of reasons. To begin with, it is only when someone is recognised as a subject, rather than a thing, that we usually feel obliged to think about who he is and what we are doing to him, and to care about what the consequences of our actions are for him. More importantly, it is only when we have the subject in mind that negotiation even begins to be relevant. The image also presents what many in the gay male community today perceive to be the physical ideal. In fact, the flier could easily be taken from any number of "soft" gay male pornographic magazines presently available throughout Australia. This type of imagery, which is ubiquitous in gay male pornography, sends a very clear message about what the idealised gay male is in today's society: young, muscular, "good looking," preferably white, definitely able-bodied.

Gay male pornography tells men that to be gay is to live, through sex, for the moment–to use it while they have it and to make sure that if they do not have it, they work hard to get it. Gay men are encouraged to participate in a sexual game devoid of caring and compassion, both for themselves and others, a game that focuses only on controlling or being controlled sexually. Gay male pornography encourages men to define their personal integrity through their sexual encounters–by how often they have sex and with whom. For many, the power of sex, of stimulation and arousal found in "getting off" with or as a "real" man, far outweighs any need for mutual preservation. Believing that you have no right to question, that you should get turned on when a "real" man uses you sexually, or that in order to be a "real" man you need to eroticise the sexual conquest of a sexual inferior, forces mutual respect and safety to take a backseat–often with catastrophic results. Inequality is made sexy, and unsafe sex becomes normative.

This eroticisation of inequality is part of a broader problem of identification. Even when gay men do "come out," their sexuality remains anonymous. They fail to own it. It is not a part of them, but rather something they treat as separate from their individuality. When they sexually interact with others, they see themselves as operating only on a sexual basis. They do not interact as individuals. Sex becomes anonymous, through which objectification is permitted and made sexy. Given this, why worry about someone you see only in sexual terms? Indeed, why ask that he care about you?

Stychin (1995) has argued that, "rather than focusing on sexual practices and representations, as gay men we need to examine how we treat our employees, students, co-workers and friends, as well as our sexual partners in our everyday lives and the extent to which our dealings undermine (or reinforce) systems of gender, racial and sexual oppression" (p. 90). This is not an either/or matter. To the extent that Stychin's analysis calls on us to examine how we treat each other, I agree, although I believe we also need to reflect on how we treat ourselves. I fail to see, however, how gay men can do so without *also* examining, questioning and ultimately rejecting the reasons why we treat people the way we do. That is, how can we even begin to understand ourselves and the ways in which our actions reinforce oppressive gender, racial and sexual constructs, without first focusing on our sexual and interpersonal practices and the means by which we are taught the tools of oppression? In essence, Stychin's analysis assumes that gay male pornography does *not* affect our everyday lives, and that we can simply examine our actions as gay men without also examining *why* we act the way we do.

Whether it be within the confines of the gay bar, gym, bathhouse, cruising park, or even on the street, gay male identity today is concerned less with compassion and any commitment to others than with self-gratification and the satisfaction of knowing that gay men can reap the benefits afforded "real" men as long as they are willing and able to become these men. I have often heard gay men boast that they have redefined manhood by cloning their oppressors, such that it is now difficult to distinguish between straight and gay. This is not redefinition, but rather mimicry and assimilation. Pro-pornography advocates argue that gay pornography acts as a learning tool in a society in which homosexuality remains taboo and in which learning tools are rare. Perhaps, but is this a lesson worth learning? Given what gay male pornography says about appropriate gay male behaviour and identity generally, should we not be concerned about its role in a community in which gay men have excelled at becoming, or want desperately to become, the straight men society has told them they should have been all along?

The gay male entering a gay bar or seeking sexual contact in gay zones such as bathhouses is confronted with a community quick to define his status, his role in that sexual "game" we call cruising. Cruising relies heavily on the type of role-play offered in gay pornography. Specifically, gay men in bars cease to be people. They are denied a human identity and are instead offered a predetermined sexual identity void of humanity. They become the chests, buttocks and bulging biceps meant to turn others on, and if they fail to meet the sexual standard, they simply cease to exist. The result for many is a concerted effort to become the embodiment of physical perfection. They follow a recipe for success in which masculinity is the main ingredient and soon define, and are defined, according to what they think their bodies are going to do *to* others or *for* others.

This point is made clearly in Signorile's (1997) overview of contemporary trends in the gay male community and, in particular, its commitment to "body fascism," which he describes as:

> the setting of a rigid set of standards of physical beauty that pressures everyone within a particular group to conform to them. Any person who doesn't meet those very specific standards is deemed physically unattractive and sexually undesirable. In a culture in which the physical body is held in such high esteem and given such power, body fascism then not only deems those who don't or can't conform to be sexually less desirable, but in the extreme–sometimes dubbed "looksism"–also deems an individual completely worthless *as a person,* based solely on his exterior. In this sense it is not unlike racism or sexism or homophobia itself. In this worst-case scenario, the only way one can become valued *as a person* is if one conforms to the set of standards–if one is lucky enough, from a genetic perspective, to be able to do so. (p. 28)

I would add that the basis of body fascism is homophobia, racism and sexism in that it penalises, through rejection, those who do not conform to the standards that ensure heterosexual, white male dominance. As Rotello (1997) notes, gay culture "has developed a powerful, even merciless system of rewards and penalties based on body image" (p. 254). Conformity is sexualised under this model with gay male invisibility and inequality being the end result.

Adherence to the dictates of hyper-masculinity promises the gay male the self-confidence that many homosexuals evidently lack–a point best demonstrated in the words of one of Signorile's (1997) interview subjects. This young man explains:

> I want to be physical perfection in the eyes of gay men–totally physically appealing, like the ultimate. The perfect tits and butt, bulbous biceps. I want to achieve symmetry, big and in proportion. I would look like the cover of an *HX* [*Homo Xtra*, a New York bar giveaway known for its covers of hot men]–lean, sculpted, muscular, virile, a stallion, a guy that would make your mouth water.
>
> I'm hoping it will boost my self-esteem. I don't know how to boost my self-esteem now. My feeling is, 'Get a great body and people will admire you. Get a great body and everything will be okay.' There's that voice inside me that, of course, says that all of that is full of shit. But it's not powerful enough to overcome this magnetic pull, the promise of what the perfect body might bring. It's this belief that if I can just get the perfect body, then I wouldn't be insecure. I would feel more confident. I wouldn't be afraid of certain gay environments. (p. 4)

And what of those who do not conform? This need to "blend" and be all that a community obsessed with manliness says a man should be can result in incredible self-loathing. The standard set is neither easily met nor easily maintained. As Harris (1993) explains, "porn videos–with [their] tired images and stereotypes of perfect pumped up blondes and smooth dark men with large penises–can only compound feelings of poor self-image" (p. 49). Dr. Richard Quinn, a Sydney-based physician, agrees. He argues that:

> people can develop serious psychological problems from images presented to them, and images in porn videos contribute to this. So many gays feel they haven't got anything to offer because they can't live up to the expectations that are thrown at them on how they should look. They feel that because they don't have that certain look, nobody wants them. (Harris, 1993, p. 49)

For many gay men–men who have been denied participation in a society quick to suppress their self-expression and individual development–the sexual models the gay male community offers as identity result in an overwhelming sense of non-belonging. As Ford (1992) explains:

when Sexland spills over into the real world–at clubs, say, or at the gym, or in the Castro–I once again feel an outsider, same as I did when I was the only queer boy (that I knew of) in a straight high school class. I feel excluded by my community, or a piece of it; on bad days, my self-image nose-dives. (p. 9)

Should it surprise us then that such rejection, when combined with the effects of homophobic rejection generally, has already taken its toll on our community and the community at large? The spectre of AIDS has shown us that we can and must care. We have not, however, carried this over into our sexual relationships and, perhaps ironically, this has only worsened the reality of AIDS in our community. Gay men assert that we are not to blame for AIDS. I agree. We cannot, however, state with the same certainty that we offer our youth any incentive to care about themselves, to look to the future and to recognise that their lives are worth preserving. This is evident in the words of one of the gay men interviewed by Signorile (1997). Larry, a twenty-seven-year-old Miami nurse who, at five foot nine and 220 pounds, describes himself as "tubby," finds that he is willing to have unsafe sex if it means going home with someone better looking than himself:

I've allowed men to fuck me without condoms on more occasions than I can count, quite honestly. . . . It's like this: I'm high. But not always–I've even allowed it to happen when I was on nothing at all. I meet someone who's really, totally attractive, someone I've always wanted–which is not very often, but enough of the time. I let him call the shots, tell him we'll do whatever he wants to do. My goal is to get the guy to go home with me, and I'll do whatever it takes. I can't believe he'd even consider having sex with me. And when he does, it's anything goes. I just don't think about it. I'm too caught up in it. And he is too, because he doesn't think about it either. (p. 24)

While it is true, of course, that pornography alone cannot be held accountable for the insecurity–the hierarchy–so evident in the words of these men and the sexual stereotypes they embody, it also is true that pornography cannot be excluded as a source of these feelings or the actions that result from them. One American pornography "star" is quoted as saying "people who have problems about their appearance or weight shouldn't blame pornography videos or magazines for their problems" (Harris, 1993, p. 50). Really? If, as those appearing before the Supreme

Court of Canada in *Little Sisters* assert, gay pornography is the sole sexual outlet for many gay men, then why should it surprise us that for many, gay pornography videos and magazines–with their presentation of "pumped up blondes and smooth dark men with large penises"–reinforce socially created feelings of poor self-image? Of course, the argument can be made that gay men do not have to use gay pornography. They can find validation elsewhere. But where exactly? Bars and dance clubs, perhaps? Social arenas that disseminate the same message as the one actively promoted in gay pornography, and which remind gay men that they fail to meet the expectations of an image-conscious scene obsessed with muscle and beauty? If not these places, where? Should gay men avoid being judged and sneered at by others and instead resort to that "sole outlet" of positive imagery (read: pornography) where the only ones sneering at and judging them are themselves?

This, of course, also offers a response to those who argue that the private enjoyment of erotica provides an opportunity to practice the "safest sex" possible (i.e., masturbation). To this argument one need only ask: Where is the safety in self-denigration or in the use of materials that encourage you to treat yourself and those around you with contempt? The choices offered are far from appealing or equality promoting. Criticism, from others or self-inflicted, takes its toll. For many, it results in the silence found in disempowerment–empowerment being the very thing needed by a minority community in search of equality.

CONCLUSION

'Faggot!' 'Pooftah!' 'Fairy!' They kept yelling it at me as I left the schoolyard. When some stones flew in my direction–one hit my head–I started to run. Earlier that week I had received an anonymous death threat by e-mail on the school's computer system, which said someone would bring a gun to class and shoot me. I guess my enemies were extra mad because I took a copy of it to the (principal) . . . (Callaghan, 2000, p. 11)

Chris Grant, now 21, was 17 when the schoolyard bullying he describes occurred. It happened because he needed to talk about what it means to be gay and risked confiding in friends. As he explains, "I'd been living with it in my head for years; it reached the point where I needed to tell a couple of friends." Unfortunately, his friends were unwilling or unable to help him. "Most of my friends deserted me once word got out: they found that if they continued to socialise with me, they got abused as well" (Callaghan, 2000, p. 11).

Anyone who has grown up gay, who has risked telling anyone, or who simply does not fit the model of masculinity offered gay male youth knows that events like those above, resulting in considerable pain and humiliation, are not infrequent. Indeed, they are commonplace. As any high school counsellor will tell you, Chris's story is all too familiar: "daily assaults of teasing, bumps and shoves in the corridor, being spat on, steely-eyed glares, which often graduate to kicks, punches, beatings, even death threats" (Callaghan, 2000, p. 11). This is the reality for today's gay youth and while some "survive" it, many do not.

It was within the context of this reality that the *Little Sisters* trial assumed considerable significance. Held up by activists and academics alike as a decision which would determine the right of gay men to distribute the types of life-affirming materials that would give Chris Grant the support and self-confidence he needed to survive the insecurities our society dumps on us, *Little Sisters*, we were told, would either save or further ostracise our gay youth, depending on the Court's willingness to embrace pornography as liberation.

If we look at what happens to young men like Chris Grant within a broader social context–a context in which gender conformity or nonconformity determines one's status and peer group placing–the question needs to be asked whether the materials defended in *Little Sisters* as pro-gay, pro-youth and pro-equality can in fact do anything to ensure that gay youth do not hide, inflict self-harm or mimic a sexuality which asks only that they cease to care about their futures. Gay activists have argued vociferously that gay and lesbian adolescents need to know about gay sex. I agree. But what if the sex we offer them does little more than reinforce the notion that some of us *are* "faggots," "pooftahs" or "fairies"? *Little Sisters* was a case about pornography, and while youth support workers can and do argue about the need for safer-sex education, anti-homophobia strategies, government support and equal rights, the fact remains that *this* case, a case these same people were quick to hold up as crucial to the struggle for rights, required the defence of materials which are *not* about breaking down gender barriers, ensuring safety, self-preservation and community support.

Undoubtedly, much will be achieved by ensuring that men like Chris Grant are able to access sexuality information that combat the guilt and shame thrust on him as a boy. Indeed, such materials would probably go some way in saving his life. But to link affirmation with the pornography defended in *Little Sisters* is to link equality with the types of abuse that result from the harms of rigid, polarised, socially enforced gender stereotypes. And to do so, I would argue, is to risk ridiculing everything for which gay liberation should stand. What happened to Chris Grant would not have happened in a world in which gay youth are not taught to loathe and quash sexual equality. But they *are* taught to do so, and no amount of pornography (gay or straight) will combat this fact of life.

If we are truly committed to protecting our youth, to helping them develop the confidence and self-esteem needed to ensure their survival, it is clear that multiple, often overlapping, education strategies need to be developed and promoted. While it is beyond the scope of this work to provide a comprehensive strategy here, if one thing is clear from the arguments presented thus far, it is that any education campaign must have at its core the eradication of gender as an expectation. In this regard, efforts must be made to address those early childhood dynamics that form the politics of adolescent masculinities and male dominance at school and at home.

Admittedly, the breaking down of sex-based stereotypes is but a first step in a very long process. Gay youth still need to know that 'gay' exists, that we have a history, a community and that there is nothing deviant about or wrong with sexual relations between men. Without this, as many of the interveners in *Little Sisters* rightly argue, self-esteem cannot be assured. In addition to a safe space within which to have such a discussion, the discussion itself will require a level of openness not foreign in schools but all too often ignored by educators when dealing with gay sexuality. Similar tactics will need to be employed when dealing with the issues of HIV/AIDS and safer sexual practices. The question that remains unanswered, however, is: Why pornography? That is, if gay youth need to know that gay sex exists, why is the sexuality we offer them one created by and for pornographers? More importantly, why does gay sex, as marketed through pornography, tend to embrace the inequalities characteristic of male/female relations?

There seems to be an assumption now rampant in our community that people need to see sex in order to know and feel valid about sex and that pornography is the only way to educate and validate an ignorant and self-loathing mass of gay men longing to be sexually active. While I have no doubt that young gay men need to feel less threatened by their sexual feelings and attractions, I fail to see how exposure to pornography achieves this goal. It is disappointing that a community priding itself on creativity, innovation and perseverance has abandoned sexual creativity for pornographic monotony–thereby abdicating sexual self-definition for definition by pimps. I find it difficult to believe that we cannot do better, cannot offer a sexuality that builds self-esteem and integrates sexual arousal and equality. If a frank, open discussion is needed, then let us provide *that*, rather than a deceptive array of sexual messages and stimuli that regulate desire through the threat of exclusion and promote desire through domination. Moreover, silencing those in need of a voice so that others can "know" sex cannot stand as a pillar of gay liberation. Similarly, if the effective use of condoms requires that they be seen then let us actually do that. Let us not, however, masquerade the call for safer sexuality with the use of "educative" media that suggest that only physical perfection merits safety and that once the physical ideal is achieved, safety is not needed because we are, as men, invincible.

NOTES

1. A 1993 report by the San Francisco Health Commission found that "almost 12% of 20 to 22-year-old gay men surveyed were HIV positive, as were 4% of 17 to 21-year-olds. If those figures are not quickly reversed, the current generation of young urban gay men will have as high an infection rate by the time they reach their mid-30s as middle aged gay men are thought to have today–close to 50% (Bull, 1994).
2. *R. v. Butler* concerned the constitutional interpretation of Canada's *Criminal Code* obscenity provisions. In that case, the Court defined pornography as a practice of discrimination on the basis of sex and found that pornography violated the equal rights protections guaranteed under the *Canadian Charter of Rights and Freedoms*. For an overview of the Court's findings in *R. v. Butler*, see Hunter (1993), MacKinnon (2001), McAllister (1992), and Noonan (1992).
3. In making this claim, EGALE relied on the work of Stychin (1995).
4. In making this claim, EGALE relied on the work of Cossman and Ryder (1996).
5. CAS continued:
   There is a need for safer sex educational messages to be tailored to the realities of the sexual practices of men who have sex with men; such messages need to be eroticised in order to be effective in not merely informing but encouraging behavioural change. (Factum of the Intervener Canadian AIDS Society, 1999, paragraph 9)
6. The Little Sisters trial exhibits were viewed and summarised by me, via tape recorder, in the British Columbia Court of Appeal, Civil Exhibits Division, Vancouver, British Columbia, on 27/9/99 to 30/9/99. In some cases, complete bibliographic referencing was not available, due to the printed or audio quality of some exhibits. For the purposes of this paper, I have attempted to provide publishers and dates of publication where this information was available. In some cases, however, only titles and content were available, without reference to the producers, publishers, publication date, or specific page numbers. I have transcribed the specific content of the exhibits as best as is possible given the strict legal conditions under which I was permitted to access these materials.
7. Specifically, Sherman (1995) notes:

The issue in a young man's quest for self-acknowledgement and self-acceptance is not holding hands or hugging or kissing or running through a meadow in slow motion. The issue is the sexual act. A gay adolescent encounters many examples of male-male affection, but they fail to provide the validation he needs if they do not explicitly acknowledge male-male sex. (p. 683)

8. As Dotson (1999) explains, gay porn is not simply an issue of showing us oral and anal sex. There is often a very clear message attached to the penetrative sex demanded by men like Sherman. For example, in his book, *The Culture of Desire*, Frank Browning (1993) writes:

A few minutes into almost any gay leather porn flick, one encounters the macho dudes who "beat" their boys into submission, slapping them hard across the jaw and the ass, yanking a mouth to a macho crotch, as the yanked-on one moans, "Yeah, daddy, yeah!" In many of these videos, men who sometimes look more like young boys than mature adults are forced into submissive, helpless situations such as being tied facedown on a bed or a hammock with their legs spread wide apart, while a group of stronger men, often dressed in leather and carrying whips or riding crops, stand in a circle and masturbate. Eventually, the submissive man is penetrated with a large artificial penis or a man's fist and lower arm. Next, the men standing in the circle each takes their turn at having intercourse with the man who is tied down. When the camera shows the submissive man's face, it is difficult to determine if his expression is one of excitement and pleasure or one of fear and pain. (p. 133)

9. After a brief stint in the heterosexual pornography market, Jeff Stryker regained his preferred status as a top man in his gay male pornography films. At the height of his "stardom" (late 80s-early 90s), he refused to be penetrated by others and refused to identify as gay (Koffler, 1989).

10. Criticising the rise in unsafe sexual practices in gay pornography videos, one writer notes:

... there is a move among some in the porn industry to depict unsafe sex–they say viewers want it. The problem is viewers may want to imitate it. In a *Frontiers* survey, 92 respondents said they do not imitate unsafe sex practices, 39 said they do, and 66 said they do sometimes; while it's encouraging that 92 respondents do not imitate on-screen unsafe sex practices, when you add 39 and 66, that's 105 respondents risking their lives and the lives of their sex partners, and who knows how many others.... Safer sex practices and clean-needle exchange programs are what will help save lives–to give out any other message is unconscionable. The porn industry is a billion [dollar] a year industry. If first one company and then another turns to unsafe sex practices, they will drive others to follow suit. And if fans rent and buy more videos featuring unsafe sex than videos featuring safer sex, they will send a message to the porn industry to keep depicting unsafe sex. Without the porn industry's help, fewer people will adhere to safer sex guidelines and the statistics will soon show that HIV among gay and bisexual men is again on the rise. (Anon, 1997, p. 10)

11. Other pro-barebacking arguments are outlined by Nary (1998) and Valenzuela (1999). Both authors cite numerous pro-barebacking Internet sites.

REFERENCES

Anon. (1995, January). My first lesson. *Manscape Magazine*, 111-113.
Anon. (1997, August). The serious side of porn. *Frontiers Magazine*, 10, 53.
Bagely, C. (1997). Suicidal behaviors in homosexual and bisexual males. *Crisis, 18(1),* 24-34.
Browning, F. (1993). *The culture of desire*. New York, NY: Crown Publishers.
Bull, C. (1994, May). The lost generation: The second wave of HIV infections among young gay men. *The Advocate*, 36-42.
Burger, J. (1995). *One-handed histories: The eroto-politics of gay male video pornography*. New York, NY: Harrington Park Press.
Butler, J. (1990). *Gender trouble: Feminism and the subversion of identity*. New York, NY: Routledge.
Callaghan, G. (2000, April 10). Worst days of their lives. *The Australian*, 11.
Chambers, D. (1994). Gay men, AIDS and the code of the condom. *Harvard Civil Rights–Civil Liberties Journal, 29,* 353-385.
Cole, S. (1989). *Pornography and the sex crisis*. Toronto, ON: Amanita Press.
Cossman, B., & Ryder, B. (1996). Customs censorship and the Charter: The Little Sisters case. *Constitutional Forum, 7,* 103-118.
Cranston, K. (1992). HIV education for gay, lesbian and bisexual youth. *Journal of Homosexuality, 22(3),* 247-259.
de Bruyn, T. (1998). *HIV/AIDS and discrimination: A discussion paper*. (http://www.aidslaw.ca/elements/disc/DISCdiv.html).
Dines, G., Jensen, R., & Russo, A. (1998). *Pornography: The production and consumption of inequality*. New York, NY: Routledge.
Dotson, W.E. (1999). *Behold the man: The hype and selling of male beauty in media and culture*. New York, NY: Harrington Park Press.
Dyer, R. (1985). Coming to terms. *Jump Cut, 30,* 27-29.
Edmonson, R. (1998). *Boy in the sand: Casey Donovon–All American sex star*. Los Angeles, CA: Alyson Publications.
Factum of the Appellant, Little Sisters Book and Art Emporium in the case of Little Sisters Book and Art Emporium. (1999). Supreme Court of Canada, Court File No. 26858.
Factum of the Intervener Canadian AIDS Society (CAS) in the case of Little Sisters Book and Art Emporium. (1999). Supreme Court of Canada, Court File No. 26858.
Factum of the Intervener Equality for Gays and Lesbians Everywhere (EGALE) in the case of Little Sisters Book and Art Emporium. (1999). Supreme Court of Canada, Court File No. 26858.
Factum of the Intervener Women's Legal Education and Action Fund (LEAF) in R v Butler. (1991). Supreme Court of Canada, Court File No. 22191.
Factum of the Intervener Women's Legal Education and Action Fund (LEAF) in the case of Little Sisters Book and Art Emporium. (1999). Supreme Court of Canada, Court File No. 26858.
Ford, D. (1992, September 24). The way we bore. *Bay Times*, 9.
Franke, K. (1995). The central mistake of sex discrimination: The disaggregation of sex from gender. *University of Pennsylvania Law Review, 144,* 1-48.

Frye, M. (1983). Lesbian feminism and the gay rights movement: Another view of male supremacy, another separatism. In M. Frye (Ed.), *The politics of reality*. (pp. 110-127). Freedom, CA: The Crossings Press.
Fuss, D. (1991). *Inside/out*. New York, NY: Routledge.
Harris, W. (1993, December). Porn again. *Campaign Magazine*, 49-50.
Hunter, I. (1993). R. v. Butler: Feminism trumps morality. *Criminal Law Quarterly*, 35, 147-176.
Isherwood, C. (1996). *Wonder bread and ecstasy: The life and death of Joey Stefano*. Los Angeles, CA: Alyson Publications.
Island, D., & Letellier, P. (1991). *Men who beat the men who love them*. New York, NY: Harrington Park Press.
Itzin, C. (1992). *Pornography: Women, violence and civil liberties*. London, UK: Oxford University Press.
Jeffreys, S. (1993). *The lesbian heresy*. Melbourne, AU: Spinifex Press.
Jennings, J. (1994). *Becoming visible*. Boston, MA: Alyson Publications.
Kendall, C. (1993). Gay male pornography and the pursuit of masculinity. *Saskatchewan Law Review*, 57, 21-58.
Kendall, C. (1997). Gay male pornography after Little Sisters Book and Art Emporium. *Wisconsin Women's Law Journal*, 12, 21-82.
Kendall, C. (1999). Gay male pornography/gay male community: Power without consent, mimicry without subversion. In J. Kuypers (Ed.), *Men and power* (pp. 157-172). Halifax, NS: Fernwood Press.
Kendall, C. (2001). The harms of gay male pornography. *Gay and Lesbian Law Journal*, 10, 43-80.
Kendall, C., & Funk, R. (2004). Gay male pornography's 'actors': When 'fantasy' is prostitution. *Journal of Trauma Practice*, 2(3/4), 93-114.
Kleinberg, S. (1980). *Alienated affections: Being gay in America*. New York, NY: St. Martin's Press.
Kleinberg, S. (1987). The new masculinity of gay men and beyond. In M. Kaufman (Ed.), *Beyond patriarchy* (pp. 120-138). Toronto, ON: Oxford University Press.
Koffler, K. (1989, September). Sex, videotape and maybe lies: An interview with gay icon Jeff Stryker. *The Advocate*, 26-30.
Linden, R.L. (1982). *Against sadomasochism: A radical feminist analysis*. San Francisco, CA: Frog in the Well.
Little Sisters Book and Art Emporium v Canada (Minister of Justice) (2000) 132 DLR (4th) 672.
Little Sisters Trial Exhibits, Exhibit 48, *Dungeon master: The male S/M publication*, 39, 1990, Desmotis Publishers.
Little Sisters Trial Exhibits, Exhibit 49, *MAC II: A drummer super publication*, 19, 1990, Desmotis Publishers.
Little Sisters Trial Exhibits, Exhibit 192, *Headlights and hard bodies*, A Zeus Video Production.
Little Sisters Trial Exhibits, Exhibit 197, *Bear: Masculinity without the trappings*, 9, 1989 COA Publishers.
Little Sisters Trial Exhibits, Exhibit 198, *Advocate Men*, 12, 1989, Liberation Publications.

Little Sisters Trial Exhibits, Exhibit 213, *Juice: True homosexual experiences.*
Little Sisters Trial Exhibits, Exhibit 216, *Mr. S/M 65.*
MacDonald, R., & Cooper, T. (1998). Young gay men and suicide. *Youth Studies Australia, 17(4)*, 23-27.
MacKinnon, C. (1989). *Toward a feminist theory of the state.* Boston, MA: Harvard University Press.
MacKinnon, C. (2001). *Sex equality.* New York, NY: Foundation Press.
MacKinnon, C., & Dworkin, A. (1997). *In harm's way: The pornography civil rights hearings.* Boston, MA: Harvard University Press.
Martin, A. (1992). The stigmatisation of the gay and lesbian adolescent. *Journal of Homosexuality, 16*, 163-183.
McAllister, D. (1992). Butler: A triumph for equality rights. *National Journal of Constitutional Law, 2*, 118-142.
Menadue, D. (1999). *The nouveau cowboys of barebacking.* (http://gaytoday.badpuppy.com/garchive/viewpoint/031599vi.html).
Men Against Rape and Pornography. (1993). *Looking at gay porn.* New York, NY: Men Against Pornography.
Myrick, R. (1993). *AIDS, communication and empowerment: Gay male identity and the politics of public health messages.* New York, NY: Harrington Park Press.
Nary, G. (1998). *The risks of bareback sex.* (http://www.japoc.org/policy/viewpoints/jun98edit.html).
Noonan, S. (1992). Harm revisited: R. v. Butler. *Constitutional Forum, 4(1)*, 12-19.
Pereira, D. (1999). *HIV/AIDS and its 'willing executioners': The impact of discrimination.* (http://www.murdoch.edu.au/elaw/issues/v6n4/pereira64.html).
R. v. Butler, (1992). 1 SCR 452 (Supreme Court of Canada).
Reti, I. (1993). *Unleashing feminism: Critiquing lesbian sadomasochism in the gay nineties.* Santa Cruz, CA: Her Books.
Reynolds, D. (1995). I'm ready for my cum shot Mr. De Mille. *Outrage, 147*, 12-15.
Rich, A. (1980). Compulsory heterosexuality and lesbian existence. *Signs: Journal of Women in Culture and Society, 5(4)*, 63-87.
Rotello, G. (1997). *Sexual ecology: AIDS and the destiny of gay men.* New York, NY: Dutton.
Russell, D.E.H. (1993). *Pornography: The evidence of harm.* Berkeley, CA: Russell Publications.
Sanatioso, R. (1999). A social psychological perspective on HIV/AIDS and gay or homosexually active Asian men. *Journal of Homosexuality, 36*, 76-89.
Scarce, M. (1997). *Male on male rape.* New York, NY: Insight Books.
Sherman, J. (1995). Love speech: The social utility of pornography. *Stanford Law Review, 47*, 661-705.
Signorile M. (1997). *Life outside: The Signorile report on gay men.* New York, NY: Harper Collins.
Stoltenberg, J. (1989). *Refusing to be a man.* New York, NY: Meridian Books.
Strossen, N. (1995). *Defending pornography.* New York, NY: Scribner.
Stychin, C. (1992). Exploring the limits: Feminism and the legal regulation of pornography. *Vermont Law Review, 16*, 857-898.

Stychin, C. (1995). *Law's desire: Sexuality and the limits of justice.* London, UK: Routledge.
Sunstein, C. (1994). Homosexuality and the Constitution. *Indiana Law Journal, 70,* 1-56.
Torres, F.G. (1989). Lights, camera, actionable negligence: Transmission of the AIDS virus during adult motion picture production. *Hastings Communications/Entertainment Law Journal, 13,* 89-124.
Urbine, V. (1992). Addressing the needs of lesbian, gay and bisexual youth. *Journal of Homosexuality, 24,* 9-26.
Valenzuela, T. (1999). Bareback sex and HIV: A young man's choice. (http://gaytoday.badpuppy.com/garchive/viewpoint/031599vi.html).
Waugh, T. (1985). Men's pornography: Gay vs. straight. *Jump Cut, 30,* 30-38.
Waugh, T. (1996). *Hard to imagine: Gay male eroticism in photography and film from their beginnings to Stonewall.* New York, NY: Columbia University Press.
Wilcox, W. (1995, January). That old time religion. *Manscape Magazine,* 15-18.

The Queer Sensitive Interveners in the *Little Sisters* Case: A Response to Dr. Kendall

Karen Busby, LLM

University of Manitoba

SUMMARY. Three queer sensitive organizations intervened before the Supreme Court of Canada in *Little Sisters v. Canada*, a case that challenged whether and how Canada Customs treated cross border shipments to a gay and lesbian bookstore. This paper reviews the queer sensitive organizations' arguments on some of the issues in the case, espe-

---

Karen Busby is Professor of Law at the University of Manitoba. Her teaching and research interests focus on constitutional, administrative and procedural law with a special emphasis on law and sexual violence, sexuality, sexual representations and prostitution. She was very active with LEAF (the Women's Legal Education and Action Fund) from 1989 to 2000. She was a member of the *Butler* case committee and she was lead counsel on LEAF's intervention in *Little Sisters*. She is currently on the board of EGALE (Equality for Gays and Lesbians Everywhere). The author would like to thank Jillian Boyd (for preparing extensive bibliographies); Lindsay Waddell (for wading endlessly through the *Little Sisters* trial transcript); Mariana Valverde (for her practical insights); Jennifer Scott, Doug Melynk, Larry Glawson, and her family (for keeping her honest and sane); the Court Challenges Program (for funding a consultation paper and cross-Canada consultations); Janine Fuller (for her willingness to engage with LEAF); and the Gender, Law and Sexuality Research Group, Department of Law, Keele University (for providing her with a research fellowship in March 2002 to work in issues related to obscenity law). Correspondence may be addressed: Faculty of Law, University of Manitoba, Winnipeg, MB, R3T 2N2, Canada.

[Haworth co-indexing entry note]: "The Queer Sensitive Interveners in the *Little Sisters* Case: A Response to Dr. Kendall." Busby, Karen. Co-published simultaneously in *Journal of Homosexuality* (Harrington Park Press, an imprint of The Haworth Press, Inc.) Vol. 47, No. 3/4, 2004, pp. 129-150; and: *Eclectic Views on Gay Male Pornography: Pornucopia* (ed: Todd G. Morrison) Harrington Park Press, an imprint of The Haworth Press, Inc., 2004, pp. 129-150. Single or multiple copies of this article are available for a fee from The Haworth Document Delivery Service [1-800-HAWORTH, 9:00 a.m. - 5:00 p.m. (EST). E-mail address: docdelivery@haworthpress.com].

http://www.haworthpress.com/web/JH
© 2004 by The Haworth Press, Inc. All rights reserved.
Digital Object Identifier: 10.1300/J082v47n03_07

cially the scope of obscenity law, and challenges misconceptions about their positions, including those presented in Dr. Kendall's paper (appearing in this volume). *[Article copies available for a fee from The Haworth Document Delivery Service: 1-800-HAWORTH. E-mail address: <docdelivery@haworthpress.com> Website: <http://www.HaworthPress.com> © 2004 by The Haworth Press, Inc. All rights reserved.]*

KEYWORDS. Obscenity, pornography, Canada, gay and lesbian legal advocacy

A Vancouver-based bookstore, Little Sisters Book and Art Emporium, and BCCLU (British Columbia Civil Liberties Union) sued the governments of Canada and British Columbia in 1988, asserting that Canada's obscenity laws and, in particular, how these laws were enforced at the borders violated the equality and free expression rights of gay men and lesbian women. Twelve years later, the Supreme Court of Canada (hereafter "the Court") heard the final oral arguments in the case, based on the written facta filed months earlier. The Court not only heard arguments from the original parties but also from six interveners supporting Little Sisters and BCCLU, as the appellants (CAS–Canadian Aids Society; Canadian Civil Liberties Association; Canadian Conference on the Arts; EGALE–Equality for Gays and Lesbians Everywhere; LEAF–Women's Legal Education and Action Fund; and PEN Canada) and two interveners supporting the defendant governments (Equality Now and the Ontario government).

In this paper I will provide a brief overview of the Little Sisters litigation. Then I will challenge Kendall's understanding of the positions taken by CAS, EGALE, and LEAF,[1] the interveners who were most sensitive to the equality rights of queer[2] people, as set out in his paper (appearing in this volume). In particular, I will review what these interveners said about the appropriate balance, in law, between acknowledging the liberating and oppressive aspects of sexual expression and on the issue of whether Canada should have an obscenity law.

BIG BROTHER WATCHING LITTLE SISTERS: AN OVERVIEW

Little Sisters' inventory includes "gay and lesbian literature, travel information, general interest periodicals, academic studies relating to homosexuality, AIDS/HIV safer sex advisory material and gay and lesbian erotica. It was not in the nature of an 'XXX Adult' store. . . . It is considered something of a 'community centre' for Vancouver's gay and lesbian population" (*Little Sisters*, 2000, paragraph 1). This description of the bookstore, written by Mr. Justice Binnie in his *Little Sisters* (2000) decision, should be contrasted with Kendall's description of the case as one where "the defence of gay male pornography outlined in *Little Sisters* was made in the context of a court case aimed at ensuring the production and distribution of lesbian and gay male pornography." In reducing the case to a simple defence of "pornography," a term which Kendall does not define but which seems to include most sexually explicit imagery and not just imagery which would be classified as "obscene,"[3] he misses the central reason why CAS, EGALE and LEAF intervened in the case: to defend the constitutional equality and free expression right of queer people to access materials which acknowledge and foster our diverse identities, communities, cultures and sexualities. He also ignores the threat posed by the Customs regime to the very existence of Little Sisters, a vital social institution for the queer community, at a time when few bookstores even had a gay and lesbian section.

So what was the threat? Under the *Customs Act* and *Customs Tariff*, Canada Customs has the right to detain and prohibit material being imported into Canada which might be "obscene" under the *Criminal Code* obscenity provisions. Canada Customs is a much more significant regulator of sexually explicit material through border controls than the criminal justice system is through obscenity prosecutions. The evidence tendered at trial established that in British Columbia between 1989 and 1992 only 14 charges (convictions were not noted) were laid under the obscenity provisions of the *Criminal Code*. However 34,748 shipments were prohibited under the Customs Tariff! Criminal charges have never been laid against Little Sisters and the owners and manager testified that they had never had any contact with the police regarding the content of its inventory. (The police, however, were aware of the bookstore, as it had been firebombed twice.)

Unlike the criminal justice system, the Canada Customs regime–especially at the time the Little Sisters litigation commenced–is inscrutable. For example, proceedings are not public and a government-generated list of prohibited materials is not publicly available. Basic procedural protections, like timely decision making or notice of the information the government is relying upon in making its decision, are not available to importers. Customs has refused to allow importers or their lawyers to see materials before preparing seizure appeals. Customs officers testified at trial what Little Sisters had suspected all along: that Canada Customs had targeted for routine inspection virtually all shipments to the bookstore since it opened in 1984; that shipments to other lesbian and gay bookstores in Toronto and Montreal and from distributors of lesbian and gay publishers also were methodically identified and scrutinized by Canada Customs; and that "there was no such blanket surveillance of heterosexual erotica even in the case of so-called 'adult' bookstores that sold nothing else" (*Little Sisters*, 2000, paragraph 11). The evidence at trial also established that the same materials cleared Canada Customs, even if inspected, when destined for general interest bookstores. The significant delays (months, even years) and damage caused by these inspections as well as the outright refusal to permit many goods into Canada threatened the viability of Little Sisters. The absence of mechanisms for public accountability coupled with the denial of basic procedural protections and, as will be discussed, an unclear obscenity law permitted a regime that fostered systemic discrimination against gay men and lesbian women.

Given Kendall's reduction of this case to a defence of pornography, it is important to note the wide range of materials seized and/or prohibited by Canada Customs when destined for lesbian and gay bookstores or exported by distributors of lesbian and gay materials. From 1984 until just before the 1994 trial, Canada Customs prohibited materials, written or otherwise, that referred to anal penetration. As the CAS factum (1999, paragraph 11) notes, this prohibition had a direct impact on HIV/AIDS transmission education in the gay community. A sampling of the seizures (as noted in the LEAF factum [1999, paragraph 6]) included:

a. the artwork and commentary on the artwork of visual artists including Kiss and Tell, Tom of Finland and Della Grace;
b. sex education manuals including Wendy Caster, *The Lesbian Sex Book*; Charles Silverstein, *The Joy of Gay Sex*; Pat Califia (Ed.), *The Lesbian S/M Safety Manual*; and Jack Hart, *A Manual for Men Who Love Men*;
c. novels and other works by internationally acclaimed authors including Marguerite Duras, *The Man Sitting in the Corridor*; Jean Genet, *Querelle*; Jane Rule, *Contract with the World* and *The Young in One Another's Arms*; Sarah Schulman, *Girls, Visions, and Everything*; Pauline Réage, *The Story of O*; Dorothy Allison, *Trash*; Joe Orton, *Prick Up Your Ears*; and Kathy Acker, *Empire of the Senseless*;

d. anthologies and edited collections of essays including Sarah Holmes and Karen Barber, *Testimonies: Lesbian Coming Out Stories*; Carol Beder, *Unbroken Ties: Lesbian Ex-Lovers*; bell hooks, *Black Looks, Race and Representation*; Joseph Beam, *In the Life: A Black Gay Anthology*; Richard Mohr, *Gay Ideas; Outing and Other Controversies*; Henry Abelove, Michele Barale, and David Halperin, *The Lesbian and Gay Studies Reader*; and Hannah Alderfer, *Caught Looking: Feminists, Pornography and Censorship*;
e. anthologies and edited collections of short stories including David Leavitt, *A Place I've Never Been*; Susie Bright (Ed.), *Herotica*; Karen Barber (Ed.), *Bushfire: Stories of Lesbian Desire* and *Afterglow: More Stories of Lesbian Desire*; and Pat Califia (Ed.), *Melting Point*;
f. periodicals including *The Advocate, Deneuve, The New York Native, Bad Attitude*, and *Hothead Paisan*.

Canada Customs even seized *Belinda's Bouquet*, a children's picture book by Lesléa Newman, which has a single line referring to the protagonist's "moms." While the seizure of *Belinda's Bouquet* is obviously wrong, it demonstrates Canada Customs' insidious pattern of seizing of all things queer.

Little Sisters commenced the 1988 court action, with the support of the BCCLU, because internal administrative appeals against individual seizures were not an effective way to counter Canada Customs' systemic discrimination against queer bookstores. The case took 12 years to get to the Court including pre-trial proceedings where the government contested the bookstore's right to start the case; the last minute cancellation of the 1993 trial (the dates for which had been set a year before); a trial spread over four months in 1994-95 (one of the longest non-criminal trials in Canada in a *Charter* case); a year long wait for the trial court decision, and an appeal to the British Columbia Court of Appeal (Fuller & Blackley, 1995).

Complicating the law and politics of the *Little Sisters* litigation was the Court's 1992 decision in *R. v. Butler*. In 1987, the police seized 85 videos, some magazines and some sex toys from a store owned by Butler and charged him under the obscenity provisions of the *Criminal Code*. Most of the videos involved heterosexual sexual activity but a few involved men having sex with men. Butler argued that obscenity law violated his constitutional free expression rights and that this violation could not be justified. The Court held that while the *Charter's* free expression protections included sexual expression, obscenity law could be justified because the government had a reasoned apprehension that harm flowed from the use of some sexually explicit materials. In particular, materials combining sex and violence would almost always be harmful and materials containing "degrading or dehumanizing" depictions or descriptions would likely be harmful.

The *Butler* decision seemed to adopt a feminist harms-based equality analysis, which was advocated by LEAF as an intervener in the case. Yet, the *Butler* decision also used the language of "moral corruption," "moral desensitization," and "anti-social conduct" (*Butler* 494, 481, 485, respectively) as rationales for obscenity law. Richard Moon (1993) and Mariana Valverde (1999, 2003) have noted that various constituencies, from antipornography feminists and religious conservatives to judges and other government officials, have selectively read the decision to find a justification for the law that they liked. (Even Kendall focuses on passages in *Butler* supporting his assertion that the decision was founded on feminist principles.) Others like Brenda Cossman (1997) and Jamie Cameron (1992) argue that, feminist rhetoric aside, *Butler* rests on profoundly moralistic underpinnings that could be used to justify the suppression of queer materials. Tensions percolated throughout the *Little Sisters* litigation about whether and how *Butler* was affecting access to gay and lesbian materials and what contributions feminist organizations, like LEAF, would make to the case.

WHAT DID THE SUPREME COURT OF CANADA DO?

By the time Little Sisters reached the Supreme Court of Canada, the case presented three different issues on whether the bookstore and its owners' *Charter* rights had been violated. Had Canada Customs treated the queer bookstore in a discriminatory manner? Were the procedures used by Customs to make obscenity determinations fair? Were Canada's post-*Butler* obscenity laws unconstitutional? While interveners are often seen as supportive of one side or the other, their arguments for advocating a particular outcome may be quite different from that of the other parties or interveners. The interveners on Little Sisters' side all agreed, for similar reasons, with the bookstore that it had been treated with discrimination and that the procedural regime was unfair. However, while the appellants and its supporting interveners all were troubled by the post-*Butler* state of Canadian obscenity laws, they differed on the problems identified and the desired outcomes. As this paper will describe, Kendall washes over the significant differences in the positions taken by Little Sisters (*Little Sisters*, 1999) and the three queer sensitive interveners who were generally supportive of them on the constitutionality of Canada's obscenity laws.

The Court had no trouble concluding that the bookstore had been treated in a discriminatory way. It held that:

> Government interference with freedom of expression in any form calls for vigilance. Where, as here . . . such interference is accompanied "by the systemic targeting" of a particular group (in this case individuals who were seen as standard bearers for the gay and lesbian community), the issue takes on a further and more serious dimension. Sexuality is a source of profound vulnerability, and the appellants reasonably concluded that they were in many ways being treated by Customs officials as sexual outcasts. (*Little Sisters*, 2000, paragraph 37)

Later in the decision, the Court stated that

> . . . The adverse treatment meted out by Canada Customs to the appellants and through them to the Vancouver gay and lesbian community violated the appellants' legitimate sense of self-worth and human dignity. The Customs' treatment was high handed and dismissive of the appellants' right to receive lawful expressive material which they had every right to import. When Customs officials prohibit and thereby censor lawful gay and lesbian erotica, they are making a statement about gay and lesbian culture, and the statement was reasonably interpreted by the appellants as demeaning gay and lesbian values. (*Little Sisters*, 2000, paragraph 123)

The evidence on discriminatory treatment was so overwhelming that the Court, like the lower courts before it, could hardly have come to a different conclusion.

The Court's decision on the issue of whether Canada Customs used fair procedures when making obscenity determinations is confusing (Berger, 2002). Stated simply, a majority of the judges on the Court held that, while there were a number of problems with administration of the regime, the legislation underpinning the regime was sound. Moreover, since Canada Customs *might* have remedied these problems in the six years that had elapsed since the 1994-95 trial in the case, it was not appropriate to order changes that may have already occurred. (Four of the nine judges in the case dissented on this point and would have struck down the procedural regime as too flawed to meet constitutional requirements.) Hence, the Court listed these problems, advised Canada Customs to make the changes (if they had not already done so) and stated that Little Sisters could start another case if the changes were not made. The Court did find that the "reverse onus" requirement, that is, the importer's obligation to prove that materials were not obscene, was unconstitutional as constitutional free expression rights required that the government is obligated to prove that materials are obscene.

The parties and interveners expected that the Court would revisit and clarify its 1992 *Butler* decision on the constitutionality of Canada's obscenity laws. This expectation arose not only because the constitutionality of the *Criminal Code* obscenity provisions had been raised in the court documents filed in 1988 when the *Little Sisters* case began but also because, in part, the practical problems of interpreting and applying *Butler* by lower courts had become apparent. The LEAF factum in the *Little Sisters* case (1999, paragraph 35) notes instances of lower courts applying the *Butler* case to gay and lesbian materials in ways that were "reminiscent of the morality testing [used] in the past." In particular it notes that, "the broad principles articulated in *Butler*, especially the 'degrading and dehumanizing' test, have at times been used to justify thinly disguised attacks on gay and lesbian materials" (paragraph 33). As well, questions had arisen about what, precisely, must be proven at an obscenity trial.

Surprisingly, as the evidence at trial established, Canada Customs had simply ignored the *Butler* decision. Canada Customs' internal guidelines, which purported to set out obscenity law and which were the only reference Customs officers used, were not changed after *Butler* was issued and therefore this case had not had any impact, positive or negative, on border enforcement of obscenity law! These guidelines did not even require Canada Customs to consider if the impugned materials had any artistic, scientific or educational merit. Customs officers at every level of the internal Customs appeal process testified at trial that they did not even attempt to assess the merits of the materials they were judging as they were not qualified to do this and did not consider it part of their job. Canada Customs likewise ignored other important cases on obscenity law, such as the 1983 *Rankin* decision, which held that depictions and descriptions of anal penetration were not by themselves obscene.

While the Court did make some comments on obscenity law, it took a rather technical approach to the obscenity issue, stating that the *Butler* case could not be reconsidered because a formal "Notice of Constitutional Question" had not been properly filed in the case. As will be discussed in more detail later, the Court held that the principles articulated in the *Butler* case were sound and applied with equal force to opposite and same-sex materials.

Given the inconclusive outcomes before the Supreme Court of Canada on the procedural and obscenity definition issues, it is hardly surprising that Little Sisters commenced new court proceedings in 2002 against Canada Customs (*Little Sisters v. Canada*, 2003). On the surface, the new proceeding considers whether two book editions of *Meatman: Special S & M Comics*, a well-known comic series, are obscene. More significantly, the bookstore also is contesting whether Canada Customs has taken the necessary steps to remedy the systemic problems that were identified in the lower courts and the Supreme Court of Canada and it is, again, raising the constitutionality of Canada's current obscenity law, especially as it affects the queer community. Given that these issues are before the courts (once again), it is timely to address misconceptions about the positions taken by the queer sensitive interveners in the *Little Sisters* (2000) case.

SEXUAL EXPRESSION: LIBERATION OR OPPRESSION?

The *Butler* decision has been fairly characterized as sex negative (Cossman, 1997; McCormack, 1999; Strossen, 1995). Yet, that decision marked an important step in the decriminalization of sexual expression as the Supreme Court of Canada recognized that sexual expression was included within the *Charter's* free expression protections. In contrast, the Manitoba Court of Appeal's 1990 decision in the *Butler* case, which was more consistent with judicial thinking at that time, held that the *Charter* only protected the expression of "hearts and minds" not "loins and glands" and, therefore, did not protect "base" sexual expression. The Supreme Court of Canada also held in *Butler* that works with literary, scientific or educational purposes could not be obscene and any doubt as to the merit of the work should be resolved in favour of not prohibiting it.

As LEAF's *Butler* factum (1990) and Equality Now's *Little Sisters* factum (1999) illustrate, feminists who are critical of sexually explicit materials pay little attention to the question of utility. Kendall insists that the *Little Sisters* (2000) case is about the defence of *all* gay and lesbian sexual expression. He fails to consider the range of materials that Canada Customs suppressed and the distinctions made by the interveners about various kinds of sexual expression. Therefore, I will describe what the queer sensitive interveners actually argued in the case about the sorts of material that should be protected and why.

The CAS factum (1999) focused on the need for safer sex and HIV/AIDS information. It talked about materials "*designed* to educate men on safer sex practices" [emphasis added] (paragraphs 51, 53, 57) and how materials "containing *positive* representations of gay and lesbian sex foster a healthy sexuality" [emphasis added] (paragraph 8). It described how Canada Customs' prohibition of materials depicting or describing anal penetration had adverse effects on HIV/AIDS education (paragraph 16). It also noted that Little Sisters had the largest inventory of HIV/AIDS materials in Canada (paragraph 7). CAS does not mention materials on sadomasochism (s/m) in its factum nor does it make sweeping generalizations about the defensibility of any and all materials depicting or describing men having sex with men. Yet, in spite of these arguments, all of which were supported by the evidence in the case, Kendall is sceptical about CAS's assertion that *Little Sisters* (2000) was, in part, about the suppression of safer sex and HIV/AIDS materials.

The EGALE factum (1999) opens by asserting that the case must be examined in the context of a society where "cultural representations of heterosexuality are ubiquitous, and our lesbian, gay, and bisexual sexualities are largely invisible" (paragraph 3). Since mainstream media present our sexualities as "unnatural, deviant and perverse" (paragraph 4), "sexually explicit lesbian, gay and bisexual materials . . . resist [our] enforced invisibility . . . reduce our sense of isolation . . . and provide affirmation and validation of our sexual identities by normalizing and celebrating homosexual and bisexual practices" (paragraph 5). These materials enable us to claim agency over our sexuality, document our history and provide education on "healthy and safe sexual" practices (paragraph 8). Some of the materials imported by Little Sisters depict what Kendall describes as "sexualized, large, hyper-masculine men . . . who are sexually aroused by inflicting pain on sexual subordinates . . . . who, in turn, are described as enjoying it." However, like CAS, EGALE did not say anything about s/m materials in its factum.

LEAF was criticized extensively for its failure to acknowledge the importance of sexual speech to women in its factum and oral argument in the *Butler* case, and some asserted that its arguments were homophobic (Fuller & Blackley, 1995; Gotell, 1997). Shortly after *Butler* was released, LEAF committed to developing arguments to address widely held concerns that obscenity law would have a disproportionate impact on lesbian materials (Busby, 1994; LEAF, 1993).

In a significant shift *in emphasis* from the Butler factum, almost a third of LEAF's Little Sisters factum describes why materials by, for, and about lesbian women, including sexual materials, are important for the development of identities, sexualities, and communities. When magazines like *Deneuve* and *The Advocate* and works by Jane Rule, the Kiss and Tell Collective, bell hooks, Sarah Schulman, Dorothy Allison, Susie Bright and Pat Califia, to name just a few, are seized repeatedly by Canada Customs, lesbian and feminist culture are clearly under attack. This point is lost on Kendall.

The *Little Sisters* (2000) decision is disappointing because it doesn't say much about the utility of sexual speech. As noted already, the majority recognized that using obscenity laws to target sexual minorities added a serious dimension to the free expression violation and demeaned gay and lesbian values. It also says that obscenity law should not be used to "suppress sexual expression in the gay and lesbian community in a discriminatory way" (paragraph 58). The minority decision is somewhat more explicit, although still brief, stating (paragraph 247) that:

> Homosexual literature is an important means of self-discovery and affirmation for gay, lesbian and bisexual individuals. In a society that marginalizes sexual difference, literature has the potential to show individuals that they are not alone and that others share their experience. To ban books carrying these messages can only reinforce the existing perceptions gay and lesbian individuals have of their marginalisation by society.

But having expressed disappointment, I should note that the Court made it clearer in *Little Sisters* than it did in *Butler* that sexual expression, including queer sexual expression, is not, per se, obscene but rather is protected by the *Charter's* free expression and equality guarantees.

THE QUANDARY OF CRIMINAL PROHIBITION

There has been a long, divisive and heated controversy (often called the "sex wars") among feminist (especially lesbian) academics, writers, cultural workers and antiviolence activists on the acceptability of various forms of sexually explicit materials, especially those materials involving s/m (Boyd, 1999a, 1999b). The debate has been much less divisive among gay men, as most are supportive of access to sexually explicit materials (Stychin, 1995; Waugh, 1996). Only a few men (Kendall, this publication; Stoltenberg, 1989) present a sustained critique of gay male pornography.

Yet, amidst all the controversy, one point of agreement seems to have been reached. Almost no socially progressive North Americans, writing on this issue in the last decade–including the feminists cited by Kendall as critical of pornography–have advocated that criminal law be used to prohibit access to sexually explicit materials involving adults, except in very specific circumstances like snuff films (Boyd, 1999a, 1999b). In preparation for the *Little Sisters* intervention, LEAF held consultations[4] across Canada in 1999 asking participants whether it should continue to advocate for a criminal obscenity law. Almost no participants supported this view, because such laws were either unnecessary or too susceptible to abuse. Even those most critical of s/m practices, like Didi Herman (1995), or pornography, like Catharine MacKinnon (1993) and Andrea Dworkin (1989), do *not* advocate reliance on criminal prohibitions. MacKinnon and Dworkin (1994), in response to a *New Yorker* article on Canadian obscenity law (Toobin, 1994), stated that they "did not advocate criminal approaches to pornography [as] they empower the state rather than victims with the result that little is done against the porn industry." They went on to say that "criminal law has not been used effectively to stop the porn industry. This we predicted." (Admittedly these statements are hard to reconcile with MacKinnon's active support for the retention of Canada's criminal obscenity law and the Customs regime through her work on the interventions with LEAF in the *Butler* case and Equality Now in the *Little Sisters* case.) Even Kendall does not unequivocally state that criminal or importation prohibitions are necessary to deal with the problems he identifies.

In light of this agreement among lesbians, other feminists and gay men, including both scholars and activists, it is somewhat surprising that, *contrary* to the argument advanced by the bookstore, CAS, EGALE, and LEAF all took the position that criminal law should *continue* to be used to prohibit some sexually explicit materials for adults. Moreover, while the bookstore argued that a categorical exemption for queer materials should be created if a criminal obscenity law were to be retained, queer sensitive interveners did *not* support this position. Finally, while the bookstore and the queer sensitive interveners all argued that the current Canada Customs system was unconstitutional, the bookstore argued that *no* system of border restraint could be constitutional whereas the queer sensitive interveners were silent on the issue of whether the government could or should develop another system with better procedural safeguards. Kendall fails to appreciate these key differences between the arguments made by Little Sisters and three of the "supporting" interveners. The latter's arguments should be examined in more detail to consider what, precisely, was said about the retention of an obscenity law, the use of a categorical exemption for queer or s/m materials, and the proof of harm.

Criminal Prohibition

Kendall describes "LEAF's rather unfortunate and inexplicable decision . . . to reject . . . [the] sexual equality analysis" it advanced in the *Butler* case. Yet the LEAF *Little Sisters* factum (1999) does not reject this analysis. It states, for example, that:

> The Court held in . . . *Butler* . . . that obscenity law had to be focussed on the harms posed by some sexual representations to women and children . . . Thus, this Court's *Butler* decision signals an important shift from the traditional morality rationale for obscenity law towards a harms-based equality analysis. . . . (paragraph 27)

> LEAF submits that materials which appear to eroticise exploitation or subordination or which appear to entrench discriminatory stereotypes based upon, for example, sex, sexual orientation, race, disability or age are much more likely to be harmful . . . (paragraph 31).

These are but two examples of LEAF's articulated support for retention of a harms-based criminal obscenity law. This point was repeated in oral argument. As noted earlier, LEAF also identified that the *Butler* decision was ambiguous on some key points and that these ambiguities opened the way for homophobic applications of obscenity law. In oral argument, as counsel for LEAF, I stated that the *Butler* decision should be refined to recognize the insights of a decade of its implementation, including an acknowledgement by the Court of the importance of sexual speech and the significant potential for discriminatory treatment.

CAS (1999) "conceded that some material with a 'safer sex' message might be obscene. Given the important social utility of safer sex materials, this should be determined in the context of an open trial . . ."

(paragraph 24). EGALE (1999) states, "a legislative vacuum would not be occasioned by striking down the Customs legislation, since the relevant provisions of the *Criminal Code* would continue to apply" (paragraph 49).

Thus, while all three queer organizations devoted space to arguments on the utility of sexual expression, Kendall's implication that they advocated unfettered freedom for such expression is inaccurate. While collectively made decisions are not usually motivated by singular reasons, CAS, EGALE and LEAF likely supported continued reliance on criminal prohibition because people with particular influence in these organizations were not prepared to advance a no-criminal prohibition position or because they recognized that the organizations' energies would be better spent concentrating on crafting a more workable obscenity law.

Categorical Exemptions

On the day before the Little Sisters hearing, a *Globe and Mail* (2000) editorial criticized LEAF for making a queer material exemption argument. Even though interveners are rarely asked questions, one justice of the Court asked me, as counsel for LEAF, during oral argument whether LEAF supported this position. I answered, "I do want to make *absolutely clear* that LEAF is not making an argument that gay and lesbian materials should be exempt from obscenity law."

Contrary to the impression given by Kendall, none of the queer sensitive interveners sought to exempt queer materials from obscenity law. All three, however, made arguments concerning the disparate impacts of Canada Customs' censorship of queer expression, including enforced invisibility, expression chill and stigmatization. Disparate impact arguments are the foundation for constitutional equality claims when the law in question does not contain explicitly discriminatory provisions, like the *Criminal Code, Customs Act* and *Customs Tariff*. For example, EGALE (1999) argues that:

> ... The way in which we experience the violation of our freedom of expression is not identical to the way in which the mainstream heterosexual population experiences that violation . . . Customs censorship . . . perpetuates that oppressive invisibility of our communities. (paragraphs 27-29)

CAS (1999) states that:

> Sexual orientation is the defining difference between homosexuals and heterosexuals. This difference, which requires consideration when evaluating homosexual publications for obscenity, is clearly not taken into account by the Customs legislation. (paragraph 32)

The LEAF factum (1999) states that:

> ... Obscenity law must be sufficiently inclusive to prevent harm to disadvantaged groups, yet, must be tailored so as not to entrench disadvantage. Without the requirement that harm be articulated, obscenity determinations may be filled with little more than discrimination dressed up as morality further dressed up as undue exploitation. Such inappropriate applications promote harm to lesbians and gay men by silencing legitimate sexual expression and by encouraging the view that this expression is less worthy of respect and more deserving of prohibition. (paragraph 32)

Neither the CAS nor EGALE facta specifically consider how obscenity law should treat s/m materials. On this issue, the LEAF factum (1999) asserted that:

> ... As with any sexually explicit materials, conclusions cannot be drawn that [s/m] materials are harmful and without merit and therefore obscene and prohibited without proper consideration of the factors discussed above and any other evidence which may be relevant to the question of harm or merit. (paragraph 34)

During oral argument, following my response on the categorical exemption question, I was asked, "What about s/m materials?" In response, I stated

> When it comes to the specific question of s/m materials, again a full contextual analysis is required ... First, the definition of what exactly is s/m is open to debate. Then you need to ask, "What is the purpose of the materials?" ... For example, a question a decision maker should ask is: "Does it assist people in engaging in s/m practices in a safe way?" ... Moreover, given the biases and misunderstandings that exist around why and how people engage in s/m, a decision maker would have to be aware of [his/her] own bi-

ases and the potential for misunderstanding before making an obscenity determination.

The Supreme Court of Canada stated in the *Little Sisters* (2000) decision, that "LEAF took the position that s/m performs an emancipating role in gay and lesbian culture and should therefore be judged by a different standard from that applicable to heterosexual culture" (*Little Sisters*, 2000, paragraph 63). There was nothing, *nothing at all*, in LEAF's factum, oral argument or any other representation to support this statement by the Court. The Court erred in making this statement and Kendall perpetuates the error by repeating this quote in his paper.

In short, the disparate impact arguments led the queer sensitive interveners to two more modest arguments than that of a categorical exemption from obscenity law for queer or s/m materials, which Kendall asserts they advocated. First, these interveners argued that decision makers have to recognize the differential impact that obscenity law has on queer and s/m materials when developing and applying obscenity jurisprudence to take into account the fact that the materials are not understood by most readers or viewers. The EGALE factum (1999) best states this argument:

> Due to the... deficiencies in the Customs Legislation... the protection of our freedom of expression and equality rights is effectively left to the whim of Customs officers, who are not impervious to the heterosexist ideology that permeates our culture, and who are no less prone to homophobic tendencies than the rest of society... Their decisions are influenced by their own prejudices, as well as their personal sense of morality, hence heterosexism often taints the exercise of their discretion, whether consciously or not, intentionally or not. (paragraph 22)

The second point flowing from the disparate impacts discussion is that Canada Customs' procedural regime is very poorly suited to making obscenity determinations concerning queer materials because it is "opaque, wholly unsuited to making the necessary factual and legal determinations, and fails to provide any mechanisms to guard against misuses of the censoring power. Thus it is impossible for Customs officers within the current regime to perform the task of prohibiting materials in a constitutionally satisfactory manner" (LEAF, 1999, paragraph 26).

Whenever *Charter* rights are violated, as clearly occurs whenever expressive freedom is curtailed, the government is required to establish that the limits it imposes are in response to a pressing and substantial objective and that the means used to achieve this objective are rationally connected to the objective and minimally impair the rights of those affected. In the context of a rational connection argument, both CAS and EGALE noted that the government had not presented evidence to establish that the harms-based analysis of heterosexual pornography used by the Court in the *Butler* case was applicable to queer materials. Kendall devotes much of his paper to challenging the assertion as to whether this analysis should apply to queer materials. The fact remains, however, that the government presented very weak evidence on the "pressing and substantial" objective of needing to deal with the harms caused by same-sex pornography. Further, this argument did not lead these interveners to pursue a categorical exemption of queer materials from the customs regime (except in the alternative by CAS) or criminal obscenity law. Rather the lack of rational objective *coupled* with "a draconian legislative regime, which suppresses a disproportionately large amount of homo-erotic publications, including an alarming quantity of materials that do not satisfy the statutory definition of 'obscene'" (EGALE, 1999, paragraph 38) provided the justification to strike down the whole regime.

The Court was quick to reject the categorical exemption argument presented by Little Sisters and rightly so. The argument relies on a stable category of "gay and lesbian" materials; a category that is not sufficiently precise given the slippery margins of sexuality, desire and gender. But in its haste to dismiss this argument, the Court missed the more subtle arguments on heterosexism and homophobia in obscenity determinations and the procedural protections that could help counter these pervasive problems. The Court stated, in spite of numerous examples to the contrary, that lower courts and other decisions makers did not have trouble applying the *Butler* tests; it refused to acknowledge that its own jurisprudence leaves room for morality based arguments to enter the analysis; and simply ignored homophobic applications of the law.

Proof of Harm

The "harm" of pornography is at issue in two very different points of analysis in obscenity law. Although Kendall's paper focuses on harm, he does not make this distinction clear and as it has important practical implications for obscenity determinations, I will describe it.

As already noted, whenever a rights claimant establishes that *Charter* rights are impacted, the burden then shifts to the government to show pressing and substantial reasons to justify the infringement. The Court stated in *Butler* that, "while a direct link between obscenity and harm to society may be difficult, if not impossible, to establish, it is reasonable to assume that exposure to images bears a causal relationship to changes in attitudes and beliefs" (p. 502). Thus, it was willing to hold in *Butler* and, again, in *Little Sisters* that there was reasoned apprehension of harm to equality rights that justified the criminal and border controls for some sexual expression. Other cases involving expression curtailment have considered justifications like protection of the French language (*Ford v. Quebec*), advancing public health through cigarette warnings (*RJR-MacDonald v. Canada*), and undue influence on voting (*Harper v. Canada*).

The Court was not called on in either *Butler* or *Little Sisters* to judge whether a *particular* book, magazine or video was obscene. The Court stated that sexually explicit materials were obscene if the particular materials in question created a substantial risk of harm and if they lacked merit. More particularly, it held that materials depicting sex and violence would almost always be harmful and those depicting sex activities that were degrading and dehumanizing would likely be harmful. These are a different harm analysis from the "pressing and substantial" justification analysis because, as a practical matter, *every time* a decision maker determines that particular materials are obscene, that decision maker *needs evidence* on the harm created by, and the merits of, the material being judged. As the Court noted in *Little Sisters* (2000, paragraph 60):

> The phrase "degrading and dehumanizing" in *Butler* is qualified immediately by the words "if the risk of harm is substantial." This makes it clear that not all sexually explicit erotica depicting adults engaged in conduct, which is considered degrading and dehumanizing, is obscene. The materials must also create a substantial risk of harm.

Relying on the *Hawkins* case (1993) (which the Court cited with approval in *Little Sisters* on another point), LEAF argued that "mere assumptions about harm and merit without an evidentiary foundation are not sufficient to justify a violation of expressive freedoms . . . Instead, specific and compelling evidence is required which must establish that the elements of obscenity, including substantial risk of harm and absence of merit, have been made out . . ." (1999, paragraph 29). If the Court had adopted the Ontario Court of Appeal's decision in *Hawkins* (and LEAF's submission) on this point, criminal and border prohibitions would be rare as the "specific and compelling" evidentiary requirement would be difficult to meet. Unfortunately the Court's decision is silent on the key issue of what kinds of evidence on harm and lack of merit are required before materials can be prohibited.

CONCLUSION

The Little Sisters litigation revealed that laws prohibiting access to sexually explicit materials have adverse effects on sexual minorities and that the *Butler* case made little difference on access to pornography. Consequently, most feminists and equality seeking organizations like CAS, EGALE, and LEAF worked hard to find ways to move forward with the issues and to avoid polarization in the "sex wars" debates. We have found points of agreement, like the limited utility of criminal prohibition, a willingness to acknowledge the importance of free sexual expression, and a gendered critique of some sexually explicit imagery, both straight and queer. Little is to be gained through an analysis, such as that offered by Kendall, which perpetuates that polarization by offering inaccurate accounts of this work.

NOTES

1. CAS is "an umbrella organization comprising over one hundred AIDS service organizations across Canada . . . CAS serves all communities infected and affected by AIDS/HIV, including women, First Nations and injection drug users" (CAS, 1999, paragraph 2). EGALE is "a national advocacy organization committed to the advancement of equality for lesbians, gays and bisexuals" (EGALE, 1999, paragraph 1). LEAF is a national organization "committed to advancing women's equality through public interest interventions and legal education" (LEAF, 1999, paragraph 10).
2. I prefer to use the word "queer," as it is the most inclusive term to describe people who are gay, lesbian, bisexual, transsexual, transgendered, intersexed, two spirited, or questioning. However, I will use other terminology like "gay and lesbian" if it reflects the composition of the group being referred to by me or by another author.
3. I use the terms "obscene" when referring to materials which are prohibited under the obscenity provisions of the *Criminal Code*, and "sexually explicit" when referring to materials that have sexual content. I avoid using the word "pornography" because it has different meanings for different people, unless it is the term someone I am referring to seems to prefer, like Dr. Kendall.
4. Consultations were held in Vancouver, Winnipeg, Toronto, and Halifax. I wrote a background paper (Busby, 1999) for these consultations and I attended all of them. The discussion paper was made widely available and people who could not attend the consultation were invited to give feedback on the paper.

REFERENCES

Berger, B. (2002). *Equality in an administrative state: A Report on Little Sisters Book and Art Emporium v. Canada* (Minister of Justice). Unpublished report prepared for EGALE.
Boyd, J. (1999a). *Annotated bibliography - R. v. Butler*. (Unpublished manuscript prepared for and on file with the author).
Boyd, J. (1999b). *Lesbian sadomasochism: An annotated bibliography*. (Unpublished manuscript prepared for and on file with the author).
Busby, K. (1994). LEAF and equality: Litigating on equality and sexual representations. *Canadian Journal of Law and Society, 9*, 165-191.
Busby, K. (1999). *LEAF and Little Sisters: Some issues to consider during cross-Canada consultations*. Manuscript available from author.
Cameron, J. (1992). Abstract principle v. contextual conceptions of harm. *McGill Law Journal, 37*, 1135-1157.
Cossman, B. (1997). Feminist fashion or morality in drag? The sexual subtext of the *Butler* decision. In B. Cossman, L. Gotell, & B. Ross (Eds.), *Bad attitude/s on trial: Pornography, feminism, and the Butler decision* (pp. 13-56). Toronto, ON: University of Toronto Press.
Dworkin, A. (1989). *Pornography: Men possessing women*. New York, NY: E.P. Dutton & Co.
Fuller, J., & Blackley, S. (1995). *Restricted entry: Censorship on trial*. Vancouver, BC: Press Gang Press.
Globe and Mail. (2000, March 15). Editorial, p. A8.
Gotell, L. (1997) Shaping Butler: The new politics of anti-pornography. In B. Cossman, L. Gotell, & B. Ross (Eds.), *Bad attitude/s on trial: Pornography, feminism, and the Butler decision* (pp. 57-110). Toronto, ON: University of Toronto Press.
Herman, D. (1995). Law and morality re-visited: The politics of regulating sadomasochistic pornography/practice. *Studies in Law, Politics, and Society, 15*, 147-172.
LEAF (Women's Legal Education and Action Fund) (1993, June 21). Press Release.
MacKinnon, C.A. (1993). *Only words*. Cambridge, MA: Harvard University Press.
MacKinnon, C.A., & Dworkin, A. (1994, August 26). Statement by Catherine A. MacKinnon and Andrea Dworkin regarding Canadian Customs and legal approaches to pornography. Available from: http://www.nostatusquo.com/ACLU/dworkin/ordinanceCanada.html
McCormack, T. (1999). Must we censor pornography? Civil liberties and feminist jurisprudence. In K. Petersen & A. Hutchinson (Eds.), *Interpreting censorship in Canada* (pp. 178-193) Toronto, ON: University of Toronto Press.
Moon, R. (1993). *R. v. Butler*: The limits of the Supreme Court's feminist re-interpretation of s.163. *Ottawa Law Journal, 25*, 361-392.
Stoltenberg, J. (1989). *Refusing to be a man*. New York, NY: Meridian Books.
Strossen, N. (1995). *In defence of pornography: Free speech and the fight for women's rights*. New York, NY: Simon and Schuster.
Stychin, C. (1995). *Law's desire: Sexuality and the limits of justice*. London, U.K. Routledge.
Toobin, J. (1994, October 3). X-Rated. *New Yorker*, pp. 15-24.
Valverde, M. (1999). The harms of sex and the risks of breasts: Obscenity and indecency in Canadian law. *Social and Legal Studies, 8*, 181-204.

Valverde, M. (2003). *Law's dream of a common knowledge*. Princeton, N.J.: Princeton University Press.
Waugh, T. (1996). *Hard to imagine: Gay male eroticism in photography and film from their beginnings to Stonewall*. New York, NY: Columbia University Press.

COURT DOCUMENTS

CAS (1999). *Factum of the Intervener CAS (Canadian Aids Society) in Little Sisters Book and Art Emporium v. Canada*. Supreme Court of Canada File No. 26858.
EGALE (1999). *Factum of the Intervener EGALE (Equality for Gays and Lesbians Everywhere) in Little Sisters Book and Art Emporium v. Canada*. Supreme Court of Canada File No. 26858. Available at: http://www.islandnet.com/%7Eegale/legal/littlefactum.htm
Equality Now (1999). *Factum of the Intervener Equality Now in Little Sisters Book and Art Emporium v. Canada*. Supreme Court of Canada File No. 26858.
LEAF (1990). *Factum of the Intervener LEAF (Women's Legal Education and Action Fund) in R. v. Butler*. Available in Women's Legal Education and Action Fund (1996), *Equality and the Charter: Ten Years of Feminist Advocacy Before the Supreme Court of Canada*. Emond Montgomery, Toronto.
LEAF (1999). *Factum of the Intervener LEAF (Women's Legal Education and Action Fund) in Little Sisters Book and Art Emporium v. Canada*. Supreme Court of Canada File No. 26858. Available at: http://www.leaf.ca/facta/littlesisters.pdf
Little Sisters (1999). *Factum of Appellants' in Little Sisters Book and Art Emporium v. Canada*. Supreme Court of Canada File No. 26858. Available at: http://www.bccla.org/othercontent/lsfactum.html

STATUTES

Canadian Charter of Rights and Freedoms.
Criminal Code, Revised Statutes of Canada 1985, c. C-46.
Customs Act, Revised Statutes of Canada 1985, c. 1 (2nd Supp.).
Customs Tariff, Revised Statutes of Canada 1985, c. 41 (3rd Supp.); Statues of Canada 1987, c. 49, Sch. VII, Code 9956(*a*); Statutes of Canada 1997, c. 36.

CASES

Ford v. Quebec 1988 2 Supreme Court Reports 712.
Harper v. Canada 2000 2 Supreme Court Reports 764.
Little Sisters Book and Art Emporium v. Canada (Commissioner of Customs and Revenue) 2003 British Columbia Supreme Court 148.
Little Sisters Book and Art Emporium v. Canada (Minister of Justice) (1996) British Columbia Judgments No.71 (Supreme Court) (Q/L); (1998) British Columbia

Judgments No. 1507 (Court of Appeal) (Q/L); 2000 Supreme Court of Canada 69.
RJR-MacDonald Inc. v. Canada 1995 3 Supreme Court Reports 199.
R. v. Butler 1990 Manitoba Judgments No. 519 (Q/L) (Manitoba Court of Appeal).
R. v. Butler 1992 1 Supreme Court Reports 45.
R. v. Doug Rankin Co. 1983 36 Dominion Law Reports (3rd) 154.
R. v. Hawkins 1993 15 Ontario Reports (3rd) 549.

In the Slammer:
The Myth of the Prison
in American Gay Pornographic Video

John Mercer, PhD

Buckinghamshire Chilterns University College

SUMMARY. The purpose of this paper is to discuss the significance of the prison scenario and its various permutations in the texts of American commercial pornographic video. The paper will identify the prison as a highly eroticised all male environment, an arena where the active/passive dichotomy of gay pornography is staged and re-staged. The significances of the prison are multiple. The prison draws on a gay mythology of homosexual desire that has its origins in sources as diverse as the literature of the Marquis de Sade and Jean Genet and the erotic illustrations of Tom of Finland and Etienne. Prison scenarios take many

---

Dr. John Mercer is Field Chair in Media Studies at Buckinghamshire Chilterns University College in the United Kingdom. His doctoral research into the iconography of commercial American gay pornography was undertaken in the Department of Film and Cultural Studies at Staffordshire University. The theoretical basis of his doctoral thesis was published in *Men's Bodies* (Ed: Judith Still), a special issue of *Paragraph: A Journal of Modern Critical Theory*. He is currently undertaking research into online presentations of the self in gay chat rooms and completing the film studies volume *Melodrama: Genre, Style, Sensibility* for Wallflower Press. This essay is adapted from a paper delivered at the *Dangerous Representations* conference held at the University of Sussex in June 2001. Correspondence may be addressed: Department of Arts and Media, Buckinghamshire Chilterns University College, High Wycombe, HP11 2JZ, United Kingdom (E-mail: john.mercer@bcuc.ac.uk).

[Haworth co-indexing entry note]: "In the Slammer: The Myth of the Prison in American Gay Pornographic Video." Mercer, John. Co-published simultaneously in *Journal of Homosexuality* (Harrington Park Press, an imprint of The Haworth Press, Inc.) Vol. 47, No. 3/4, 2004, pp. 151-166; and: *Eclectic Views on Gay Male Pornography: Pornucopia* (ed: Todd G. Morrison) Harrington Park Press, an imprint of The Haworth Press, Inc., 2004, pp. 151-166. Single or multiple copies of this article are available for a fee from The Haworth Document Delivery Service [1-800-HAWORTH. 9:00 a.m. - 5:00 p.m. (EST). E-mail address: docdelivery@haworthpress.com].

http://www.haworthpress.com/web/JH
© 2004 by The Haworth Press, Inc. All rights reserved.
Digital Object Identifier: 10.1300/J082v47n03_08

shapes in gay pornography such as the American penitentiary, the military brig, and the fantasised dungeon of the leatherman. I see these scenarios as performing an important function within gay porn by offering idealised spaces for the acts of pornography: voyeurism, narcissistic display and active/passive role-play. *[Article copies available for a fee from The Haworth Document Delivery Service: 1-800-HAWORTH. E-mail address: <docdelivery@haworthpress.com> Website: <http://www.HaworthPress.com> © 2004 by The Haworth Press, Inc. All rights reserved.]*

KEYWORDS. Gay pornography, pornography, homosexuality, gay men, hegemonic masculinity, discourse

In August 2002, Titan Video released *Slammer*, a gay pornographic video located in an unspecified American correctional facility where inmates and prison guards alike submit to the libidinous urges of the sinister, sexually aggressive prison warden played by the video's star, a muscular and tattooed performer using the name Dred Scott. Advertised with promotional literature bearing the slogan, "Don't do the crime if you can't do the warden," *Slammer* is the latest in a long line of gay pornographic videos that use the location of the prison as a venue in which homoerotic desires are played out.

The intention of this paper is to identify ways in which one might theorise about the scenarios of contemporary gay pornographic video and the prison scenario in particular. At this point, I should emphasise that my focus is mainstream American gay video pornography. A consistent problem with studies of pornography is the tendency to conflate modes of pornographic production and, subsequently, to suggest that they all serve broadly the same ideological agenda: that there is, as Andrea Dworkin (1991) has suggested, a *sameness* across a range of pornographic texts. This is not the case. I believe there is a difference between observing the narrative, thematic or rhetorical conventions of a specific genre and deterministically arguing that, due to these conventions, all modes of representation within any given genre are fundamentally the same. It is equally important to emphasise that this essay deliberately does not engage in the ongoing and intractable feminist debate around pornography. Academic attempts to discuss pornography all too frequently seem overburdened with an ostensibly self-imposed responsibility to either justify or condemn this medium; to provide exhaustive overviews of the volatile and often contradictory nature of debate on the subject; to either apologise, or endlessly qualify, the validity of academic interest in such an area; and/or to stray into the treacherous and muddied semantic quagmire that surrounds definitions of the term *pornography*. At specific points, such as the heated climate generated by Dworkin and Mackinnon's ascendancy during the 1980s, for example, these scholarly practices have undoubtedly been necessary. However, it strikes me that they also have resulted, too often, in a failure to fully engage with, or address, the manifest content of the pornographic materials supposedly under discussion. Before we can begin to explain the function of pornography within both gay and non-gay culture and fully understand the positive and negative implications of such a highly charged form of cultural production, we first need to establish what it is that constitutes pornographic text in the first place. This endeavour will not be realised through rhetoric but rather through a frank engagement with the manifest content and formal characteristics of commercial American gay pornography.

In the essay "Men's Pornography: Gay vs. Straight," originally published in 1985, the author, Thomas Waugh, developed a structural analysis of gay pornographic video comparing it to heterosexual pornography. In his foreword to the essay reprinted in 1995, Waugh acknowledges the limitations of the scope of his essay and the changes that have taken place in the intervening period:

> The cultural and political context has muddied considerably since those days of clarity in the early eighties when I was writing this piece. For one thing, the pandemic and the universal presence of home video have radically altered the sexual landscape; though each gets a mention or two in the text, it is obvious how this alteration requires that we look at 'Men's Pornography: Gay vs. Straight' as much as a historical document as an entry in our ongoing debates. (p. 307)

Though these limitations are evident, Waugh's (1995) essay is of significance as, perhaps, the first attempt to conduct a formal analysis of the conventions of gay pornography as a genre. In fact, this essay acted as the catalyst for me to try and theorise about the discursive realm of the gay pornographic video. In his analysis, Waugh identifies the conditions of production, consumption and modes of representation in both gay and straight pornography as a way of identifying the similarities and differences between them. Though Waugh's textual analysis is detailed, his attempts to identify what he describes as "common narrative formulae" (1995, p. 320) are, perhaps, a little too prescriptive or limited to be useful in the analysis of the huge proliferation of commercial gay pornographic videos that occurred subsequent to the writing of his original essay. Given these reservations, I have taken Waugh's invaluable first attempt as the starting point for a discussion of the arenas in which the prototypes of gay pornography operate and hope here to construct a model that more effectively accounts for the wide variety of scenarios that are deployed by contemporary video producers.

The first point that I want to make concerns the generic nature of the scenarios most frequently presented in gay porn videos; scenarios that can be seen as actively contributing to the construction of a gay mythology. This statement requires some qualification. By using such terminology, I am referring simultaneously to the Structuralist concept of myth as an ideological process and a more traditional articulation of the term, referring to the "fictional, fantastical, even allegorical realm" (Kipnis, 1996, p. 163) within which pornography operates.

In reference to myth's Structuralist inflection, Roland Barthes (1982) observed the function of myth in contemporary culture as twofold. Firstly, Barthes proposes that myth has a normative function (i.e., it explains the way the world is). Secondly, Barthes sees myth in narrative as performing the function of masking the repetitious ideological qualities of cultural texts.

Whilst being wary of the determinism of Structuralist concepts, I am interested here in the identification and application of these two aspects of myth in the conceptualisation of a gay mythology in pornography. Drawing on Barthes, I am suggesting that gay porn is normative and concerned with repetition. In *Bound and Gagged: Pornography and the Politics of Fantasy in America*, Laura Kipnis (1996), ambitiously conflating Freud and Marx, attempts to account for the repetitious nature of pornography:

> But why is there so much pornography? Why the sheer repetition? It may be that there's something inherent in human desire that defeats the capacity of anything to satisfy it. For Freud that's because any sexual object is always a poor substitute for the original one you couldn't have, with that unfulfillable wish taking the form of a succession of substitute objects. (Freud also related repetition to trauma, to the need to master psychic injury through the compulsive return to the scene of its origin.) It may also be that within consumer capitalism, our desires have to be endlessly activated to keep us tied to the treadmill of the production-consumption cycle:

if we ceased having unfulfillable desires and stopped trying to quell them with a succession of consumer durables and unnecessary purchases, instant economic chaos would soon follow. (1996, p. 202)

By the use of the term mythology, I also am referring to a more traditional sense of the word, drawing on ideas of the fantastic and the metaphorical. Again, Kipnis (1996) is useful here, identifying pornography as:

... a fictional, fantastical, even allegorical realm; it neither simply reflects the real world nor is it some hypnotising call to action. The world of pornography is mythological and hyperbolic, peopled by characters. It doesn't and never will exist. (p. 163)

Gay porn's principle function is the production of fantasy and the solicitation of desire. A potential contradiction appears to emerge in this specific articulation of myth as both normative and fantastical. However, this contradiction should not be regarded as a peculiarity of gay pornography but rather more as a fundamental feature of mythology as a narrative form. The mythologies of the ancient cultures of Classical Greece and Rome and the fairytale, for example, operate in a similar fashion. These narrative traditions function to explain power relations, to validate or condemn specific forms of conduct and to articulate the shared values of the culture from which they emerge. These ideological agendas often have been expressed through the use of allegory or within the context of a fantastical realm. Similarly, gay porn videos not only perform a normative function, in that they construct norms of sexual conduct, desire and power relations, they also posit a range of fantastic and subversive tableaux, which attempt to structure and, to some extent, articulate the consumer's desires. Gay porn constructs a fantasy of what the gay world should (or could) be like; who takes on what role in sexual encounters, what constitutes good or bad sex, and how the ideal gay man lives his life. Furthermore, contradiction and paradox must be regarded as integral features of popular culture more generally. This is especially true of gay pornography, a genre that exists within the Capitalist system of production and consumption yet also challenges the dominant, heterosexual ideology that underpins Capitalism, through its celebration and articulation of desires and sexualities that are widely regarded as taboo.

I will not attempt to construct an exhaustive list of the scenarios deployed in gay pornographic video, an endeavour that could never be fully realised due to the constant evolution of the genre. Rather, I propose that it is more useful to identify a range of discourses that operate in the narratives of gay pornography. These discourses are normative; they situate gay desire and construct the locus of a gay mythology. I contend that six broad categories can be detected in the majority of commercial gay pornographic videos.[1] They can be seen to operate singularly or simultaneously and their deployment aids in constructing a mythology of homosexual desire.

The first two categories explore the "hidden" indicants of potentially oppressive environments.

THE ALL MALE ENVIRONMENT

This is, perhaps, the most recurrent discourse in operation in gay pornographic videos. The fetishisation of the sailor, the soldier, the prison inmate, etc., is a recurrent feature of gay pornography. The discourse of the all male environment posits scenarios where the restrictions of the heterosexual world no longer apply, where, in the absence of females as objects of sexual desire and release, men are compelled to use each other as substitutes, or where men's *true* sexual desires for each other can be articulated. Army barracks, prisons, locker rooms, dormitories; all are familiar settings. In his exhaustive study of pre-Stonewall gay male eroticism, Waugh (1996) discusses the significance of the all male environment:

> Take for example the myth of team sports . . . These images, like that of the barracks, or the dormitory or swimming hole, offer a dream of community. They are an embodiment, not of the secret rites of an underground subculture . . . but of belonging to the mainstream of homosocial normalcy. (p. 228)

Examples of the all-male environment are almost too numerous to mention, as this is the discourse most frequently invoked in commercial gay pornography. Sporting themes are recurrent in videos such as *The New Coach* (Mustang, 1997), *The New Pledgemaster* (Jocks, 1994) and *The Coach* (Pacific Sun Entertainment, 2001). *Powertool* (HIS Video, 1986) is set in a prison where both inmates and, finally, prison guards engage in homosexual contact. *Pumped Up* (Titan Media, 2000) is set in an all male gym where bodybuilders, aroused by the exertions of physical exercise, engage in sexual play. Similarly, the proliferation of videos with military themes such as *Whatever You Say Sir* (Studio 2000, 1998) and *Marine Crucible* (Centaur Films, 1997) invoke the discourse of the all male environment.

HETEROSEXUAL SCENARIOS

Paradoxically, heterosexual scenarios are a prominent feature of gay pornography. Such a discourse manifests itself as either the supposedly straight man being inducted into the joys of gay sex or, in conjunction with the discourse of the all male environment, the red-blooded heterosexual male using the opportunity of gay sex as an outlet for his uncontrollable sexual urges. *Powertool* draws upon this discourse explicitly. In the first sex scene, Jeff Stryker watches and masturbates as an inmate in the opposite cell becomes sexually aroused after reading a letter from his girlfriend and uses a younger prisoner as a sexual substitute. In *The Bridegroom's Cherry* (All Worlds Video, 1993), a bachelor party becomes an orgy of initiation into the world of adult sexuality with the bridegroom occupying the surrogate position of his bride as his friends teach him how to make love to a woman. In both *Married Cops Do* (Big Blue Productions, 2000) and *Total Corruption* (VCA/HIS Video, 1993), repressed homosexuality among the closeted members of the police force is used as a theme to fetishise sexual play based on the exercise of authoritative power dynamics.

This discursive category can be regarded as homophobic as it appears to celebrate and affirm hegemonic masculinity by eroticising the heterosexual male and his milieu. Indeed, evidence can be found to confirm this supposition. In the opening scene of *The Bridegroom's Cherry*, for example, Ted Matthews is depicted in a sexual encounter with an anonymous gay pick-up. The sexual scene that occurs is confined solely to oral sex, and Matthews is a non-reciprocal participant throughout. The episode culminates with Matthews ejaculating on the face of his kneeling partner. Matthews then dresses and leaves. When asked if they can meet again at some point, Matthews tells the man that he doesn't "hang out with fairies."

Whilst many other examples of the type mentioned here exist, there are, equally, instances when heterosexual scenarios are deployed that are not necessarily homonegative. In *Steele Ranger* (Rascal Video Productions, 1999), for example, heterosexual scenarios are used in a rather more complex or ambiguous fashion. In the first scene of the video, macho park ranger Chris Steele encounters a group of three supposedly straight men masturbating with girlie magazines in a picnic area. Steele's punishment for this flagrant disregard of appropriate conduct is to order the aroused group to give him oral sex. This initial exchange escalates into a full-blown sexual encounter in which the "gay" Steele and the "straight" trio participate. Steele, the insistently macho, predatory, gay park ranger, is presented not as passively giving pleasure to the eroticised straight man but, rather, as actively pursuing men who can provide *him* with the sexual release *he* demands. Later in the video, a scene between Paul Carrigan and Eric Scott problematises the heterosexual scenario even further. Carrigan and Scott, presented as married men, search the forest for firewood whilst their wives, waiting for them on the porch of their log cabin, complain about their inadequacies. The two "straight" men, meanwhile, begin discussing their sexual tastes. Scott tells Carrigan that he prefers to have anal sex with his wife, an experience Carrigan claims never to have tried. Before long, cross-cut with scenes of the increasingly angry wives, the two men begin to have sex with each other in a forest clearing. Carrigan fellates Scott, who tells him, "My wife never does this," an expression that is repeated, in some form or other, throughout their sexual play. The scene indicates not so much the theme of sexual substitution that is often suggested by heterosexual or all-male scenarios, but what might be described as the theme of conversion, where the straight man discovers, sometimes to his surprise, that gay sex is different from, and possibly better than, its heterosexual equivalent.

The next two categories can be seen as validating, in that they offer (albeit highly idealised) representations of an autonomous gay lifestyle.

THE URBAN GAY LIFESTYLE

This discourse is marked by a celebration of the contemporary urban gay lifestyle. Of course, it is a very particular gay lifestyle; one that is situated in the West Coast of America and one that revolves around youth, physical beauty, sexual availability and promiscuity. Within the terms of this discourse, the gay lifestyle depicted becomes synonymous with an idealisation of the lives of urban, affluent, Californian, white gay men: men who are always young, always good-looking, always muscular and, of course, always horny. The gay porn industry, prostitution, street life, bar and club culture as well as luxuriously appointed domestic arrangements are the scenarios regularly identified. Catalina's *Score* (1999) and *All About Steve* (HIS Video Gold, 1993), located in the world of the "legitimate" Hollywood film and the adult video industries, respectively, are good examples. Similarly, *Driven: No Turning Back* (Falcon Studios, 1996), *Sit Tight* (Jocks, 1998) and *Basic Plumbing II* (Jocks, 1998) are situated in San Francisco's gay community, a setting where the videos suggest attractive, gym-toned, gay men lead an autonomous lifestyle that is predominantly concerned with the pursuit of new sexual experiences. Titan Media's *Detour* (2002), for example, begins with title credits superimposed over the rainbow flag and a panning landscape shot of the Golden Gate Bridge. The video is situated in the Castro district, a location that becomes a mythologised arena where gay men can encounter sexual partners on every street corner.

As in the case of the heterosexual scenario, the discourse of the urban gay male is not unproblematic. The overwhelming emphasis that is placed on the coterminous relationships between sexual desirability and both youth and physical beauty is a specific cause for concern. In *One-Handed Histories: The Eroto-Politics of Gay Male Video Pornography*, John R. Burger (1995) identifies ageism as a negative development in gay pornographic video, noting what he describes as the "unfortunate looks-ism practised to satisfy consumer demand for idealised sexual fantasy" (p. 57). Burger believes that the ageism (and racism) that he observes in contemporary video pornography should be addressed by the creation of more socially responsible forms of erotica. He contends that "as liberationists, the gay communities must not practise an erotics of segregation or subjugation" (p. 57).

It might be argued that this articulation of the ideal, urban, gay utopia populated by men that epitomise ideals of physical desirability may well provoke consumers to question, rather than take pleasure in, their own physicality. Further, that exposure to images of gay men with perfect bodies may result in low self-esteem, or even, in extreme cases, body dysmorphia. Although no empirical research can be produced at this stage to either back up or refute this suggestion, the significant body of feminist research into the relationship between advertising and body image amongst women, for example, would seem to suggest that this line of argument may have some validity. I wish to emphasise at this point that it is equally important to acknowledge the empowering potential of gay pornography realised in this specific discursive formation. Through the discourse of the urban gay lifestyle, gay porn offers a utopian fantasy of a world free from societal pressures and the mundane day-to-day prejudice that many gay men encounter in their "real" lives.

In any analysis of pornography, it is important to remember that the genre is primarily concerned with the production of fantasy and, as such, pornography cannot (and some may well argue should not) be expected to reproduce politically correct orthodoxies.

THE LUXURY FANTASY

The luxury discourse is frequently deployed in conjunction with the discourse of the urban gay lifestyle. Its tone is often sybaritic, deploying a mise-en-scène imbued with either pseudo-classical conceits or, more often, the signifiers of a wealthy and indolent California lifestyle. Poolside luxury, glamorous locations, beaches, tennis courts, ski lodges and the requisite jacuzzi are all devices used in the construction of this discursive formation. Falcon's long running *The Other Side of Aspen* series, set in the exclusive ski resort, *Heatwave* (Falcon, 1998) and *Men Only* (Jocks, 1996), both set in luxurious gay holiday resorts, and *Voyager* (Catalina, 2001), based around the exploits of passengers on a gay cruise liner, all draw on this discourse. The work of Kristen Bjorn, one time porn performer and stills photographer for publications such as *Men* magazine and *In Touch*, fits easily into this category. Often filmed in Latin America with relatively high production values, using casts of handsome, Hispanic men in highly choreographed sexual scenes, Bjorn's luxurious videos might be described as gay travelogue pornography. Videos operating within this discourse frequently draw on elements of mise-en-scène borrowed from the representational traditions of heterosexual, soft-core pornography, in particular the exotic locations and lavish settings of cinematic erotica such as Just Jaeckin's *Emmanuelle* (1974). The luxury fantasy articulates an economy of abundance in gay pornography. Laura Kipnis (1996) notes that abundance, in its various manifestations, is "an inherent aspect of the genre" (p. 202) and acts as an expression of a profound psychological human need that she identifies as the "primary desire for plenitude" (p. 202). Kipnis notes that, "Pornography proposes an economy of pleasure in which not only is there always enough, there's even more than you could possibly want" (p. 202).

The final two categories operate in a more fantastic or metaphysical arena of sexual discourse. Both are often characterised by a far less prominent emphasis on narrative and, in some cases, the deployment of more elaborately stylised or codified mise-en-scène.

THE IDYLL

As a corollary to the above, the discourse of the idyll is articulated around "back to nature" scenarios where nudity and exposure to the elements arouse the gay man's "natural" sexual instincts. Scenarios can range from the all male farmhand fantasy of *Big River* (Falcon, 1995) or *Ripe for Harvest* (Jocks, 1995), both set in a mythological, agrarian, American homeland, to the more esoteric and utopian idylls of *Desert Train* (Titan Media, 1997), *Absolute Arid* (Falcon, 1999) and *Absolute Aqua* (Falcon, 1999), which invoke elemental forces of nature and spectacular landscapes as backdrop for the display of equally spectacular bodies and sexual performances. The utopian videos of George Duroy and his production company Bel Ami, such as *Frisky Summer* (1996) and *Lucky Lukas* (1996), featuring casts of young, boyish Eastern European models in idyllic rural locations, also fit into this category.

SADOMASOCHISM

The final identifiable discourse is that of the sadomasochistic (S&M) fantasy, which is invoked in conjunction with almost all of the other discursive categories presented in this paper. Its principle characteristics are the use of dungeon settings, the overdetermined iconography of the leatherman and the fetishisation of anonymous and/or group sexual encounters. The more extreme sexual practices depicted in gay porn videos frequently occur within this discursive framework. The most obvious examples are Titan Media's *Fallen Angel* series, All Worlds Video's *Link* series, Falcon's *Abduction* and *Code of Conduct* series and Forum Studios' *Leather Obsession* series.

The six discursive categories identified constitute the basis of what I have described as a gay mythology in pornographic video. These categories identify and articulate the paradigm of discourses and social settings in which homosexual desire can be situated and manifest itself. In some cases, these discursive formations are deployed singularly, but more often (as will be observed in the final section of this paper), they are used in conjunction with each other; the discourse of the all male environment and the S&M fantasy in military-themed videos, for example. The deployment of these discourses demonstrates, in the fantasised world of the porn video at least, that articulations of gay desire and gay eroticism are by no means uniform. The mythology constructed by gay pornography tells viewers that there is more than one form of gay sexual conduct, there are many sets of circumstances in which homosexual desire can manifest itself and, perhaps most significantly, that there is more than one "type" of gay man. The mythology constructed by gay pornography suggests that there is a plurality to the nature of gay desire. The deployment of the discursive categories that I have identified articulates the arenas in which gay sexuality can be situated and facilitates the celebration of masculinity as a homoerotic spectacle.

THE PRISON AND GAY PORNOGRAPHY

How then do prison scenarios 'fit' within the paradigm of discourses identified previously? Further, why is the prison a motif of the American gay pornographic video?

The first point is that prison scenarios enable several of these discursive frameworks to operate simultaneously. Prisons are all male, self-contained environments where the social conventions of the outside world (i.e., the heterosexual world) do not apply and where hierarchical power relations can be played out. Prisons afford opportunities for characters identified as heterosexual to channel sexual energies through homosexuality, and the power dynamics implicit in prisons enable the S&M discourse to be articulated. In gay pornography, the prison becomes a fetishised space of danger, sexual tension and desire.

The prison scenario, then, has the potential to conflate three of the discourses of gay pornography simultaneously. Through an analysis of videos that incorporate prison scenarios, it is possible to discern three broad prison spaces that emerge in gay pornography. For the final section of this paper, I will identify these scenarios and offer some suggestions as to their function and origin. It should be noted that I am not offering a deterministic genealogy of the myth of the prison in gay porn. By its very nature, pornography is a genre that draws promiscuously on a disparate range of sources, historical and artistic precedents, urban myth and fantasy. Instead, I would suggest that there are several key catalysts for the recurrence of certain types of prison scenarios in gay pornographic videos.

The Penitentiary

The penitentiary is, perhaps, the most recurrent of prison scenarios in gay pornography. This may be due, in no small part, to the notoriety of Jean Genet's foray into the world of pornographic cinema, *Un Chant*

D'Amour. Made around 1950, *Un Chant D'Amour* is a short silent film in which a prison warden spies on inmates in varying degrees of undress and suggested sexual activity. The film, subsequently, follows the attempts at communication and metaphorical sexual union between two prison inmates interspersed with what the viewer is to infer are either idyllic dream sequences or the recalled memories of one of the prisoners. The film suggests themes of isolation and alienation, the impossibility of communication and the disparity between dreams and reality. The romanticism of *Un Chant D'Amour* is ostensibly absent from the fantasy prison spaces invoked by contemporary American gay pornography; however, themes of voyeurism and narcissism, the sexualisation of seeing and being seen are always evident.

The most notable example of the penitentiary scenario in contemporary commercial gay pornography is William Higgin's *Powertool* (1987), which is reputed to be the best-selling gay pornographic video of all time. Though this hyperbolic claim is difficult to verify, it is undeniably the case that *Powertool* is one of very few gay pornographic videos that most gay men will have either heard about or seen. In the video, Jeff Stryker is jailed for 30 days for an unspecified crime, which the viewer is to assume is some form of soliciting. Whilst in prison, he is involved in a succession of sexual encounters with prison inmates culminating in his sexual conquest of a similarly voyeuristic prison guard. The video deploys a constantly shifting point of identification for the viewer, utilising the various ways of looking and being seen that characterise pornographic representation; namely, voyeurism and narcissistic display. Whereas *Un Chant D'Amour* is concerned with isolation, metaphorically realised through the device of the confined prison cells, *Powertool* deploys the caged cells of US penitentiaries as a device to afford what Linda Williams (1989) describes as the motivating goal of pornography: maximum visibility. We can see the prisoners and their every action as they offer their bodies to us narcissistically for our voyeuristic delight. This dual viewing position, shifting between voyeurism and narcissistic display, is best exemplified by the first action scene in *Powertool* where Stryker watches as two prisoners, after reading letters from girlfriends, begin to engage in sex. Our point of identification is initially with Stryker: we see what he sees. As he undresses and begins to masturbate while watching this erotic spectacle, his self-obsessed performance of his own sexual excitement alters the dynamic of the viewing position. The viewer alternates between observing the two cellmates through Stryker's eyes and witnessing Stryker's narcissistic display of his own body, which is focussed on the spectacle of the star's famously prodigious endowment.

The Military Prison or Brig

The second identifiable prison space owes a significant debt to the work of the so-called physique artists of the 1950s onwards and in particular to the illustrations of Etienne and Tom of Finland. The latter demonstrated an enduring fascination with military iconography, especially the uniforms of the Nazi troops who occupied Finland during World War II, and who became something of a sexual fixation for the young artist. The uniform of the stormtrooper combined with the accoutrement of 1950s bikers formed the basis of the leatherman iconography with which Tom is, perhaps, most clearly associated. In Tom's work, military figures abound, as do scenarios based on sexual relations marshalled around power dynamics and their subversion. It is this rich and relatively complex source material that is drawn upon in the deployment of the military prison in gay pornography. The brig offers the opportunity for power relations to be played out and articulated through the passive/active dichotomy of gay sexual representation that is presented in gay pornography. In the brig scenario, the prisoner is nearly always the passive *bottom*, often identified as heterosexual, and forced to submit to the sexual desires of the fetishised, active *top* military figure.

One example may be found in *Code of Conduct 1: Stripped* (Falcon, 1996) in which a young sailor is arrested for procuring a female prostitute and is imprisoned by military police dressed in the pseudo-fascist regalia of Tom's leathermen. The sailor's response to homosexual stimuli is tested over a succession of days. The structure of the video's narrative references simultaneously a prison journal, a military report and the catalogue of sexual practices listed in the Marquis de Sade's *120 Days of Sodom*; as each day progresses, the sailor is subjected to even more elaborate and rigorous tests of his homosexual response.

The Dungeon

The final identifiable prison space frequently operates within a highly stylised, nonlinear narrative construction. The dungeon scenario, yet again, draws inspiration from Tom of Finland's and Etienne's homoerotic illustrations. Tom's realisation of the iconography of the leatherman has effectively provided a generic paradigm of iconography and types that populate the abstract realm of the dungeon. The dungeon also has a literary origin in the work of the Marquis de Sade. Just as Sade's cumulative excess can be seen adopted elsewhere within pornographic narrative, so in the dungeon scenario, one can observe the deployment of motifs that suggest an, albeit metaphorical, descent into the depths of hell or the deepest recesses of animalistic sexual drives. Whereas a clear linear narrative is always evident within the context of penitentiary or brig scenarios, the deployment of the dungeon offers the opportunity to construct fantasies that eschew linear narrative conventions. Montage editing, dream sequences, flashbacks and visual metaphors are but some of the filmic strategies deployed in the context of this scenario.

An example of the dungeon scenario is offered by Titan Media's *Fallen Angel* series, advertised with the strap line 'Hell Never Felt So Good.' *Fallen Angel I* (1997) focuses on the leather clubs of Chicago and events surrounding the 1997 *International Mr. Leather* (IML) competition. In this video, scenes of fisting and other assorted S&M activities are united by stylised montage sequences of the protagonist. The fallen angel of the title, tattooed, pierced and moustachioed Steve Cannon, wears leather gear based on Tom of Finland's illustrations and acts as an observer of, and occasional participant in, the various scenes. In the second video of the series, the stylisation and visual metaphors contained in *Fallen Angel I* (1997) are heightened with a mise-en-scène that evokes a plethora of hellish connotations. Dean Coulter is seen sporting fetish gear and black wings in a wilderness location on the outskirts of San Francisco. He follows a stream of similarly clad leathermen to an underground dungeon presided over by a demonic leathermaster, Kyle Brandon, who is presented in stylised close-ups against blazing furnaces and nightclub laser beams before he initiates a lengthy series of fetish sex scenes. The video is distinguished by the absence of a conventional plotline in favour of extremely stylised and abstract filmic strategies. It is notable that, even within the constraints of pornographic videos driven by a conventional narrative, the deployment of the leatherman is often accompanied by scenes of somewhat more extreme or outré sexual practices, the use of a highly stylised mise-en-scène and by filmic techniques (montage editing, for example) that disrupt narrative progression. In *Fallen Angel 2* (1998), the leathermaster is rhetorically positioned as the ultimate fantasy figure for the viewer both as the focus of the viewer's desiring gaze and also by his facility to disrupt a sense of linear narrative progression. In accordance with Laura Mulvey's (1975) controversial suggestion that the strategies used to represent women in classical Hollywood cinema (the close-up and the fractured body, for example) halt narrative progression, so, too, it might be argued (though this is clearly an observation that would require further research) that the leatherman has an equally significant function in gay pornographic video.

In closing, it is tempting to suggest that prison scenarios act as metaphors for the alienated and marginalized position of gay men within culture. It would be equally tempting to suggest that the deployment of the prison suggests an underlying masochism or homophobia enshrined within pornographic representation. I contend that both of these lines of argument are essentially flawed and far too simplistic and reductive to account for the relatively complex range of discourses at play within these scenarios. Rather, I would suggest that prison scenarios offer spaces that draw on a mythology of homosexual desire and offer arenas in which the active/passive dichotomies of gay pornographic representation can be staged, problematised and explored.

NOTE

1. Whilst I cannot claim to have used representative sampling, my observations here are based on a textual analysis of 110 commercially available gay pornographic videos produced between 1987 and 2002, collected as part of a larger study into the iconography of gay pornography.

REFERENCES

Barthes, R. (1982). *Selected writings.* London, UK: Fontana.
Burger, J. R. (1995). *One-handed histories: The eroto-politics of gay male video pornography.* Binghamton, NY: Harrington Park Press.
Dworkin, A. (1991). Against the male flood: Censorship, pornography and equality. In R.M. Baird & S.E. Rosenbaum (Eds.), *Pornography: Private right or public menace* (pp. 56-61). New York, NY: Prometheus.
Kipnis, L. (1996). *Bound and gagged: Pornography and the politics of fantasy in America.* Durham, NC: Duke University Press.
Mulvey, L. (1975). Visual pleasure and narrative cinema. *Screen, 16(3),* 6-18.
Waugh, T. (1995). Men's pornography: Gay vs. straight. In C.K. Creekmur & A. Doty (Eds.), *Out in culture: Gay, lesbian, and queer essays on popular culture* (pp. 307-327). Durham, NC: Duke University Press.
Waugh, T. (1996). *Hard to imagine: Gay male eroticism in photography and film from their beginnings to Stonewall.* New York, NY: Columbia University Press.
Williams, L. (1989). *Hard core: Power, pleasure and the frenzy of the visible.* Berkeley, CA: University of California Press.

"He Was Treating Me Like Trash, and I Was Loving It..." Perspectives on Gay Male Pornography

Todd G. Morrison, PhD

National University of Ireland-Galway

SUMMARY. As the topic of gay male pornography has received limited attention from social scientists, little is known about how gay men perceive this medium. In the current study, a focus group methodology was used whereby participants examined specific scenes from commercially available gay pornography in terms of the messages they disseminate about the body and gay sexuality, in general. Findings suggest that discussants tended to view the medium from a utilitarian perspective. They saw pornography as a masturbatory aid, and did not believe that it possessed much significance vis-à-vis gay men's attitudes and behaviours. Those who identified potentially negative influences of this medium saw them as transitory and most likely to occur among gay men other than themselves. *[Article copies available for a fee from The Haworth Document Delivery Service: 1-800-HAWORTH. E-mail address: <docdelivery@haworthpress.com> Website: <http://www.HaworthPress.com> © 2004 by The Haworth Press, Inc. All rights reserved.]*

Correspondence may be addressed: Department of Psychology, National University of Ireland, Galway, Ireland (E-mail: Todd.Morrison@nuigalway.ie).

[Haworth co-indexing entry note]: " 'He Was Treating Me Like Trash, and I Was Loving It...' Perspectives on Gay Male Pornography." Morrison, Todd G. Co-published simultaneously in *Journal of Homosexuality* (Harrington Park Press, an imprint of The Haworth Press, Inc.) Vol. 47, No. 3/4, 2004, pp. 167-183; and: *Eclectic Views on Gay Male Pornography: Pornucopia* (ed: Todd G. Morrison) Harrington Park Press, an imprint of The Haworth Press, Inc., 2004, pp. 167-183. Single or multiple copies of this article are available for a fee from The Haworth Document Delivery Service [1-800-HAWORTH, 9:00 a.m. - 5:00 p.m. (EST). E-mail address: docdelivery@haworthpress.com].

http://www.haworthpress.com/web/JH
© 2004 by The Haworth Press, Inc. All rights reserved.
Digital Object Identifier: 10.1300/J082v47n03_09

KEYWORDS. Gay male pornography, gay men, attitudes, pornography, focus groups, body image, heterosexual men, masculinity

My "relationship" with gay male pornography is somewhat conflicted. On the one hand, I admit without reservation or embarrassment that I find some (much?) of it to be highly erotic. I can remember seeing a photograph of Ken Ryker from *The Other Side of Aspen IV*, and thinking "I *have* to see that body (or, in truth, a more specific part of his anatomy) fuck something!" Exposure to that image resulted in the purchase of my first gay pornographic video–surprisingly enough, the fourth instalment of the *Aspen* series. Buying another Ken Ryker "sextravaganza" entitled *Big River* led to my discovery of "super-bottoms" Scott Baldwin and Christian Fox. Mr. Ryker was summarily buried in the graveyard of abandoned masturbatory fodder, as these performers (and the various "films" in which they appeared) received my undivided attention. Since then I have moved on to (and, in many cases, past) Clay Maverick, Lane Fuller, Anthony LaFont, George Vidanov, Brett Mycles, Travis Wade, Matthew Rush, and a host of pornography actors/models whose names I didn't bother committing to memory. All of these individuals have been a source of sexual pleasure either directly through masturbation or indirectly through erotic fantasy. I cannot deny their aesthetic appeal or the physical response they trigger in me.

And yet, there are aspects of gay male pornography that I see as problematic. On a minor note, I find the medium's efforts to create an erotic interchange between consumer and performer patently manipulative and somewhat irritating. For example, in *Men* magazine (January 2003), the text accompanying a pictorial layout of Blake Harper reads:

> Look into my eyes and tell me what you want. Would you like to watch me take my clothes off? Do you want to see me naked? Perhaps you'd like to see me in leather–or maybe latex. That's OK, baby... So come on, handsome. Let loose. Let's get wild. (p. 67)

Are the imaginations of most gay male readers so impoverished that they need this kind of textual assistance in order to create and sustain a masturbatory fantasy about Blake Harper? Do most gay men respond to generic sexual overtures, ones that are mass-produced and distributed (e.g., "You wanna suck my cock–you wanna fuck my ass?"–*Men*, January 2003, p. 67)? Do we find this ersatz intimacy titillating?

Of greater concern is the hyper-masculinity that is rampant in gay male pornography. For example, in a recent layout for *Men* magazine (January 2003), cover model Nate Christianson reports that his favourite exercise is squats. The reason he offers for liking them isn't because they firm one's buttocks, a motivation that is aesthetic and, thus, clearly "feminine," but rather because "working those muscles makes me able to fuck a guy's tight ass good and hard for a real long time" (p. 33). In popular gay men's pornographic magazines such as *Blueboy*, *Dude*, and *Jock*, there is a surfeit of cocks that are "fist-sized," "huge," "big," "enormous," "massive," "fat," "thick," and "monstrous"; testicles that are "egg-sized"; and ejaculate that is "super-blasting," "thick," "hot," "juicy," and "heavy." Gay pornographic actors/models are described as "masculine muscle stud[s]," "outdoor men," "tough guys," "super-masculine jock bodybuilder[s]," "rough and tough bad boys," and believe it or not, "super-macho manly men."

The medium's determination to be fiercely "masculine," and its eschewal of anything remotely feminine may explain its misogynistic elements and its disturbing tendency to conflate pleasure and pain. For example, "this month's ass pounder [Just Dragon]" is characterized as:

> ... A hard fuck, he takes you down and pounds your ass with such relentless repetition you find yourself just letting go ... When he pulls out of you, your hole is so pitifully trashed it can't even squeeze close. (*Blueboy*, April 2002, p. 50)

In an erotic story appearing in the same issue of *Blueboy*, author "Tad Tramp" writes:

> He held me down hard, slapping the back of my head and calling me a bitch, demanding me to tighten my 'loose fucking cunt' and take his cock even deeper ... He held me down like the pig whore I was and fucked me hard and filthy. I was a slut in his mind. He was treating me like trash, and I was loving it ... Just when I thought I couldn't take another thrust, he ripped his fist-sized prick from my torn, trashed hole and spit a cupful of hot, thick cum all over my back. ... (p. 69)

Finally, in a pictorial layout entitled "Doin' it up the butt," "Jet Set Productions dude" Dane Colt reports that: "When I first took it in the butt, it was a pain I can't describe. It was like I was being ripped open, but after a while I couldn't get enough ..." (*Jock*, April 2002, p. 50). Directly above this statement are a series of photographs accompanied by the caption: "take that nasty fucking hole hard."

By identifying elements of gay male pornography that I find problematic, I am not subscribing to the "pious hysterics of such prophets of doom as Andrea Dworkin and Catharine MacKinnon, who presume an absurdly literal relation between fantasy and reality" (Harris, 1997, p. 157). I recognize that pornography often serves as a convenient scapegoat, one which individuals can self-righteously attack and in so doing protect against self-criticism and more meaningful and complex analyses of gay male culture. I am not blaming this medium for internalized homonegativity and its sequelae such as substance abuse and unsafe sex. Nor am I advocating that text and images of "hard man-meat" and "waiting, hungry butt-holes" be censored.

Instead, what I am asking is that gay men explore their responses to this medium. Dyer (1994) reports that pornography "participates in the cultural construction of desire" (p. 49). Yet, if one assumes that, like any commercial enterprise, pornography also responds to the demands placed upon it by the consumer, then it is incumbent upon us to examine why we want certain kinds of images and text. For example, why do some of us find "barely legal pretty boys spread[ing] their firm butt cheeks" erotic? What is about it "nasty bum-slamming," "nipple-biting," and "throat-stabbing blowjobs" that turns some of us on? [All quotes taken from *Dude*, November 2001, p. 67.] Why is masculine authenticity granted iconic status in gay male pornography? And why do many of us sexualize performers such as Just Dragon who "likes his men on their back, legs spread wide and taking his hard, pounding cock, deep and wet in their hole all the way down to the nuts, his bush grinding hard into [their] asslips" (*Blueboy*, April 2002, p. 52)? (Incidentally, how many gay men who consider the preceding sentence unobjectionable would do so if it described a woman in a supine position, legs spread wide?)

The purpose of this study is to explore gay men's attitudes about commercially available pornography, as represented by sexual scenes taken from three popular titles: *Absolute Aqua* (Falcon Studios, 1999), *An Officer and His Gentleman* (Celsius Films, 1995), and *The Naked Highway* (Big Video Entertainment, 1997). A number of issues were explored; however, for the sake of concision, only the following will be outlined in detail: (a) the medium's portrayal of the "ideal" homosexual body and the possible implications of exposure to that type of imagery; and (b) its depiction of gay sexuality.

Given the sensitive nature of this topic (i.e., participants would be answering questions about gay male pornography and viewing sexually explicit material), a focus group methodology was used. Grogan and Richards (2002) suggest that, when discussing issues that are considered personal or private, individuals may talk more freely in a group setting than in one-on-one interviews. As well, these authors report that the depth of self-disclosure tends to be greater in focus groups, and that they generate interactive data (i.e., discussants converse with both the facilitator and each other using language that is fairly naturalistic). Finally, focus groups may lessen the power differential between researcher and subject–creating a non-hierarchical climate in which the "free exchange" of ideas is encouraged.

METHOD

Participants

Ten individuals[1] were recruited using chain-referral sampling (i.e., two acquaintances of the author were asked if they would be interested in participating in a focus group on gay male pornography, and were instructed to locate other volunteers).

Materials

Each discussant received a two-page sheet outlining a number of questions that would be explored during the focus group. Pens and paper also were distributed so that discussants could write down any observations made while watching the three pornographic scenes (which were shown on a large screen using an LDC projector). Participants' conversations were recorded using a tape recorder with a directional microphone.

Procedure

Those expressing interest in the study were informed that: (a) in a group setting, individuals would watch three scenes from commercially available mainstream gay male pornography; (b) after each scene, a variety of trigger questions would be explored to generate group discussion; (c) discussants' conversations would be tape-recorded and transcribed–however, no identifying information would appear on the transcriptions and the tapes themselves would be available only to the author; and (d) each focus group would last for approximately 90 minutes. In addition, potential discussants were informed that the study had received ethical approval from the Human Research Ethics Committee at the institution where the study took place. Those who were still interested in participating were then given the date, time, and location of the focus group.

Three focus groups were conducted (*n*s were 4, 2, and 4, excluding the author who served as facilitator). Each focus group was held in a small conference room, located in a relatively private part of the college, and contained a large circular table, several chairs, an LDC projector, and a movie screen. On the table, in front of each chair, were placed a two-page sheet of questions, a pen and a pad of paper.

The protocol for each focus group was as follows. Upon arrival, participants were greeted by the facilitator and informed to "help themselves" to refreshments (e.g., bottled water, granola bars, etc.) located on a side table. They were, again, informed of the purpose of the study and reminded that their conversations would be tape-recorded and transcribed. As well, the author stressed the confidential nature of all discussion occurring in the focus group.

After 10 minutes of preliminaries, the study proper began. The scenes were presented in the following order (*Absolute Aqua*, *An Officer and His Gentleman*, and *The Naked Highway*),[2] and group discussion followed *each* scene. Conversation about a given topic was terminated when it appeared to "dry up" naturally (Grogan & Richards, 2002). At the end of the focus group, discussants were thanked for their participation and informed to contact the author should they have any further questions about the study.

RESULTS

The Gay Body in Pornography

When asked to identify the constituent parts of the ideal male body, as represented by mainstream gay pornography, discussants evidenced remarkable consistency in their responses. They emphasized that the ideal gay physique embodies a "butch" aesthetic in which one is "tanned," "muscular," and "hairless," and possesses "tattoos," "short hair," "a v-shaped build," "broad shoulders," and "six-pack abs." The level of body image investment associated with being depilated, defined, and devoid of "[even] an ounce of body fat" would suggest a level of corporeal preoccupation that might be perceived stereotypically as feminine. However, discussants appeared to ignore this contradiction. The investment required to achieve and maintain this "butch" body may deviate from the strictures of hegemonic masculinity; yet, ironically, the body itself possesses unassailable masculine credentials.

Despite participants' awareness of the various properties of the "ideal" physique, as represented in gay pornography, there was disagreement about this body's erotic value. Some felt that the unreal status of the performers' bodies enhanced their appeal.

Facilitator: Does this [sex scene with Anthony LaFont and Lane Fuller] map onto the body gay men want to possess and want to fuck?

Group 3a: Yes. Absolutely . . . you want to have sex with him because he's young and hot and [sex with] the other one because he's so masculine and manly and you want to be like him . . .

Group 3b: If you saw a real body up there then you wouldn't want it. You'd be like "Oh, look, he's got a paunch or he's got hair . . . look at how small his dick is" . . . or me making fun of, you know, it's limp. [Gay men] want that perfect body. Even if you can't have it, you still don't want to watch real people have sex because that's not fun.

Conversely, others maintained that the absence of corporeal authenticity or realness diminished the performers' erotic value.

Group 1a: To me, it's the ideal fashion model. It portrays more of the gay clone image . . . that everyone should [possess] the perfect body. In that way, I don't find it as appealing as if [he] had 5 percent body fat versus 1 percent.

Facilitator: So, you're saying it's almost generic? It's so perfect that it's not interesting?

Group 1a: It's not real.

Group 3c: [Being hairless] gives the illusion of plastic, too. It doesn't look like a real person . . .

Group 3b: Ken and Barbie.

Facilitator: So, for this group, realistic bodies constitutes more erotic?

Group 2a: I think so . . . Those [individuals appearing in a scene taken from *An Officer and His Gentleman*] are guys that I could actually imagine having sex with, you know . . . People that you think "Oh, yeah, I've had someone who looks like that or I have a good chance of having sex with someone who looks like that."

Participants expressed divergent views on whether exposure to the "ideal" body contained in pornography affects gay men's perceptions of their appearance. Of those contending that it has little influence, most simply stated that viewers are able to differentiate between "fantasy" bodies and "real" bodies. However, some discussants offered specific explanations for this position. One maintained that pornography doesn't necessarily trigger a motive of emulation ("I'm not so sure that's how we want to look; I think that's who we want to have"–Group 1b), and others felt that specific characteristics of the viewer such as age needed to be taken into consideration:

Group 1c: It depends on how old you are, where you live, how long you've been out, and how comfortable you feel with your sexuality.

Group 2a: I've seen this in friends of mine that aren't 25 anymore; they go into this really nice space of not being concerned. They don't look for it in a partner; they don't want it for themselves. They just want to be healthy . . .

Finally, one discussant said the influence of pornography was mitigated by the utilitarian relationship between the medium and its consumers, which he believed distinguished it from other media/viewer interchanges.

Group 1c: When women open a magazine, they're told they can look like this, if they do this. We [put] in the videotape because we're going to get our rocks off. There is nothing being sold. We're not going into it with a–preconceived notion is a bad way to put it, I think–but we're going in with a purpose. We're only pulling from the images what we want. The people behind the images aren't telling us anything.

Facilitator: So, you're saying that's an important distinction between women's magazines where they're pitching a product—saying you can get slim thighs in thirty days if you take this pill . . . whereas with [gay porn] we're just sort of watching this, and it's just to have fun with.

Group 1c: Yeah.

A few discussants, however, felt that exposure to the "idealistic" imagery contained in gay male pornography had the potential to influence viewers' perceptions of their bodies.

Group 1d: Yeah, I definitely feel a bit more inadequate [after watching the scene from *Absolute Aqua*]. Well, I know I'm not going to look like that, but it may drive me to look a bit better . . . like, try and work out.

Group 2a: Well, I think even if people don't accept this as an ideal [or] attainable body image, they'll still say things like "I don't have a porn star body," so they still use that as a comparison to their more normal, realistic body. There's always that comparison: "You know, I'm fine, but I'm not hot."

Gay Sexuality

Discussants observed that the three pornographic scenes, especially the one from *Absolute Aqua*, did not embody a new model of sexuality. Rather, the sequences shown appeared to promulgate the view that gay sex is mimetic; that it simply reflects the "transferring of heterosexual culture to gay people" (Group 2a), and the reproduction of a traditional "male/female model." A key signifier of this gendered view of gay sexuality was the differential representation of "tops" (i.e., those engaging in insertive anal intercourse) and "bottoms" (i.e., those engaging in receptive anal intercourse).

Facilitator: How is the top represented in [*Absolute Aqua*]? How is the bottom represented?

Group 3b: [The top was] older . . . tanned . . . taller.

Group 3a: More masculine, more aggressive . . . much more aggressive.

Group 3d: More straight.

Group 2b: I think, yes, the top was portrayed more as the aggressor. He was the taller one, the one with the larger dick. He was definitely the one in control. He was doing this because it was what he wanted to do.

Facilitator: Do you think there was an attempt to make it . . . reciprocal . . . ?

Group 2a: Well, it was pretty transparent. The top was giving him head for a while there, but he didn't kneel. The bottom kneeled the whole time, the top stood with his legs far apart. And even when [the top] was blowing him, it was like he spent more time rubbing his dick on his face then he did actually putting it in his mouth.

Group 3b: Even when [the top] was semi-licking him, which isn't as intimate as kissing, [the top] was always pushing [the bottom's] head down . . . like, "OK, I don't really want to be looking at you right now, get down there."

Some discussants observed that even the act of ejaculation was differentially represented based on whether the porn performer was a "top" or a "bottom."

Group 2a: Although [the top] didn't actually cum on [the bottom's] face, that was entirely accidental. They had lined up for that, you know. And then the bottom came on himself.

Group 3c: [The top] comes first. He's higher up on the hierarchy, and the [bottom's] beneath him . . .

Group 3a: And he rubs his cummy cock all over the [bottom's] face . . . [it's like] and *then* you're allowed to cum . . .

Group 3d: On yourself.

Group 3b: Alone.

Despite these differential representations, the discussants did not necessarily perceive the gay performers engaging in receptive anal intercourse as "feminine." Possessing myriad visual indicants of masculinity (muscles, short hair, and tattoos), they remained "quote unquote, straight looking" and "were not femmy by any means" (Group 3a).

Rather, the performers appearing in the three sequences appeared to occupy different spaces on a continuum of masculinity, with "tops" being considered more masculine than "bottoms."

The retention of performers' masculine status whilst engaging in gay sex would appear to be somewhat challenging. However, discussants suggested that some gay male pornography accomplishes this feat by excising intimacy from performers' sexual repertoire.[3]

Facilitator: Why don't they have a thirty second scene of [the performers] hugging after the cum shot or one nestling his head on the other . . . ?

Group 1c: Because the viewer wouldn't watch it anyway . . .

Group 1a: Intimacy is associated as well with the female role. So, portraying your masculine role, you don't want to touch intimacy too much.

Discussants commented on the absence of "kissing," "touching," "hugging," "caressing," and "[anything] post-coital." As well, one discussant remarked on the silence of some performers: "there was no moaning or groaning . . . throughout the entire process except until the cum shot . . ." (Group 3a). The removal of these sorts of sounds, which are often non-volitional, may serve to reinforce the idea that masculine men remain in control, even when engaging in sexual activity.

The contrast between performers representing "gay" and "straight" characters[4] (albeit ones remarkably willing to engage in homosexual activity) may further reinforce the idea that when men have sex with other men, a stereotypic "male/female pattern" is evoked in which "one is subordinate to the other" (Group 2a).

Group 1b: I figured out the gay guy [in a scene from *An Officer and His Gentleman*] was the shorter guy; the weaker guy; the whiner. The gay guy is the only one who doesn't say a word during sex.

Gay characters were seen as "weaker," "more servile," and "prissy"; they had "well done hair," and wore "white uniforms [and] white socks" (both of which denote tidiness). In contrast, straight characters were described as "dirty looking," "ultra-butch," "traditional," "tough," and "aggressive." Variations in sexual agency also were observed, with gay men's pleasure being secondary and, in some instances, irrelevant to the sexual scenario.

Group 1a: I found there was a fair bit of the gay guy [when he was performing fellatio] looking up with his eyes almost like he was asking "Is this OK?"

Group 1c: The [straight] guys gave it. They were there serving their own pleasure. And the gay guy was there to provide it ... The straight guys were treating the gay guy the same way they would treat a woman.

Group 1a: [In reference to a scene from *An Officer and His Gentleman*], it was kind of, pat him on the head; we're done; we've cum; we're out.

Finally, some discussants reported that this type of imagery contributes to the belief that gay men are "sexually insatiable" and "exist to service straight men."

Group 2a: ... there is that belief that gay men will ... you give them a cock, and they will suck it. They just won't even question it. ... I think every gay man has been in those situations where a straight man makes that sort of [assumption]. It always just baffles me. You don't honestly think that do you? That because we've had two drinks, I'm going to suck your dick. No. Life doesn't work that way.

In *Absolute Aqua*, *An Officer and His Gentleman*, and *The Naked Highway*, condoms were used when the performers engaged in anal intercourse. Although discussants observed that condoms were used (i.e., no one reported operating from the assumption that a given sequence depicted unsafe sex), none of them felt that safer sex had been emphasized or depicted in an erotic manner.

Facilitator: What about the whole notion of safer sex?

Group 1d: Kind of hid it as much as they could, I thought.

Group 1b: It was kind of interesting, I mean you see ... he's perched [above someone's penis], and there's no condom, and then the camera cuts away, and ... magically the condom is on. It's kind of invisible.

Further, some discussants expressed concern with gay male pornography's restriction of condom use to the practice of anal intercourse.

Group 3b: The danger of that particular porn [scene] is the fact that they did have the condom, but they only put [it] on for the actual intercourse. I mean, [the scene] portrayed like giving head and everything. You could still have gotten something. There are still things that are transferable [via] mouth to genital contact. And I thought that's kind of interesting, like you guys can play around with things orally as much as you want. You don't have to worry about condoms until the very end.

Group 3a: And that's such a common thing in gay porn. Like there are no condoms at all until penetration.

Group 3b: Yeah, and that doesn't seem very safe.

DISCUSSION

The results of this study suggest that gay male pornography, as represented by three scenes taken from popular titles released in the 1990s, is rife with masculine iconography. Bodies were described as embracing a butch aesthetic, and the absence of physiques deviating from the muscular mesomorphic "ideal" was noted. Sexual interactions between performers appeared to simulate a traditional (read: nonegalitarian) heterosexual model, in which one or more partners assumed a subordinate role. Somewhat paradoxically, though, even individuals represented as subordinate on the basis of genital size, muscularity, or sexual orientation were perceived as masculine. Therefore, it would appear that the world of gay male pornography is one characterized by differential placement on a continuum of masculinity and eschewal of anything feminine.

A few discussants expressed the desire for greater variability with respect to the bodies and activities represented in this medium. However, most of the participants considered the pornographic scenes shown to be fairly erotic, and thought that efforts to deviate from the masculine status quo[5] likely would be rejected.

Group 2a: I remember once watching a porn with some friends of mine . . . and there was dialogue, and the performers were so gay. We all started laughing. They sound like we do. They sound like the four of us sitting around planning a gang-bang or something... You never actually hear the men talking to the point where you can acknowledge that they might sound a little bit gay. It's that whole "sissyphobia" or whatever... it's just the fantasy of, you know, making everyone feel more masculine, just devaluing the sort of femininity that gay men have.

Facilitator: Why is it [masculinity] such an important element of gay porn?

Group 1b: I think it comes from our growing up that homosexuals are sissies. If you don't screw women, well, you're not a real man. This seems to say that, yes, you are masculine . . .

Group 1d: It gives them a secure image of their sexuality, I guess. Reassures them . . . almost.

Facilitator: That they're real men?

Group 1d: Yeah.

These comments suggest that, as consumers of this medium, gay men are culpable for the dearth of imagery that reflects "the sort of femininity that gay men have" (Group 2a). As pointed out by discussants 1b and 1d, some viewers may use the hyper-masculinity evident in gay pornography as "proof" that they are "real" men and, thus, reject images that present gay men as more feminine or androgynous. However, discussants stressed that the medium would serve this purpose for a minority of viewers only; many reiterated that, like *most* gay men, they saw pornography as a masturbatory aid and little else.

Group 1a: [Gay pornography] is a show. It's physical. Masturbatory viewing.

Group 1b: [Pornography] is a visual medium. You're looking at nice bodies and that's what you're doing, and that's what you're getting out it.

Facilitator: So, you're saying for gay men, in particular, or maybe for men in general, [pornography] is very utilitarian. You watch it for 10, 12 minutes, whatever so you can ejaculate and that's it.

Group 3a: Yep. And it's not this big fantasy . . . It can be, but [that's] not essential.

Group 3c: It [is] like a vibrator . . . a visual vibrator.

In conclusion, the results of this exploratory study suggest that the predominant discourse on heterosexual pornography (i.e., a harm-based feminist analysis) may not serve as a suitable analytic framework for sexually explicit materials targeting gay men. Discussants appeared to minimize the potential significance of this medium, with respect to individuals' perceptions of their sexuality and construction of a sexual repertoire. Although they could articulate potentially beneficial and negative aspects of gay male pornography, they did not appear to conceptualize it in those terms.[6] Rather, discussants saw the medium through a lens of utilitarianism, and regarded it with nostalgic fondness.[7]

Group 2a: I remember the first time I saw gay porn. I was about nine. I happened to [come across] a magazine in a back alley, and it was so validating. It was like, "Yeah, that's it. That's what I am. And, look, there's other people doing it; they're having sex; they don't look embarrassed; they don't look grossed out . . ."

Additional research is needed to determine whether other gay men share the opinions raised in these focus groups. As well, social scientists should explore the possibility that discussants' minimization of gay pornography's influence reflects adherence to the belief that "real men" are impervious to mass media.

NOTES

1. The sample size is admittedly small and, thus, the opinions expressed herein are not necessarily representative of many (or even some) members/supporters of the gay and lesbian community. However, it should be noted that locating even 10 individuals willing to participate in a study on gay male pornography was a rather arduous process. This difficulty may be attributed to the conservative environment in which the study was conducted (i.e., a small comprehensive college located in what has been referred to as the "bible belt" of Canada). For example, prior to entering the room in which the focus group was being held, one gay male informally told the author that he waited until "the hallway was clear." He was fearful that if others knew he was participating in this sort of research, they would assume he was gay. In addition to the location of the study,

the topic itself may have been a deterrent. Indeed, one discussant told the researcher that two of her gay male friends refused to participate because they felt "porn was private" and shouldn't be discussed in a public forum.

2. The sequences were shown in fixed order because they seemed to reflect variations in "raunchiness." The first sequence, from *Absolute Aqua*, is pure vanilla–it depicts hairless, sculpted bodies engaging in sanitized sex; the next scene (*An Officer and His Gentleman*) shows three men performing oral and anal intercourse in a prison setting, and contains a scintilla of coercion; the final scene, taken from *The Naked Highway*, focuses on three men being "serviced" by a hustler (whom they have drugged) and was described by a discussant as "just fucking vile."

3. A few discussants observed that the language used to describe ejaculate in gay male pornography serves to increase the masculinity of the medium.

Group 3a: In gay porn, it's not sperm. In gay porn, it's cum. And I think there is [a] real difference. Sperm is what you use to conceive a child, whereas [cum] is . . .

Group 3b: Man juice.

Group 3c: From my big man cock [laughter].

4. Gay male pornography often depicts sexual encounters between "gay" individuals and men signified, either directly or indirectly, as "straight." When asked to explain why this scenario possesses enduring appeal, most discussants remarked that it's akin to "straight men's obsession with lesbian women"; it represents the "unattainable, " "the notion of getting what you can't have."

5. Many discussants found the "realistic" bodies contained in the scenes from *An Officer and His Gentleman* and *The Naked Highway* to be more erotic than the "perfect" bodies depicted in *Absolute Aqua*.

Group 2b: I found it interesting to just see body hair . . . Those bodies were still attractive, still in shape, but certainly more accessible bodies.

These comments suggest that (somewhat) greater latitude is afforded gay performers in terms of their physical appearance than in terms of their level of masculinity.

6. Any substantive influence of gay male pornography on the viewer was regarded as transitory and most likely to occur among younger individuals.

Group 1c: Maybe if they're younger and they haven't had a lot of experience, it may sort of influence what they do for a little while until . . .

Group 1b: Reality sets in. And then you find what makes you comfortable, and then you just sort of respond and behave sexually in whatever way works for you.

7. Discussants acknowledged that, due to modern technology and the greater visibility of non-heterosexuals, gay male pornography's importance as a source of validation (and information), especially during the "coming out" process, has likely decreased.

Facilitator: It's interesting how gay men of my age have the same erotic referent points. It's like *Blue Lagoon, All the Right Moves* . . . we had, like, three or four movies. There was nothing [else], and I think that's difficult for young [gay men] to understand. You couldn't type in the word "cock" on some wonder box, and have 8000 pictures at your disposal. There was *Playgirl*, which was too frightening to buy . . .

Group 2a: And it wasn't talked about in the media at all. I can remember watching a horrible movie with Christopher Reeves and Michael Caine [*Deathtrap*] . . . When they kissed in it . . . I was about 8 years old sitting in a theatre, and it was like a lightning bolt from the top of my head to my toes; it was like someone slapped me . . .

REFERENCES

Blueboy (2002, April). New York, NY: Global Media Group Ltd.
Dryer, R. (1994). Idol thoughts: Orgasm and self-reflexivity in gay pornography. *Critical Quarterly, 36*, 49-62.
Dude (2001, November). Pompano Beach, FL: Dugent Corporation.
Grogan, S., & Richards, H. (2002). Body image: Focus groups with boys and men. *Men and Masculinities, 4*, 219-232.
Harris, D. (1997). *The rise and fall of gay culture*. New York, NY: Hyperion.
Jock (2002, April). New York, NY: Global Media Group Ltd.
Men (2003, January). Los Angeles, CA: Specialty Publications LLC.

Sex Pigs:
Why Porn Is Like Sausage, or The Truth Is That–Behind the Scenes– Porn Is Not Very Sexy

Benjamin Scuglia

SUMMARY. The author examines the gay adult video industry from an insider's perspective. The workaday reality of making porn is contrasted with the skin trade's glamorous myths, and the idea that porn consumers prefer these myths to the "truth" is outlined. *[Article copies available for a fee from The Haworth Document Delivery Service: 1-800-HAWORTH. E-mail address: <docdelivery@haworthpress.com> Website: <http://www.HaworthPress.com> © 2004 by The Haworth Press, Inc. All rights reserved.]*

KEYWORDS. Gay pornography, pornography, gay men, video, consumers, adult performers

I am a writer in the gay adult video industry. I have reviewed literally thousands of tapes, interviewed the newest models[1] and veteran direc-

---

Benjamin Scuglia is a writer based in Los Angeles. He is Editor of *Inside Porn Magazine* and has covered the gay adult video industry since 1995. Correspondence may be addressed: 7095 Hollywood Blvd., #518, Hollywood, CA 90028-8903 (E-mail: bscuglia@aol.com).

[Haworth co-indexing entry note]: "Sex Pigs: Why Porn Is Like Sausage, or The Truth Is That–Behind the Scenes–Porn Is Not Very Sexy." Scuglia, Benjamin. Co-published simultaneously in *Journal of Homosexuality* (Harrington Park Press, an imprint of The Haworth Press, Inc.) Vol. 47, No. 3/4, 2004, pp. 185-188; and: *Eclectic Views on Gay Male Pornography: Pornucopia* (ed: Todd G. Morrison) Harrington Park Press, an imprint of The Haworth Press, Inc., 2004, pp. 185-188. Single or multiple copies of this article are available for a fee from The Haworth Document Delivery Service [1-800-HAWORTH, 9:00 a.m. - 5:00 p.m. (EST). E-mail address: docdelivery@haworthpress.com].

http://www.haworthpress.com/web/JH
© 2004 by The Haworth Press, Inc. All rights reserved.
Digital Object Identifier: 10.1300/J082v47n03_10

tors, and visited porn sets. I have even tried my hand at writing and directing skin flicks. Half of my adult life has been spent immersed in erections and cum shots; I have seen how difficult it can be to light, shoot, and edit a double-penetration, which is why you rarely see them in gay porn. I have been mesmerized by a rose (not the floral variety) and been splashed with semen even whilst standing 20 feet from men in the throes of climax.

At parties, my profession is an ideal icebreaker. Most people, male or female, straight or gay, are inevitably fascinated with the idea of porn. If they do not watch it, they want to know all I can tell them. If they do consume it, they usually bubble over with questions about their favourite model. And whatever their orientation or proclivity, they always get around to The Question: What is it like on a porn set?

The short answer is it's boring. Anything repeated over and over for eight hours is boring, whether it is flipping burgers, folding sweaters, or giving someone a blow job. Making porn is definitely titillating but after an hour, one's mind starts to wander to lunch, bills, and who is going to get voted off *Survivor* tonight.

Sure, the partygoers say, but what is it *really* like? This is neither a strange nor unexpected question. After all, for most of us, sex is only shared periodically with one other person in the darkened privacy of a bedroom. To watch it happen live can be pretty damn thrilling. Which is not to imply that filmed sex is the same as *live* sex; an average scene can take up to eight hours to film. The set has to be dressed and lit properly and the director generally has a mandate to capture certain positions for a certain period of time. The usual formula for an average sex scene is kiss-kiss-suck-suck-rim-fuck-change positions-fuck-cum-cum. It's that last bit –waiting for the cum shot–that can easily derail a shoot.

I know a director of bisexual videos who swears that he will only direct lesbian porn because he can shoot the sex, have the women fake their cum shots, and be done with the scene in ninety minutes or less. Conversely, the men in his videos have been known to take hours. In an attempt to achieve orgasm, one hapless gentleman in a male-male scene took almost four hours, and even then could not quite manage it. His co-star had already provided his pop shot and was showered and dressed. Out of desperation, the director asked the co-star if he was up for another go and promised a bump in pay. The co-star agreed, unzipped his pants, and kneeled over his partner–who lay back with a camera tightly framing his upper chest and face. He faked the motions of masturbating (moans included) as his co-star quickly brought himself to orgasm and shot several ropes of semen neatly into frame and across the guy's chest. On camera, you could never tell the difference.

When I talk about the industry with non-porn civilians, it is the heterosexuals who are most fascinated. They appear highly intrigued by the concept of two strangers meeting in the parking lot, shaking hands, going into makeup, ducking into the bathroom to take off their clothes, then joining on a brightly lit set to have sex for a few hours. To gay men, the concept of screwing a stranger is not beyond the pale of everyday life.

Generally, the models don't know each other beforehand and occasionally don't even like each other. But stick around the industry long enough and you naturally begin to make friends. On one set I visited, a model balked at fucking his co-star because the pair weren't merely good friends, "we're like sisters!" There wasn't time to locate a replacement, so the performer had to make do. Later, I asked him how he got through it. He said it wasn't *really* a problem. "He's got a hot body and a big honking dick, so it wasn't like work," he explained, "but you know what we were talking about?" (They had done a lot of whispering and sharing secret smiles during their sexual encounter.) "Cyndi Lauper! I just saw her in concert with Cher."

Most directors hope for a bit of chemistry between their scene partners. Companies like Falcon Studios and Titan Media discourage their performers from fraternising beforehand in the hope of capturing, on camera, that first flame of attraction. Others, such as Eastern European director George Duroy (who runs the powerhouse studio Bel Ami) and auteur Kristen Bjorn (of Sarava Productions), labour intensely to manufacture that fire; Bjorn has been known to spend three days on a scene until he gets what he wants.

But what if the performers simply cannot stand one another? It usually does not matter. Most gay porn stars regard what they do on film as work and not as something intrinsically pleasurable. One performer, who recently retired, says his worst experience was during a scene with a straight model that couldn't manage an erection. "I was kneeling in front of him, waiting to blow him, and it was taking forever, so I closed my eyes and kind of drifted off. I woke up when he balanced a porn magazine on my goddamned head! A *straight* porn magazine! I got through that scene by totally compartmentalizing. I was so pissed, I didn't even want to pretend I was enjoying myself." And this example encapsulates the problem: porn is like sausage and politics; you don't want to see how they are made.

It is often said there are two types of "legitimate" Hollywood fans: those wishing to escape the reality of their lives for a couple of hours and those wanting to uncover every moviemaking secret, including the name of the person inside the rubber Godzilla suit. The same two groups of people watch porn. At parties, when The Question invariably arises, it is the former group that usually asks it. Consequently, I do not tell them about the sausage factory. My ready answer is: "It's great. Totally hot. You'd love it."

NOTE

1. When I say "newest models," I am not necessarily referring to "Twinks." Basically, if you are under 30 or over 45, but not quite 55, you are the right age for the job and, thus, technically could be called a "new model." (I know an early 30-something performer whose small stature and youthful demeanour have allowed him to carry off being in his "early twenties" for his entire career, and thus far no one has done the math.) Porn is not strictly for the young. Although a muscular daddy with a salt-and-pepper beard, explains one director, "is a niche. Twinks are a genre. Daddy-types are a niche." In fact, at the *Adult Video News' GayVN Awards* show, a new category was added this year: Best Specialty Release, 18-23 (translation: best non-middle-of-the-road video featuring models whose "public age" falls between 18 and 23 years). Apparently, the days of encountering any 24-year-olds in porn are now essentially over.

Alterity and Construction of National Identity in Three Kristen Bjorn Films

Clare N. Westcott, MA

Red Deer College

SUMMARY. In the gay pornographic films *Manly Beach* (1991), *Call of the Wild* (1992) and *Paradise Plantation* (1994), director Kristen Bjorn capitalises on the appeal of alterity, or "otherness." By using exotic locations and national stereotypes, he provides North American viewers with idealised sexual scenarios that are different, but not *too* different, from that with which they are familiar. *[Article copies available for a fee from The Haworth Document Delivery Service: 1-800-HAWORTH. E-mail address: <docdelivery@haworthpress.com> Website: <http://www.HaworthPress.com> © 2004 by The Haworth Press, Inc. All rights reserved.]*

KEYWORDS. Gay pornography, pornography, alterity, gay culture, nationality, community, gay men, identity, ethnicity

---

Clare N. Westcott teaches Spanish at Red Deer College. She is currently working on a PhD with the Department of Modern Languages and Cultural Studies at the University of Alberta, with a present focus on film studies and masculinity. Correspondence may be addressed: Department of Humanities and Social Sciences, Red Deer College, PO Box 5005, Red Deer, AB, T4N 5H5, Canada (E-mail: clare.westcott@rdc.ab.ca).

[Haworth co-indexing entry note]: "Alterity and Construction of National Identity in Three Kristen Bjorn Films." Westcott, Clare N. Co-published simultaneously in *Journal of Homosexuality* (Harrington Park Press, an imprint of The Haworth Press, Inc.) Vol. 47, No. 3/4, 2004, pp. 189-196; and: *Eclectic Views on Gay Male Pornography: Pornucopia* (ed: Todd G. Morrison) Harrington Park Press, an imprint of The Haworth Press, Inc., 2004, pp. 189-196. Single or multiple copies of this article are available for a fee from The Haworth Document Delivery Service [1-800-HAWORTH, 9:00 a.m. - 5:00 p.m. (EST). E-mail address: docdelivery@haworthpress.com].

http://www.haworthpress.com/web/JH
© 2004 by The Haworth Press, Inc. All rights reserved.
Digital Object Identifier: 10.1300/J082v47n03_11

Alterity, or "otherness," is a relevant concept in gay culture, as evidenced by the significant number of gay men who are attracted to sexual partners outside their own racial group, or by the sexual appeal of straight men. Gay pornography constitutes one form of cultural production in which this attraction to the "Other" (i.e., a person unlike oneself) is manifested. In *Manly Beach* (1991), *Call of the Wild* (1992), and *Paradise Plantation* (1994), director Kristen Bjorn capitalises on the desire for "otherness" of his English-speaking, North American market in a number of different ways, most of all by creating variety through nationality. I will endeavour to illustrate that, although Bjorn achieves alterity (albeit often inexact and stereotypical) in these three videos, the cinematic result is safe and watered-down.

Kristen Bjorn, of British and Russian descent, was born in London, England, in 1957 and grew up in Washington, D.C. He reports always being "fascinated by physical beauty and exotic faraway places" (Jamoo, 1997, p. 13); has travelled extensively; and asserts that "most of my [sexual] experiences with men have been out of the [United States]" (Jamoo, 1997, p. 16). These personal experiences and predilections are evident in his work; Bjorn has distinguished himself by producing videos that are international in scope, offering variety of a geographical and ethnic nature. Director William Higgins writes of this diversity in his foreword to *The Films of Kristen Bjorn*: "These unique, otherworldly qualities for me represent a large aspect of the appeal of Bjorn's videos: their total avoidance of the bland sameness that permeates the American gay porn scene" (Jamoo, 1997, p. 10). Similarly, erotic film star and author Jamoo (1997) contends that Bjorn's work "goes beyond sucking and fucking and hot male bodies; it's the sensuality and exoticism he creates" (p. 11).

I have chosen to examine *Manly Beach* (1991), *Call of the Wild* (1992), and *Paradise Plantation* (1994) because they feature three different continents and, therefore, may be viewed as representative of the geographic scope of Bjorn's work. While he has directed many other films, my discussion focuses on the material contained in these three videos only.

Bjorn's employment of alterity is evident when reading the covers of these videos. For example, the synopsis of *Call of the Wild* begins with the following:

> Far out in the wilderness of French Canada, the long winter melts into spring and the Call of the Wild begins. It's the call of nature; it's what drives both man and beast with lust. For the first time

ever, you will see 11 hot French Canadian men just as they are–rough and untamed . . .

The use of the word "they" draws attention to the fact that this video is targeting a non-French Canadian audience, showing what "they" are like, as opposed to "us" (presumably, the viewer of the film). This use of the third person plural embraces the core of alterity: the "us" vs. "them" dichotomy.

Bjorn presents alterity in a variety of different spheres in these films. As is done in most gay pornographic videos, "otherness" is established through the use of "masculine" professions. *Manly Beach* showcases lifeguards, *Call of the Wild* focuses on loggers, hunters and law enforcers, and *Paradise Plantation* depicts ranch hands. Since these occupations are of a stereotypical "manly" nature, and are not fields in which the "average" gay man is purportedly employed, one could say that masculinity itself has become an attractive form of "otherness" to the gay viewer.

An alterity of class also is revealed in *Paradise Plantation,* in which the "narrative" features Gustavo, the plantation owner's idle son, who seems to spend most of his time lounging against pillars, rubbing his crotch and watching ranch workers with yearning. For the majority of the video, Gustavo's sexual desires are frustrated, as a class barrier prevents him from fraternising with the labourers, who are presented as more vital and less repressed sexually.

In addition, Bjorn incorporates an alterity of sexual orientation. Various characters appear to begin the videos as straight and happen upon homosexual displays (usually whilst strolling innocently through the forest). These "straight" characters are intrigued by the erotic spectacles they encounter; masturbate as they watch; and before long are included in the activities. Their participation is somewhat reluctant, or even gently forced, but eventually they partake in the sex acts wholeheartedly. Indeed, other than the fact that they are having sex with men, there is nothing in these films to suggest that any of the men represented self-identify as gay. Thus, Bjorn seems to be eroticising straight men.[1]

The alterities of profession, class, and sexual orientation evident in Bjorn's work are, perhaps, of less importance than his use of geographical otherness. As Bjorn himself says, "That's a difficult thing when making porn; how can you make it different from all of the other thousands of porn videos? Locations are a key factor" (Jamoo, 1997, p. 114). *Manly Beach, Call of the Wild* and *Paradise Plantation* were filmed in Australia, Canada (Québec) and Brazil, respectively. Bjorn capitalizes on differences in location by including panoramic views, and by filming scenes in and amongst indigenous vegetation. In *Call of the Wild*, one notes the conspicuous presence of maple leaves (Canada's national emblem) in the frame as one lumberjack fellates another on the floor of a deciduous forest. The chirping of birds also can be heard in the background in certain sequences. In *Paradise Plantation*, the culminating love scene between Gustavo and the new ranch hand, Armando, is enhanced by the cricket-like sound of insects.

Although the flora and fauna employed in the videos are indigenous to the respective regions, the models are not. With the exception of one black man in each video–this obvious pattern compels me to refer to him as "token"–the models in *Manly Beach*, *Call of the Wild* and *Paradise Plantation* are, judging by their appearances and/or surnames,[2] of British, French and Portuguese extraction, respectively. Therefore, the primary "otherness" manufactured in these videos is not one of race, but rather one of *nationality*.[3]

As Benedict Anderson (1991) aptly illustrates, nations are not natural entities but, rather, *constructs*. A nation cannot be considered a true community because its members are not personally acquainted with one another; the sense of solidarity experienced by members of each nation has been constructed from the stories, songs, traditions, sports, and cuisine (among other things) that they have come to view as shared. We do not *sense* the defining elements of our particular nation intuitively; rather, we *learn* them. Therefore, national identity is based largely on a series of symbols and stereotypes. In addition to the physical locations of his films, Bjorn avails himself of these stereotypic national characteristics to produce a sense of alterity. Since he works with only the most obvious and, in some cases, antiquated stereotypes, the results can be quite comical. In addition, a comparison of the three videos reveals a definite formula in Bjorn's construction of national identity.

In *Manly Beach*, Australia gets off relatively lightly as far as stereotypes are concerned; there are no kangaroos, koalas or boomerangs. There are, however, (mostly blond) surfers and lifeguards, and Bjorn heavily exploits the "exotic" Australian accent in the gratuitous narration that punctuates the film. At one point, the narrator refers to a "young bloke," which is a typically Australian expression. Similarly, while the models engage in a variety of sex acts, the dubbed-over voices refer to one another as "mate." Bjorn's efforts to achieve an alterity of nationality through speech are most evident when one model moans to another, "Yeah, swallow that Aussie dick." As far as costume, the first couple shown never take off their white socks and running shoes and, just in case the viewer forgets they really are men of the surf, subsequent models leave on their matching bathing caps and wet suits throughout most of their sex scenes.

Call of the Wild (an allusion to the Jack London novel) may be the film most rife with national stereotypes, although it's possible that, as a Canadian viewer, I am simply more aware of stereotypes pertaining to my own country. Bjorn divides this film into four sections, three of which exploit Canadian archetypes: lumberjacks, hunters and "Royal Mounties."[4]

In the opening scene, one of the lumberjacks is languidly sawing a tree with a colleague, and sporting a generic North America "coonskin" cap, which stays on during much of the forest romp that ensues. The loggers are, naturally, attired in "lumberjack" shirts and blue jeans, which are eventually removed. The gradual shedding of costumes (with the exception of the work boots) is repeated in subsequent sex scenes (as it is in the other movies in question). However, the coonskin cap is replaced by a camouflage one in the case of the hunters and by a tan-coloured, broad, flat-brimmed one in the case of the "Royal Mounties." When not in the forest, the Canadian archetypes are having sex in rustic cabins, usually in front of a fireplace.

Linguistic signifiers of national identity also are employed; namely, the use of dubbed voices saying "oui" and "formidable." However, the most remarkable indication of national identity in *Call of the Wild* is the appearance of the fleur-de-lis, the blue and white flag symbolic of French Canadian nationalism. For a moment, it flutters in the whole of the frame, only to be draped by two rustics over a wooden bench in a cabin, with a pile of firewood in the background. The men then use the covered furnishing to engage in an act of fellatio. Oral sex also is performed on a fleur-de-lis laid out on a lawn. Given such imagery, one may conclude that this video targets non-French Canadians, as the Québécois would likely view these scenes as offensive.

The set-in-Brazil *Paradise Plantation* emphasises, predictably, the "Latin-ness" of its subjects and their culture. Soft guitar music plays during much of the video, replaced at times by frenzied drumming. The narrator's introduction distances the diegetic world of the film from that of the spectator both temporally and spatially with his fairy tale-like introduction: "Faraway, in the tropics of northern Brazil, there was once a plantation so beautiful . . ." In this, the most recent of the three productions, Bjorn seems to be stretching himself by setting this story at some non-specific point in the past. The contemporary technology that is casually present in *Manly Beach* and *Call of the Wild* is absent here as Bjorn attempts to recreate an idyllic world of yore. The result is an easy, laid-back atmosphere in which the workers (languidly, once again) harvest berries, dig holes, feed chickens, load bananas onto a boat, sing, drum and have sex.

For the most part, the ranch hands look and speak Portuguese, and the added cultural touches in this video are mostly of an imperial character. However, there is one allusion to the region's precolonial past: early in the film the labourers are, inexplicably, digging in the forest when they uncover a small, carved statue. They ascertain that it is "an Indian thing" and that it depicts "someone being sucked and fucked." After this brief contemplation of the ranch's indigenous past, the men go about emulating the artefact. Homage also is paid to Brazil's African heritage when the one black worker dances erotically in a vaguely African style to his colleagues' drumming (on empty liquor bottles) around a campfire. In keeping with Bjorn's formula, the majority of the sex acts in *Plantation Paradise* take place under the canopy of the Brazilian rainforest, the straw hats stay on until the very end, and the work boots are never removed.

The physiques of the models used in *Manly Beach*, *Call of the Wild* and *Paradise Plantation* are similar, as are the sex acts portrayed. Consequently, in an attempt to differentiate the three works, Bjorn has established an alterity of location and nationality, but not of race. The national identities he has created in each of the films are of an imperialist, hegemonic nature; the men, culture and language the viewer encounters are not indigenous, but rather are derived from the European power that conquered it. As North America is a place where a European imperialist culture (in this case, English) prevails, and in which many people are genetic descendants of "triumphant" colonists, Bjorn's filmic creations, while still being "exotic," are not, on a relative scale, all that different from what his target viewers know. In short, Bjorn has endeavoured to create something different, but not *too* different, for his mainstream North American audience.

This brings us to the most important factor driving the pornography industry: sales. Bjorn's most commercially successful film is *Carnival in Rio* (1989), which is along the same lines, ethnically, as *Paradise Plantation*, but with a modern, urban, Carnival setting. *Manly Beach* and *Call of the Wild* are among his least commercially successful, with *Paradise Plantation* falling somewhere in between. In accounting for why some of his films are more successful, Bjorn focuses solely on market forces. He explains the success of *Carnival in Rio* as being due to the fact that it has been out longer than his other videos: "When the video came out it sold a lot in the very beginning, and there wasn't as much competition on the market as there is now. There is even competition now between my own videos, but at the time that was the only Kristen Bjorn video" (Jamoo, 1997, p. 46). Similarly, he does not explain the disappointing sales of his Australian videos, including *Manly Beach*, in terms of content. In response to a query about the commercial success of these videos, Bjorn reports: "You have to remember at that period we had a very serious recession and sales of everything went down. The video market was doing very badly at the time, but the sale of these videos didn't compare to the sales from before, which was very disappointing" (Jamoo, 1997, p. 84). One could interpret the success of Bjorn's Brazilian movies over his Canadian and Australian ones as stemming from a quest for "otherness" greater than that of mere nationality. Although his Brazilian models are Caucasian for the most part, they are, admittedly, darker-skinned than most of the models in the Canadian and Australian movies, and therefore more *different* from most North Americans, Bjorn's target consumers. Also, Brazil is more culturally dissimilar to Anglophone North America than are Australia and French Canada. The appeal of Bjorn's Brazilian films may reside in their "Latin-ness"–a mixture of the swarthiness of their men (and their reputation for unbridled passion), and the exuberance of Brazilian/Latin culture.

Although Bjorn's films originated from his own interest in "foreign" cultures and the men they spawned, he does not deny his obedience to market forces in his filmmaking. When asked about his selection of models for *Island Fever*, one of his earliest films set in Brazil (where widespread miscegenation has resulted in a large range of racial diversity from which to draw upon), Bjorn says, intriguingly, of his American distributors: "They thought that black or white was all right but what they didn't like were all the shades in between . . . they felt that Americans were used to blacks and they were used to whites but not to these other things that couldn't be categorised as either one" (Jamoo, 1997, p. 52). This may explain why Bjorn's models, even in subsequent videos, are distinctly white or black, and suggests that the American market appreciates alterity as long as it is a *definable* and easily recognisable "otherness" that does not challenge predominant discourse surrounding "racial" categories.

Many factors influence video production and sales; thus, it is difficult to pinpoint exactly what it is that sells, and why. Analyses of film content and subsequent commercial success seem to raise more questions than they answer. One thing that cannot be denied is the attraction to alterity existent in the North American gay pornographic market, be it "otherness" rooted in sexual orientation, occupational identity, hegemonic masculinity, race and/or nationality. By catering most ostensibly to the desire for geographical/national difference, Bjorn has made himself a prominent figure on the gay pornography scene. Bjorn speaks of his work in very simple, intuitive terms, and his commercial success is best summarised in his own words:

> When it comes to business, most people don't like to take chances. They prefer to stick to tried and proven formulas . . . no one knew if there was a market for "exotic" gay videos . . . it was assumed that everyone wanted to see blond models from California and nothing else. But I knew that I liked different types of guys and was interested in exotic locations. Luckily, as it turns out, other people liked that too. (Jamoo, 1997, p. 69)

And "other people liked that too" to such an extent that the safe brand of exoticism (i.e., alterity) presented in Bjorn's videos has become yet another "tried and proven formula."

NOTES

1. Bjorn says, "Approximately ninety-five percent of my models aren't gay and don't consider themselves to be gay " (Jamoo, 1997, p. 25). Such commentary underscores the varying conceptions of sexual orientation among the models used in Bjorn's work. The models' apparent ability to differentiate what they do as erotic performers from their sexual identity would prove a fascinating topic for further study.

2. Although these surnames are fictitious, and often chosen by Bjorn himself, they tend to reflect the model's true ethnicity. Bjorn also tends to use models that are, for the most part, actually from the particular region he is showcasing.

3. "Race," like "ethnicity," is a vague and potentially problematic term. For the purpose of this article, "race" refers to the models' outward appearance, most obviously evidenced by skin colour. With the exception of the black models, the men featured in these three films are ostensibly Caucasian (i.e., belonging to the same race of European origin); thus, Bjorn resorts primarily to creating national or "ethnic" identity in order to create alterity. To clarify: for the purpose of this article, Caucasian, Black and Native North American men are considered to be of different races, and English, French, and Portuguese men, although mostly belonging to the same race (Caucasian), are of different nationalities, or ethnicities. Due to immigration, men of different races can be of the same nationality, and we see this frequently in Bjorn's work. He routinely puts one black man in each of his films, regardless of the country he is featuring. These black models display all the same "trappings" of nationality as their white counterparts.

4. I have put quotation marks around "Royal Mounties" because this term is not commonplace. In Canadian culture, these law enforcers are either referred to (officially) as "R.C.M.P." (Royal Canadian Mounted Police) or as "Mounties."

REFERENCES

Anderson, B. (1991). *Imagined communities: Reflections on the origin and spread of nationalism.* New York, NY: Verso Press.
Jamoo. (1997). *The films of Kristen Bjorn.* Laguna Hills, CA: Companion Press.

Porn Again:
Some Final Considerations

Shannon R. Ellis

University of Saskatchewan

Bruce W. Whitehead

Red Deer College

SUMMARY. Contributors were asked to respond to seven questions examining various aspects of gay male pornography. Their responses were collated with the hope that the reader may gain additional insight into this topic. *[Article copies available for a fee from The Haworth Document Delivery Service: 1-800-HAWORTH. E-mail address: <docdelivery@haworthpress.com> Website: <http://www.HaworthPress.com> © 2004 by The Haworth Press, Inc. All rights reserved.]*

KEYWORDS. Gay male pornography, pornography, gay male culture, fantasy, patriarchy, sex-trade industry

---

Shannon R. Ellis is a graduate student in the applied social psychology program at the University of Saskatchewan. Her research interests include modern prejudice, pornography, and genital perceptions. Bruce W. Whitehead is a third-year sociology student at Red Deer College, Red Deer, Alberta. His research interests include gay and lesbian identity formation, and gay men's conscious decision to practice unsafe sex as it relates to their sexual identity. He intends to pursue a doctorate in sociology.

[Haworth co-indexing entry note]: "Porn Again: Some Final Considerations." Ellis, Shannon R., and Bruce W. Whitehead. Co-published simultaneously in *Journal of Homosexuality* (Harrington Park Press, an imprint of The Haworth Press, Inc.) Vol. 47, No. 3/4, 2004, pp. 197-220; and: *Eclectic Views on Gay Male Pornography: Pornucopia* (ed: Todd G. Morrison) Harrington Park Press, an imprint of The Haworth Press, Inc., 2004, pp. 197-220. Single or multiple copies of this article are available for a fee from The Haworth Document Delivery Service [1-800-HAWORTH, 9:00 a.m. - 5:00 p.m. (EST). E-mail address: docdelivery@haworthpress.com].

http://www.haworthpress.com/web/JH
© 2004 by The Haworth Press, Inc. All rights reserved.
Digital Object Identifier: 10.1300/J082v47n03_12

Seven questions concerning gay male pornography were sent to the individuals contributing to this volume. (The editors responsible for preparing this piece also were asked to participate.) The instructions outlined that contributors: (a) could answer as many questions as they wished; (b) did not have to limit themselves to issues explored in their articles; and (c) should use a writing style that is conversational in tone. As well, contributors were informed that the accoutrements of "traditional" academic writing such as references, endnotes, and adoption of an "objective," dispassionate authorial voice were unnecessary–indeed, undesirable.

The questions are not presented in any sort of thematic sequence. The responses are simply listed in order of receipt and, aside from minor editing for typographic errors, appear as they were received.

QUESTION 1

Are there beneficial aspects to commercially available, mainstream gay male pornography? Are there harmful aspects?

Paul Hallam:

> A maddening either/or question. Is the question addressed to consumers or to participants in/makers of pornography? And since participants and makers might also be consumers, there is no either/or there either. Oh, for the day when I can separate benefit from harm. If I'm honest, it isn't a day I would wish to see.

Todd G. Morrison:

> Before answering this question, I think it's important to point out that, with respect to mainstream gay pornography, the beneficial or harmful aspects concern the viewer rather than the material. That is, for the most part, the advantages or disadvantages of porn are a product of the viewer's perceptions; a consequence of how the viewer responds to the imagery he sees.
>
> I believe that gay male pornography possesses a number of "benefits." First, it's a masturbatory aid–it's something we can use when we don't want to expend the cognitive energy required of fantasy. (Of course, this doesn't preclude the possibility of incorporating the pornographic imagery we see/read into our fantasies.)

Second, it represents the ultimate form of safer sex; the viewer simply masturbates to the imagery he sees in the magazine, on a television screen, etc.–no body fluids are exchanged. Third, it has the potential to serve an educative function–it provides a guide on how to perform certain activities, and can expand one's sexual repertoire. In the absence of pornography, how many gay men would necessarily know anything about anilingus? One would have to rely on *The Joy of Gay Sex* or the spontaneous discovery of such an activity or "instruction" from a more experienced partner. Fourth, gay pornography may help some individuals accept their orientation by reinforcing the view that being homosexual is acceptable and even desirable. Fifth, gay pornography permits one to "experience" a variety of bodies. When I use the word "experience," I don't mean in the traditional sense of pretending that one is having sex with a porn star but, rather, that the viewer can imagine he IS the individual he sees on the screen. Through pornography, I can imagine I AM [porn performers] Matthew Rush, Scott Baldwin, Ken Ryker, Travis Wade, etc.–that I am submissive AND dominant; 6'3" and muscular AND a cute "porn pup"; a twink AND a daddy; etc. Finally, I appreciate any medium that promotes the objectification of MEN for sexual purposes. Given that we exist in a patriarchal society, men (read: heterosexual men) appear oblivious to the possibility that they could be subject to the gaze. They seem to operate from the assumption that the power (indeed, the right) to scrutinize others in aesthetic terms is theirs and theirs alone. Gay pornography reveals that those in positions of power can be denied subjectivity–that they can be treated as objects. Even when the pornographic imagery depicts "straight" men treating "fags" abominably, the "power" of heterosexual orthodoxy (and more generally, patriarchy) is being subverted; the "straight" man is, after all, performing for the masturbatory pleasure of the gay viewer.

I also believe that gay pornography has the potential to be harmful. It may promote unrealistic assessments about the body required to be a "successful" member of the gay community. Impressionable consumers may believe that if they fall outside the narrow parameters of being 21, muscular, hairless, tanned, etc., they are ciphers; that being removed from this "ideal" is a punishable offense, one worthy of house arrest. Although pornography may expand the parameters of gay men's fantasies, it has the potential of increasing the homogeneity of their erotic thoughts. One begins to fantasize in "pornographic terms"–in accordance with the imagery one sees. Finally, I think there is the possibility that impressionable consumers may develop a distorted view of gay sexuality–they may assume that ALL gay men are hypersexual "sluts" who will seize any sexual opportunity that presents itself.

Clare N. Westcott:

I would say the availability of gay male pornography is beneficial for the "normalization" of homosexuality in society. Heterosexual porn is easily available, so why not gay male porn? I can't see any negative aspects of gay porn that wouldn't be shared by heterosexual porn (i.e., people could say it depicts male homosexuals in a degrading way at times, but the same happens to all kinds of demographic groups in all kinds of porn).

Benjamin Scuglia:

Yes, there are beneficial aspects to gay porn. It can serve as a release valve for sexual energy, fuel fantasies, and satiate men who are starved for gay imagery. Of course, there can be negative aspects. But whether mainstream gay porn ever becomes harmful depends entirely on you. Without balance, anything can become harmful.

Bruce W. Whitehead:

When I see the words "mainstream gay male pornography," I tend to think of the vanilla variety of porn that features hairless, pretty white boys fresh from the gym and the hairdresser. I don't find it harmful so much as boring. My biggest complaint with the sex-trade industry is that the people getting rich are not necessarily the ones that are doing all the 'work.' I think it is unfortunate that the person who is selling an image of his or her body tends to see only a short-term gain, and I do question, "Who is getting rich here?" The more available porn is, and the more mainstream it is, the more apt there is to be an immense profit generated, and in so doing, the gap widens between wages and profit. I would also question racial representations in gay porn, again considering the specification of "mainstream," and how specific racial groups (Asian, African-American, etc.) are represented in comparison to their Caucasian counterparts. The same could be said for discrepancies in the ages of the actors; the middle-aged actor doing a scene with the younger man is no accident nor does it go unacknowledged. So I do think that, as much as I enjoy gay porn, the more mainstream it is, the more likely it is to reinforce specific ideals of beauty and to promote racial stereotypes and power differentials. Granted, the individual consumer does have the choice of accepting or rejecting those representations.

Bertram J. Cohler:

The benefits are many. Gay porn plays an important role for men learning what to do sexually with other men. Boys in high school who identify as heterosexual talk together about what boys do with girls. This socialization into dating and sexuality is often accompanied by formal sex education classes (alas, too often taught by heterosexist male athletic coaches). Comparatively, gay boys have little opportunity to learn what gay men do together sexually. It is often difficult to know other gay boys in school, so gay porn replaces conversation as a means for socialization into gay sexuality. Younger gay men report that the magazine *XY* is important in that respect, as are gay porn novels and magazines. We don't realize how often gay boys are lonely, particularly in less supportive communities. (Although the Internet has helped in many respects with issues of loneliness.) Finally, there is the benefit in the time of STDs that a personal sexual encounter with the assistance of a gay porn video may be much safer than an anonymous sexual encounter.

The "downside" of gay porn is that it teaches an idealized and stylized approach to gay sex. Younger gay men just beginning their journey into gay sexuality find a model for cruising (a sexual encounter marked by a sequence of undressing and feeling each other up, then oral sex, then anal sex, pretty much in that order). Sometimes rimming and prepping the partner are shown in detail, which is informative, but which leads some young men to believe that if a sexual encounter doesn't follow this pattern then there must be problems. Some younger gay men (perhaps older ones as well) believe that an intimate encounter without penetration is not real "sex." All too often, the "models" don't seem to be enjoying the event. Gay porn star Scott O'Hara used to complain about that and wanted to show that gay sex was fun.

Shannon R. Ellis:

Unfortunately, society in general is still very naïve, uncomfortable and seldom understanding about a gay male's need and desire to explore and express his sexuality. Although I do not believe that pornography is an ideal tool to assist gay males in their quest for knowledge about their sexual desires, sometimes we have to settle for second best when the appropriate means are not available to us. Ideally, if we lived in an open-minded society that embraced and encouraged divergence in the matters of sexual identity, gay male pornography would probably appeal only to a limited audience who viewed this medium as pure entertainment.

As far as harmful aspects, all porn can have negative effects if the audience is naïve and believes that what they see on the screen is representative of real life. Speaking as a heterosexual female, I think that gay male porn may also subtly harm the audience it claims to want to liberate because it fuels the misconception that many heterosexuals have that gay men are sexually promiscuous, thinking of little else than finding their next sexual conquest.

Scott J. Duggan:

While it is true that gay male pornography idealizes and idolizes the perfect male physique, I think there are some redeeming qualities to it. One is that it functions as an educational tool for gay men. It is true that the mechanics of heterosexual sex are not well taught, but same-sex acts are given even less voice. Gay male pornography provides a "how to" for many sexual acts. Point in fact, with the advent of AIDS, gay male pornography adopted safer sex techniques and introduced them to the gay male population. From this, gay men could see how condoms could be incorporated into their sex acts.

Gay male pornography also normalizes same-sex sexual activity. Instead of limiting the places of gay sex to back rooms and darkened corners of seedy bars, gay pornography depicts sexual activities in a variety of places and settings. It brings sexual activity into the light, so to speak. It removes the stigma associated with the enjoyment of same-sex sexual activity in that the actors are often encouraged to vocalize their enjoyment of what they are doing.

QUESTION 2

What role, if any, does gay male pornography play in gay male subculture?

Paul Hallam:

Yes, we had and have the shared secrets, the shared fantasies from all manner of likely and unlikely sources. Images we subvert and are subverted to our own ends. But, in the end, it seems to me that we still keep, even with those most 'close to us,' our real porn interests quiet and private. This is probably no bad thing.

Todd G. Morrison:

I find the concept of "gay male subculture" problematic. What exactly does one mean by this term? How is this culture defined? Do all gay men partake in this culture by virtue of their sexual orientation? Are my experiences as a gay social psychologist in a small city in Ireland similar to a waiter living in San Francisco? More importantly, does gay culture even exist? Does the handful of commercial enterprises found in most "gay ghettos" constitute culture? If a book or film has one or more gay characters, does it become a thread in the tapestry of "our" culture? Because I have difficulty with this concept, I cannot really answer the question. However, I will acknowledge that gay pornography is ubiquitous– I have yet to meet a gay male who has never been exposed to this type of material. And, certainly, the objectification characteristic of porn is found in a variety of non-pornographic media directed at gay men (even safer-sex pamphlets). Finally, I believe that because it is so commonplace, gay pornography is less stigmatized than heterosexual pornography by members of their respective "communities."

Benjamin Scuglia:

Gay male pornography primarily serves as fuel for fantasies, a sexual tool, and a release valve.

Bruce W. Whitehead:

Role? You mean that gay male (sub)culture involves more than porn? Pornography is so ubiquitous in the gay community that I'm not sure you could escape it and still claim to be an active part of gay culture, at least not the consumer aspect of gay culture. I tend to think of gay culture as being gay consumerism. Pornography generates an immense amount of profit, and not only for the pornographers, but for many individuals and companies in the gay community, and this in turn facilitates many aspects of gay culture. How many gay chat lines could survive, and remain free of cost, without the revenue provided by the sale of gay pornography? It would appear that–as consumers–we are buying more porn than gay-themed calling cards. I can't readily think of the last time I walked into a "pride" store and had the books on activism dwarf the racks of porn. In many ways porn embodies gay culture. It is camp, kitsch, butch, drag, and politics all rolled into one nicely edited package complete with a cum-shot at the end.

John Mercer:

I think it plays a pretty central role. Unlike heterosexual pornography, which is a rather marginalized form of cultural expression, it strikes me that gay pornography is right at the heart of anything approaching a gay culture. The primary thing that gay men have in common is a shared sexuality. This seems like a facile observation but our identity as a group is defined by sexual choice and, therefore, I think that the cultural articulations of that form of sexuality are extremely important. Gay porn functions as documentary evidence that certain desires exist; it creates a mythology of sexual desire for the gay male community; it has played an important role in constructing and disseminating a paradigm of gay male iconography; to some extent, it determines normative sexual conduct; and it has the potential to educate viewers about sexual practices.

QUESTION 3

Is there a distinction between gay pornography and gay erotica? If so, what factors differentiate between the two?

Paul Hallam:

> Not that old chestnut. You just have to work a bit harder on the erotica. A shirt collar in a painting or on a man in the street might set me off. Where do I go from there? At times, I might "outsade" de Sade. But I don't have to make the enormous effort to write it up. At others, that collar might just be sufficient unto itself.

Todd G. Morrison:

> To me, erotica is merely a socially acceptable term for pornography. If an individual feels more comfortable using the word erotica or "scientific" terminology like sexually explicit material, fine; however, I perceive these words as synonyms. I also don't think there is a meaningful way to distinguish between erotica and pornography. Supposedly, the former depicts loving, compassionate sexual relationships; eroticizes equality; and ensures that all participants are granted subjectivity. However, it is unclear how one can unambiguously determine the existence of such intangible qualities. If a man ejaculates on another man's face, does this represent inequality; a power differential? Does context matter–strangers versus lovers celebrating their five-year anniversary? (Incidentally, why is ejaculate given the power of determination in this matter? Perhaps more importantly, why is ejaculate regarded as so obscene, so polluting by so many antiporn activists?) I remember Diana Russell reporting in one of her books that the rape scene in *The Accused* wasn't pornographic because the film was designed to increase public awareness of sexual violence (i.e., its educative function outweighed the violent nature of its sexual content). But what happens if someone masturbates to that scene–does it retain its non-pornographic status? Given the inherently personal nature of arousal (I think [porn performer] Travis Wade is sexy, others may find him unappealing) in conjunction with the amorphous-

ness of concepts like subjectivity, the clichéd statement is true: one person's erotica is another person's pornography.

Benjamin Scuglia:

Gay "erotica" is just gay "pornography" in a prettier dress.

Bruce W. Whitehead:

Erotica, for me at least, represents that which is unspoken. Gay innuendo in mainstream films, gay subtext in literature, and sexual ambiguity within a heterosexual framework; the subtlety that exists in those situations, and is open to imagination and interpretation, I can find erotic. Once sex is presented, rather than implied, it often becomes pornography. Discussions beyond that point tend to become debates around personal taste rather than actual content. Further to that, when sexuality is specifically marketed as erotica, it tends to lack in story-value or sex-value, and subsequently borders on tedious. Sex-value (pornography), or story-value (erotica), at least one should be prominent; too often the producers of "erotica" rely on both, and achieve neither.

Bertram J. Cohler:

The distinction between gay erotica and gay pornography is one of degree. Gay erotica is designed to arouse the reader or viewer (perhaps soft porn would be a better term). Abercrombie and Fitch photos are a good example of gay erotica (so coded that gay men have little difficulty recognizing these pictures). Gay porn is specific and explicit carrying through the entire course of sexual activity to orgasm.

John Mercer:

It tends to be the case that texts that commentators approve of are described as erotica and the ones they disapprove of are described as pornography. The terms nearly always imply some kind of class-based judgment of merit. I'm not keen on the term "gay erotica" for exactly this reason as I think that language, designed to afford gravitas or cachet to sexually explicit or titillating material, buys into the notion that there is this whole other debased area of cultural production that is *not* erotica, just merely pornographic. The term erotica is tied into notions of both class and taste making in this regard. However, I would say that intention plays a large part in the equation. I'm of the view that it is not possible to produce a text that is accidentally pornographic. My argument is that a text is pornographic because that was the intention of the producer of the text. This seems like a pragmatic approach to adopt in the rather thorny area of defining what pornography is. The alternative is, of course, to suggest that pornography is in the eye of the beholder, which is rather problematic as there are, no doubt, individuals who use the footwear section of mail order catalogues for their sexual gratification! History also seems to play an important role here. One epoch's scandalous pornography is another's quaint erotica. Jean Genet's *Un Chant D'Amour*, for example, was made for the specific intention to be exhibited as pornography but now tends to be regarded as an interesting and rather poetic example of avant-garde erotic gay cinema, just as Tom of Finland's illustrations have found their way into the permanent collections of prestigious art galleries.

QUESTION 4

How would you counter the argument that gay male pornography subverts heterosexual orthodoxy and is an instrument of liberation? How would you counter the argument that gay male pornography reinforces hegemonic masculinity and, thus, is an instrument of oppression?

Paul Hallam:

Much as I love porn, I do not see it an instrument of liberation. Nor do I see it as "subversive."

Todd G. Morrison:

The fact that such contradictory arguments are forwarded about gay pornography suggests that it isn't the material itself that is functioning as an instrument of oppression/liberation; rather, it is the *viewer's* response to such material that determines its effect. Consequently, blanket statements about gay porn–pro or con–are unwarranted.

Benjamin Scuglia:

I can't counter the first argument because it's true. As for the second argument, even a casual examination of gay pornography will show a kaleidoscopic variety of men, the very opposite of masculine hegemony.

Bruce W. Whitehead:

I'm more apt to give those accolades to the men that are unapologetically out, their mere presence subverts and liberates. Porn just gets watched. Which hegemonic masculinity are we referring to? The hegemonic masculinity of the skate punk, the pig, the bear, the cub, the gym bunny, the twink, the pretty boy, the pierced and tattooed phreak, or the butch daddy bottom? Media, gay or otherwise, reinforces specific "looks," with one ideal superseding the others. If the dominant ideal is an image that you reject, then the alternatives are available. Gay porn may reinforce distinct masculine representations, but there are several to choose from rather than just one, and they mirror the masculinities that are dominant in gay culture. As to whether or not that oppresses or liberates is entirely the interpretation of the individual that identifies with, or rejects, one of those ideals.

Bertram J. Cohler:

In contrast to heterosexual porn, gay porn is a more differentiated genre. Rather than an instrument of repression, it is an instrument of liberation, portraying the variety of means possible for realizing sexual satisfaction. While heterosexual pornography subjugates women to men, men in gay pornography volunteer. Indeed, if they were not deriving pleasure from the experience, it wouldn't work. Gay porn producer Aaron Lawrence has described, on his Website, the process of working on a porn movie. Outside of the boredom of sitting and waiting for his turn on the set, he describes the pleasure of being with other guys he is attracted to. There is a fascinating subculture of men who act in gay porn and many of these men know each other, have been lovers and are still friends. That aspect of the work of gay porn has never been studied. It is less clear that gay porn is a means of reinforcing the hegemony of the handsome gay man. Gay porn reflects rather than creates shared fantasies about men. Again, recognizing the many types of gay porn, it is clear that gay porn succeeds because it reflects desire, which particular men have regarding their sexual partner.

John Mercer:

My view, and it is a personal one, is that framing debate on pornography in this way, much as in the first question posed, identifies very clearly one of the fundamental problems with academic and popular discussions of pornography that seem to have failed to move beyond an impasse reached in the late '80s and '90s. Discussion of pornography always seems to be about either saying pornography is irredeemably bad or that pornography is good in a rather unquestioning fashion. It strikes me that these are ultimately the wrong questions to be asking and trying to answer in the first place and just perpetuate the entrenched positions that have prevailed for decades. Gay pornography can easily be regarded as an instrument of liberation and oppression at the same time; just as all other forms of popular culture are both exploitative and simultaneously the means by which we construct a sense of our own identities.

Were I forced into a corner, I would have to say that I think gay pornography is more positive than negative for the reasons that I identify in my response to the second question, but during the course of my own ongoing research into the area, I have made a conscious decision not to engage with these rather polarized debates which seem to lead nowhere. I'm more interested in trying to understand what gay pornography is, how it manifests itself, what kind of iconography it uses and what kinds of stories it tells and the origins of these thematic concerns. As there is no shortage of academics and commentators only too keen to make evaluative judgments, I think it's safe to let the 'porn is good or bad' debate rumble on.

QUESTION 5

If someone were to ask you to discuss your personal relationship with gay male pornography, what would you say?

Paul Hallam:

"Mind your own business" might be my first response. The second might be relief–even greater relief once the question has been addressed and the article submitted.

Todd G. Morrison:

Gay porn allows me to view a number of attractive men engaging in behavior that ordinarily occurs in private. It satisfies my voyeuristic impulses; my innate curiosity to determine what exists "underneath all those clothes." It is a source of pleasure, an "illicit" thrill. And, on those occasions, when the minutiae of my life forces my homosexuality into the background, it reminds me that "yes, I am gay!"

Benjamin Scuglia:

Like my actual sex life, porn has been a lot of fun, and also quite boring. It has taught me new tricks I can't wait to try in real life, introduced me to old ones I hadn't considered, and even helped me rule out a few things that I now know I wouldn't want to attempt in real life. Porn has been a useful tool I keep handy for when I need it.

Bruce W. Whitehead:

I like porn. I'm not sure I have ever grappled with my relationship to it. It's my vanilla and my kink. The first time I had to identify as a gay male was when I bought gay porn as a teenager, and at that time I made a conscious decision not to be ashamed of what I was doing. Gay porn triggered the first conversation I had with my parents about my homosexuality, or rather I came home from school to find them sitting at the kitchen table, arms folded across their chests, and my meager magazine collection spread out on the kitchen table. I was 15 years old before I saw a healthy gay individual represented on television; yet, at this point, I was already out to family and friends. The only other place I saw gay men was in the pages of the pornography that I no longer hid. In this medium, I saw men that didn't fit the stereotypes that I was being fed by my family, my church, my school, and my television. I acknowledge that it was a one-dimensional medium that I was free to interpret, yet the images I received from other sources did not allow for interpretation. In 'their' world, all gay men were predatory, deceptive, mentally vacuous, and laughably effeminate. In pornography, I saw men that were tender and loving, even passionate and committed, and better yet they kissed (they also hiked a lot). Porn provided me with the gay imagery that the media were unable, or rather unwilling, to offer. (It also taught me to relish a good hike.)

Bertram J. Cohler:

Like many other younger gay men, I learned about my sexuality and the meaning of being gay through available gay porn (at the time, mostly muscle magazines and cheap paperback novels). I still enjoy a good gay porn video, well acted and with a plot, with cute guys acting and enjoying themselves. I enjoy reading good gay fiction and flip through gay magazines in my local bookstore. I don't have much free time else I would enjoy some of the porn sites on the Web. The point is that gay porn is a part of life for many of us, not something to be ashamed of.

Robert Jensen:

When I came to understand my attraction to men, I had a choice to explore that, in part, through gay pornography. I chose not to, for the simple reason that I didn't want an industry dedicated to making money off other people's bodies to define my sense of my own sexuality. I look to art, literature, and politics for insights about sexuality. I continue to seek a community in which I can share such insights with others. But I see no reason to expect that the commercial sex industry will have much to offer in that realm.

John Mercer:

> I would probably say, "Mind your own business" or profess to have a purely academic interest in gay pornography. Either way my response would be evasive in the extreme!

Shannon R. Ellis:

> I would say that I have a fascination with pornography in general, whether homosexual or heterosexual. When I use the word "fascination," I am referring to an interest in why people become so engrossed in it and how that influences their perceptions of themselves as physical and sexual beings. The type and amount of pornography that individuals expose themselves to can offer an outsider looking in unique insight into how those individuals view themselves.

Scott J. Duggan:

> Gay male pornography introduced me to a variety of sexual acts, many of which I may never have had the opportunity to assess. I could entertain the idea of many acts and decide which ones I would like to experiment with in real life.

QUESTION 6

Thomas Waugh (1995) asserts that "unlike straight male porn, gay porn does not directly and systematically replicate the heterosexist patriarchal order in its relations of production, exhibition, consumption, or representation ... It subverts the patriarchal order by challenging masculinist values, providing a protected space for nonconformist, non-reproductive, and non-familial sexuality, encouraging many sex-positive values and declaring the dignity of gay people" (pp. 323-324). What are your observations about this statement?

Paul Hallam:

> I would want to write a book on notions of "dignity." Dignity, in the gay context, is worse than our acquired gay "pride."

Todd G. Morrison:

The ability of gay pornography to achieve such lofty ambitions is contingent upon the perceptiveness of the viewer (i.e., the viewer must recognize that the material in question is challenging masculinist values; promoting the "dignity" of gay people, etc.). In addition, the idea that gay pornography provides "a protected space for nonconformist sexuality" may be questioned. Certainly, gay sex is nonconformist from the vantage of heterosexuality. However, if one restricts this analysis to gay men, the representations of their sexuality offered by pornography appear to be fairly uniform (kiss-kiss-suck-suck-rim-fuck-cum- the end). On the contrary, nonconformist *gay* sexuality does not appear to be embraced by mainstream pornographers. (Incidentally, by nonconformist, I am not referring to outré sexual practices; rather, I mean the sexual depiction of various bodies, ages, etc.–representations that better reflect the diversity of the gay "community.")

Benjamin Scuglia:

I would say, "The next round is on me."

Bertram J. Cohler:

I believe that gay porn, as presently produced, does not oppress the actors. Since it is difficult to feign enjoyment of gay sex, and gay men report enjoying their participation, this seems less like exploitation than heterosexual porn where women are taken advantage of, model but do not necessarily enjoy their sexual encounters, and where the typical heterosexual stereotype of men dominating women is so often present. Gay porn shows the pleasures of gay sexuality. For me, gay sexuality is most meaningful in the context of a man with whom I am in love, but others enjoy even an anonymous tryst. What is important is that men gain pleasure out of their encounters with other men and that they do not feel shame or guilt.

John Mercer:

> I think it is important to remember that the article that this statement is taken from was written nearly 20 years ago, prior to the growth in the home video market and also largely prior to the establishment of a developed, mainstream gay porn industry. Waugh acknowledged that the essay had dated over time in a reprint in 1992/93 and, of course, another 10 years or so on things have changed again. It's rare for any commentary on cultural phenomena to become the definitive statement on the subject because porn, like all other forms of culture, changes.
>
> I understand the broad sentiment of Waugh's statement though there are several things that he says that I would take issue with or at least question. I'm not at all sure in what ways relations of production, exhibition or consumption are clearly linked to the heterosexist patriarchal order. I have recently been reminded, usefully, that the links between patriarchy, as a system of knowledge, and capitalism, as a process, are extremely complicated and often contradictory, and this is a useful thing to bear in mind as there is often a temptation to slide from talking about one to the other and inferring, therefore, that they are one and the same. In this regard, I don't know how a patriarchal form of production, exhibition or consumption manifests itself, as these are key features of capitalism as a process and, perhaps more importantly, how this supposed challenge comes about. I'm of the view that regardless of the fact that–as gay people–we live in a society in which we are marginalized and subject to oppression, it is also the very same society and culture that allows me to identify myself as gay. This is a paradox but I think that paradox is one of the recurrent features of contemporary Western societies and it's something that we do well to remember. Similarly, though I absolutely agree with Waugh that pornography opens up a cultural space for nonconformist sexuality (which it strikes me is one of its key strengths as a form), I don't really agree that it challenges masculinist ideals, or at least not fully. It strikes me that the thing that mainstream gay porn most insistently does is celebrate masculinist ideals, at an aesthetic level at least ... if it's subversive then it's at the level of presenting these ideals as the object of desire, especially male desire; eroticising the 'real' man, something that mainstream culture often (though not always) goes to extreme lengths to avoid.

QUESTION 7

Daniel Harris (1997) states that "In a world without [gay] pornography, we would be far more tolerant of the physical imperfections of our lovers, whom we now constantly appraise by means of the punitive and highly unrealistic criteria for attractiveness purveyed by an insinuatingly commercial medium that has turned intercourse into a beauty pageant, a wild dash down a runway at a fashion show. Pornography shows us how sex should look, not how it really looks. Its effect is essentially prescriptive and judgmental. It vitiates our sense of touch and exaggerates our sense of sight, promoting dissatisfaction with our real-world lovers and distancing us from the actual sensations of an experience that many now perceive exclusively through the stylized representations of it available on the store shelves" (p. 133). What are your observations about this statement?

Paul Hallam:

> I was invited to question my own article's position, by contributing to this forum. My brief answers to the interesting questions above have been spoiled by my anger at this remark. I wanted to scream at Harris.
> Harris might give me sleepless nights, and I don't mean in any ambiguous and pleasurable way. It would seem to suggest that the lover relation is the relationship that matters, that counts. "The physical imperfections of our lovers" is Harris' phrase, not mine. Interesting that he doesn't say "my physical imperfections." I've never thought of a lover in an "imperfect" list kind of way. I reject, however much porn I've watched–and I've watched a lot–the idea that porn somehow distorts or diminishes my relation with lovers–ex, present (situation vacant), or future. I reject the idea that a lover/intimate is somehow more important than other relations. Great if you have one, and that you are exclusive, open, tender, and even wild with your imperfect lover, Harris. I wish you both well. But there are more important things in life, perhaps, than waking up with your perfect arms wrapped around your perfect lover. Friendship, for example. Perhaps another anthology could focus on friendship and include the interesting relation of erotica/porn to that. And I suspect that porn viewing goes way beyond the one sense, sight. Just think of the senses involved in that porn viewing.

Todd G. Morrison:

This statement may be applicable to a small proportion of highly impressionable viewers; individuals who believe their erotic lives should emulate the "sexcapades" they see in pornography. However, I think most gay men are able to differentiate between the two. I have never met a gay man who expressed disappointment that his sexual partners/experiences didn't map onto what he saw in pornography. (Perhaps Harris has.) With regards to pornography "showing us how sex should look, and not how it really looks," is that necessarily problematic? Personally, I do not want pornography to mirror my own erotic life. I am not interested in watching individuals with splotchy skin, hair on their shoulders, and mottled buttocks. I want gay pornography to represent what I do not have (and never will have); I want it to be pure, unmitigated fantasy. Finally, I think most of us are tolerant of the "physical imperfections of our lovers" because we are cognizant of the imperfections we possess ourselves. I can hardly demand that a sexual partner look like [porn performers] Matthew Rush or Scott Baldwin unless I approximate that "ideal" myself. (And I'm well aware that I do not.)

Clare N. Westcott:

I think what Harris says may be true, but isn't it a waste of time dreaming of a utopian "world without gay pornography"? I mean, let's be realistic–there is a demand for gay pornography, like all kinds of pornography, so it will be produced and distributed. And if it's going to be produced and distributed, don't we at least want it to be aesthetically pleasing to the majority of viewers? Does Harris advocate the total abolition of porn, or would he be supportive of the production of porn that was more realistic (i.e., ugly and clumsy); that wouldn't run the risk of making us feel so badly about our partners and ourselves? What Harris says about gay porn could be said of pop culture in general–basically all the images out there in movies, TV, and magazines, etc., are capable of making a lot of us feel less than adequate if we let them. The solution is not the abolition of these media–which is impossible by the way–it is seeing them for what they are. We must watch porn with a grain of salt, remembering that it is artificial while our lives are not.

Benjamin Scuglia:

> The root of Harris's argument really has nothing to do with porn and everything to do with how people in our modern consumerist culture create self-worth: "I'm a good person if I have sex with a beautiful man," or have a fast car, expensive clothes, and a fabulous life. THAT is the root of the problem, not pornography itself.

Bruce W. Whitehead:

> I'm envisioning my naked body dashing down a runway at a fashion show and the thought is making me laugh, and not a fun laugh, but rather one of those creepy, nervous laughs. Did I see my lover? Not at all, I saw myself and my response was to evaluate myself unjustly. We are definitely affected by images of beautiful people, but our critical judgments are more apt to reflect negatively on ourselves. I tend to view the images disseminated by porn to be similar to any mass-produced cultural imagery, and as a result, try to evaluate the image critically and not my lover or myself. In many ways, the images in porn are so much more extreme than other media images that they can be easier to dismiss. These images do not sneak into my consciousness under the guise of selling me shoe polish or a new mop. These people are paid to be beautiful, and this is something I know going into the exchange. I seek out pornography because I want to see beautiful people having sex. I have no emotional investment in them, nor do I love them. When I'm intimate with a partner I am engaged with more than the physical exterior of his physique. I think Harris' point would be better directed towards media culture in general, rather than specifically at pornography, gay or otherwise.

Bertram J. Cohler:

> Harris fails to separate fantasy and reality. Each of us has our fantasies regarding our ideal lover and we seek to satisfy those fantasies through gay porn either as video or gay writing. The search for the ideal lover matching this picture inside our heads would go on in any event. Harris gives too much credit to the image taking precedence over the fantasy. Men have particular fantasies of their ideal sexual partner and there is a good deal of variation in desire. Clearly, if an intimate encounter is to "work" there has to be good

chemistry–that is, some fit between fantasy and reality. But, it is the fantasy that spurs the selection of gay porn, and not the gay porn that shapes the fantasy.

John Mercer:

I think it is very sad if this is the case and whilst it, perhaps, [is] true of the author's perceptions and may be more widely the case, I find the inclusive 'we' in the remarks slightly troubling . . . these comments are not speaking for me or anybody I know for that matter. I think that even the implicit suggestion that gay pornography is somehow instrumental in perpetuating the appearance-based prejudice that is evident in some quarters of the gay community is naïve in the extreme. I would think that attitudes more prevalent in wider society, and I'm talking about Western, capitalist society here, are more significant. The ubiquity of global capitalism, the notion that one can commodify bodies . . . that you can, through techniques such as gym training, produce yourself as the desired object (Brian Pronger talks about this) and that your body and the bodies of others become part of some economic system (Baudrillard talks about this) are just some of the factors that result in the so-called contemporary body fascism. Reducing a complex set of cultural and social determinations down to the negative effect of pornography is flawed to say the least. These kinds of arguments tend to overlook that there is a difference between the representations of pornography and reality. I find it alarming and frustrating that so many academics and commentators seem to consistently confuse and conflate the two. There is little real similarity between living, breathing, flesh and blood people who may become sexual partners and five or six inch high, flat televisual images of perfected male bodies. I doubt many people really confuse the two and it is my suspicion that quite a small percentage of people then decide that they must evaluate their real sexual partners according to the artificial world represented by pornography both gay and straight. I, like many people, can take pleasure in the fantasy world of gay porn and its milieu of improbably handsome, well-built men but I can also (like the majority audience, I suspect) recognize that these representations are neither especially representative of my experience nor do they need to be my experience; I regard them as fantasies and do not mistake them for my own reality. I seem to think that confusing fantasy and reality is a symptom of psychosis. I have no doubt that Daniel Harris is not psychotic and I also presume that he isn't suggesting that most gay men are psychotic, but his comments, though unintentional, do seem to suggest as much all the same.

Shannon R. Ellis:

It is not just pornography that portrays the human body in an idealist fashion. Every medium available at some time or another shows the human body in a stereotypically accepted 'perfect' form. If we were to judge our potential sexual partners based on the media's idea of acceptable, I fear that we would all be celibate or extremely unhappy with our sex lives. I don't think that Daniel Harris gives the viewers of pornography much credit for knowing the difference between fantasy and reality. These fantasies are not what you aspire towards; they are merely a form of escapism that allows you to take a mental sexual holiday. Very few people would want to live a holiday forever, as it would lose its appeal and what would be the sense of indulging in it?

Scott J. Duggan:

While it may be true that gay pornography exposes the viewer to near perfect bodies and while it may have some effect on the expectations the viewer has of his sexual partners, it is certainly not a perfect correlational relationship. One must take into account that pornography is only one of a plethora of places where near perfect, idealized bodies are showcased. Mainstream media are presenting an increasing number of advertisements depicting semi-naked men with whom to compare oneself.

CONCLUSION

It is unrealistic to assume that the complex questions surrounding gay male pornography can be addressed within a simple question and answer framework. However, it is hoped that delineation of contributors' personal and academic views will challenge the reader and in so doing prompt further discussion about this unjustly neglected topic.

REFERENCES

Harris, D. (1997). *The rise and fall of gay culture*. New York, NY: Hyperion.
Waugh, T. (1995). Men's pornography: Gay vs. straight. In C.K. Creekmur & A. Doty (Eds.), *Out in culture: Gay, lesbian, and queer essays on popular culture* (pp. 307-327). Durham, NC: Duke University Press.

Index

The Adonis Complex (Pope et al.), 46-47
Ageism, 159
AIDS
   gay male pornography as source for education materials for, 108-109
   in gay pornography, 14
Alterity, use of, in films of Bjorn, 190-196
Autobiographies, 10. *See also* Life-stories
Autopornography: A Memoir of Life in the Lust Lane (O'Hara), 24-25

Barbican Tapes (film), 69
Barebacking, 111-113
Barry, Kathleen, 98
Barthe, Roland, 154
Bijou (film), 18,21
Bisexual youth, suicide rates and, 89
Bjorn, Kristen, 160,187
   films of, 190-196
   use of alterity by, 190-196
Body fascism, 117-119
Body image
   gay men and, 47-48
   hypotheses about, 48
   men and, 46-47
   study of
      discussion about, 54-57
      methodology for, 48-51
      results for, 51-54
   women and, 46
Boys in the Sand (film), 18,20-21
Boys in the Sand II (film), 22-23

Brandon, Kyle, 165
Brig scenarios, gay male pornography and, 164
British Columbia Civil Liberties Union (BCCLU), 130
Burger, John, 99,159
Butler, Judith, 100

Call of the Wild (Bjorn), 191-195
Canada Customs, 131-133,136
Canadian AIDS Society (CAS), Little Sisters position of, 88-89,130,138,139-147
Canadian Civil Liberties Association, 130
Canadian Conference on the Arts, 130
Canon, Steve, 165
Carnival in Rio (Bjorn), 194
Carrigan, Paul, 158
Change. *See* Generation change; Social change
Condom Code, 109
Condoms, use of, in gay male pornography, 110-112
Coulter, Dean, 165
Criminal law, sexually explicit materials and, 140-141
Cruising, 117
Culture, life-stories and, 11-12
Culver, Cal (Casey Donovan), 20,23

Delany, Samuel, 11
Dirty Poole: An Autobiography of a Gay Porn Pioneer (Poole), 18
Donovan, Casey (Cal Culver), 20,23

Dungeons, gay male pornography and, 164-166
Duroy, George, 187
Dworkin, Andrea, 140,152,170

Eating disorders, 46-47
Equality for Gays and Lesbians Everywhere (EGALE), Little Sisters position of, 87-88,130,138,139-147
Erotica, gay, *vs.* gay male pornography, 205-207
Etienne, 164-165

Fantasy, gay porn and, 155
Feminism. *See* Radical feminism
Feminists, sexually explicitly materials and, 139-140
Fetishes, in gay porn videos, 156
Films. *See* Gay porn films; Gay porn videos
Fisting, 14,25-26
Freud, Sigmund, 154-155

Gay erotica, *vs.* gay male pornography, 205-207
Gay lifestyles, in gay male videos, 158-160
Gay male pornography. *See also* Heterosexual pornography; Pornography
  advent of AIDS and, 14
  attitudes about safe sex in, 112-113
  benefits and harmful aspects of, 198-202
  case study of gay men's attitudes about
    discussion, 179-181
    methodology, 170-172
    results, 172-179
  characteristics of, 91-97
  condoms in, 110-112
  dignity of gay people and, 212-214
  function of, 155
  gay conformity in, 117-120
  vs. gay erotica, 205-207
  gay men and, 115-116
  gay sex in, 113-114
  gender in, 97-107
  as genre, 15
  heterosexual scenarios of, 157-158
  as historical and social narratives for gay sexual identity, 14
  history of, 15
  hyper-masculinity in, 169
  as instrument of liberation or oppression, 207-209
  mythology and, 154-155
  personal relationships with, 210-212
  prison scenarios and, 162-166
  real life and fantasy of, 215-219
  role of, in gay male subculture, 203-204
  as source for AIDS education, 108-109
  structure of sexual encounter in, 14
  types of, 2
  unexamined questions about, 2
  unsafe sexual practices in, 110-112
  working on porn sets of, 185-188
Gay male youth
  HIV/AIDS transmission and, 84
  need for sexuality education and, 85-86
  self-esteem needs of, 85-86
  suicide rates and, 84
Gay men
  body image and, 47-48
  radical feminism and, 75-81
Gay porn films
  early theaters for, 15-16
  as genre, 15
  political statements in, 14-15
  structure of sexual encounters in, 14

Gay porn videos, 14
  all male environments of, 156-157
  alterity in Bjorn's films, 189-196
  "back to nature" scenarios in, 161
  fantasy and, 155
  fetishes and, 156
  generic nature of scenarios in, 154
  luxurious fantasies in, 160
  prison scenarios and, 162-166
  real life in industry of, 185-189
  sadomasochism in, 161-162
  urban gay lifestyle in, 158-160
Gender, in gay male pornography, 97-107
Generation change, 13-16
Genet, Jean, 162-163

Harm, proof of, pornography and, 145-147
Harris, Daniel, 215
Herman, Didi, 140
Heterosexual pornography, attention paid to, by social scientists, 1-2. *See also* Gay male pornography; Pornography

Identity, social and historical change and, 8. *See also* Life-stories
Identity performance, defined, 9-10
Idyll, gay male pornography and, 161
Internet, 32
  life-stories and, 12
  writing of life-stories and, 14

Kinsman, Gary, 98
Kipnis, Laura, 154-155,160

Lawrence, Aaron, 9,11,16-17,31-37, 38-39. *See also* Life-stories
Lesbian youth, suicide rates and, 89
Life-stories, gay, 8-9,37-39. *See also* Lawrence, Aaron;
O'Hara, Scott; Poole, Wakefield
  culture and, 11-12
  history and, 11-12
  as identity work, 9
  Internet and, 12,14
  plot lines of, 11-12
  sexual identity and, 37
  shifts in, 12
  social change and, 10-12
Lifestyles, in gay male videos, 158-160
Little Sisters Book and Art Emporium court case, 84-85,130
  arguments of queer sensitive interveners in, 138-147
  gay community's response to, 86-91
  overview of case of, 130-134
  Supreme Court of Canada's decision on, 134-137
  utility of sexual speech and, 139

MacKinnon, Catharine, 140,170
Manly Beach (Bjorn), 191-195
Mannheim, Karl, 13
Marx, Karl, 154
Masturbation, 60-62
Matthews, Ted, 157
Memoirs, 10. *See also* Life-stories
Military prisons, 164
Miller, Tim, 16
Monette, Paul, 12,30
Mythology, in gay pornography, 154-155

Nature, gay male pornography and, 161

O'Hara, Scott, 9,11,16-17,23-31, 38-39, 111-112. *See also* Life-stories

Paradise Plantation (Bjorn), 191-195
Patriarchy, 77
Penitentiaries, 162-164
Performance. *See* Identity performance
Plots, of life-stories, 11-12
Political statements, in gay films, 14-15
Poole, Wakefield, 9,11,16-23,38. *See also* Life-stories
Pornography. *See also* Gay male pornography; Heterosexual pornography
   defined, 9
   proof of harm and, 145-147
   user's personal tribute to, 59-74
   watching, 60-62
Powertool (Higgins), 163
Prison scenarios, gay male pornography and, 162-166

R. v. Butler, 86-87,133-134,137. *See also* Supreme Court of Canada
Radical feminism, gay men, 75-81
Rarely Pure and Never Simple (O'Hara), 24-25

Sade, Marquis de, 164,165
Sadomasochism (S&M), 161-162
Safer sex
   attitudes about, in gay pornography, 112-113
   gay male pornography as source of information for, 109
   gay sex and, 110-120
   as sexual negotiation, 113,114-115
   use of condoms and, 110-112
Scott, Eric, 158
Self, 8
Self-abuse, 60-62
Self-esteem, 85-86
Sex industry, real life in, 185-188
Sexual encounters, structure of, in gay pornography, 14

Sexual expression, Supreme Court of Canada and, 137-138
Sexual identity, 14
   gay male pornography as historical and social narratives for, 14
   life-stories and, 37
Sexuality education, gay male youth and, 85-86
Shirts and Skins (Miller), 16
Slammer (video), 152
S&M (sadomasochism), 161-162
Social change
   generations and, 13-16
   life-stories and, 10-12
Steam (journal), 16,31
Steele, Chris, 158
Stefano, Joey, 111
Stryker, Jeff, 104-105,157,163-164
Stychin, Carl, 100,116
Suicide rates
   gay male youth and, 84
   lesbian, gay, and bisexual youth and, 89
Supreme Court of Canada, 134-137. *See also R. v. Butler*
   on sexual expression, 137-138

Take One (film), 22
Theaters, for early gay films, 15-16
Tobias, Andrew, 11
Tom of Finland, 164

Un Chant D'Amour (Genet), 162-163,207
Urban gay lifestyles, in gay male videos, 158-160

Videos. *See* Gay porn films; Gay porn videos

Wanking, 60. *See also* Self-abuse
Waugh, Thomas,
    97-98,153-154,156,212
Websites. *See* Internet
Women, body image and, 46

Women's Legal Education and Action
    Fund (LEAF), Little Sisters
    position of, 88-90,130,
    138-139,139-147

Zeeland, Steven, 24

Monographs "Separates" list continued

Male Intergenerational Intimacy: Historical, Socio-Psychological, and Legal Perspectives, edited by Theo G. M. Sandfort, PhD, Edward Brongersma, JD, and A. X. van Naerssen, PhD (Vol. 20, No. 1/2, 1991). *"The most important book on the subject since Tom O'Carroll's 1980 Paedophilia: The Radical Case." (The North American Man/Boy Love Association Bulletin, May 1991)*

Love Letters Between a Certain Late Nobleman and the Famous Mr. Wilson, edited by Michael S. Kimmel, PhD (Vol. 19, No. 2, 1990). *"An intriguing book about homosexuality in 18th-Century England. Many details of the period, such as meeting places, coded language, and 'camping' are all covered in the book. If you're a history buff, you'll enjoy this one." (Prime Timers)*

Homosexuality and Religion, edited by Richard Hasbany, PhD (Vol. 18, No. 3/4, 1990). *"A welcome resource that provides historical and contemporary views on many issues involving religious life and homosexuality." (Journal of Sex Education and Therapy)*

Homosexuality and the Family, edited by Frederick W. Bozett, PhD (Vol. 18, No. 1/2, 1989). *"Enlightening and answers a host of questions about the effects of homosexuality upon family members and the family as a unit." (Ambush Magazine)*

Gay and Lesbian Youth, edited by Gilbert Herdt, PhD (Vol. 17, No. 1/2/3/4, 1989). *"Provides a much-needed compilation of research dealing with homosexuality and adolescents." (GLTF Newsletter)*

Lesbians Over 60 Speak for Themselves, edited by Monika Kehoe, PhD (Vol. 16, No. 3/4, 1989). *"A pioneering book examining the social, economical, physical, sexual, and emotional lives of aging lesbians." (Feminist Bookstore News)*

The Pursuit of Sodomy: Male Homosexuality in Renaissance and Enlightenment Europe, edited by Kent Gerard, PhD, and Gert Hekma, PhD (Vol. 16, No. 1/2, 1989). *"Presenting a wealth of information in a compact form, this book should be welcomed by anyone with an interest in this period in European history or in the precursors to modern concepts of homosexuality." (The Canadian Journal of Human Sexuality)*

Psychopathology and Psychotherapy in Homosexuality, edited by Michael W. Ross, PhD (Vol. 15, No. 1/2, 1988). *"One of the more objective, scientific collections of articles concerning the mental health of gays and lesbians. . . . Extraordinarily thoughtful. . . . New thoughts about treatments. Vital viewpoints." (The Book Reader)*

Psychotherapy with Homosexual Men and Women: Integrated Identity Approaches for Clinical Practice, edited by Eli Coleman, PhD (Vol. 14, No. 1/2, 1987). *"An invaluable tool. . . . This is an extremely useful book for the clinician seeking better ways to understand gay and lesbian patients." (Hospital and Community Psychiatry)*

Interdisciplinary Research on Homosexuality in The Netherlands, edited by A. X. van Naerssen, PhD (Vol. 13, No. 2/3, 1987). *"Valuable not just for its insightful analysis of the evolution of gay rights in The Netherlands, but also for the lessons that can be extracted by our own society from the Dutch tradition of tolerance for homosexuals." (The San Francisco Chronicle)*

Historical, Literary, and Erotic Aspects of Lesbianism, edited by Monica Kehoe, PhD (Vol. 12, No. 3/4, 1986). *"Fascinating. . . . Even though this entire volume is serious scholarship penned by degreed writers, most of it is vital, accessible, and thoroughly readable even to the casual student of lesbian history." (Lambda Rising)*

Anthropology and Homosexual Behavior, edited by Evelyn Blackwood, PhD (cand.) (Vol. 11, No. 3/4, 1986). *"A fascinating account of homosexuality during various historical periods and in non-Western cultures." (SIECUS Report)*

Bisexualities: Theory and Research, edited by Fritz Klein, MD, and Timothy J. Wolf, PhD (Vol. 11, No. 1/2, 1985). *"The editors have brought together a formidable array of new data challenging old stereotypes about a very important human phenomenon. . . . A milestone in furthering our knowledge about sexual orientation." (David P. McWhirter, Co-author, The Male Couple)*

Homophobia: An Overview, edited by John P. De Cecco, PhD (Vol. 10, No. 1/2, 1984). *"Breaks ground in helping to make the study of homophobia a science." (Contemporary Psychiatry)*

Bisexual and Homosexual Identities: Critical Clinical Issues, edited by John P. De Cecco, PhD (Vol. 9, No. 4, 1985). *Leading experts provide valuable insights into sexual identity within a clinical context–broadly defined to include depth psychology, diagnostic classification, therapy, and psychomedical research on the hormonal basis of homosexuality.*

Bisexual and Homosexual Identities: Critical Theoretical Issues, edited by John P. De Cecco, PhD, and Michael G. Shively, MA (Vol. 9, No. 2/3, 1984). *"A valuable book . . . The careful scholarship, analytic rigor, and lucid exposition of virtually all of these essays make them thought-provoking and worth more than one reading." (Sex Roles, A Journal of Research)*

Homosexuality and Social Sex Roles, edited by Michael W. Ross, PhD (Vol. 9, No. 1, 1983). *"For a comprehensive review of the literature in this domain, exposure to some interesting methodological models, and a glance at 'older' theories undergoing contemporary scrutiny, I recommend this book." (Journal of Sex Education & Therapy)*

Literary Visions of Homosexuality, edited by Stuart Kellogg, PhD (Vol. 8, No. 3/4, 1985). *"An important book. Gay sensibility has never been given such a boost." (The Advocate)*

Alcoholism and Homosexuality, edited by Thomas O. Ziebold, PhD, and John E. Mongeon (Vol. 7, No. 4, 1985). *"A landmark in the fields of both alcoholism and homosexuality . . . a very lush work of high caliber." (The Journal of Sex Research)*

Homosexuality and Psychotherapy: A Practitioner's Handbook of Affirmative Models, edited by John C. Gonsiorek, PhD (Vol. 7, No. 2/3, 1985). *"A book that seeks to create affirmative psychotherapeutic models. . . . To say this book is needed by all doing therapy with gay or lesbian clients is an understatement." (The Advocate)*

Nature and Causes of Homosexuality: A Philosophic and Scientific Inquiry, edited by Noretta Koertge, PhD (Vol. 6, No. 4, 1982). *"An interesting, thought-provoking book, well worth reading as a corrective to much of the research literature on homosexuality." (Australian Journal of Sex, Marriage & Family)*

Historical Perspectives on Homosexuality, edited by Salvatore J. Licata, PhD, and Robert P. Petersen, PhD (cand.) (Vol. 6, No. 1/2, 1986). *"Scholarly and excellent. Its authority is impeccable, and its treatment of this neglected area exemplary." (Choice)*

Homosexuality and the Law, edited by Donald C. Knutson, PhD (Vol. 5, No. 1/2, 1979). *A comprehensive analysis of current legal issues and court decisions relevant to male and female homosexuality.*

BOOK ORDER FORM!

Order a copy of this book with this form or online at:
http://www.haworthpress.com/store/product.asp?sku=5349

Eclectic Views on Gay Male Pornography
Pornucopia

___ in softbound at $ (ISBN: 1-56023-291-9)
___ in hardbound at $ (ISBN: 1-56023-290-0)

COST OF BOOKS _____	❏ BILL ME LATER:
	Bill-me option is good on US/Canada/ Mexico orders only; not good to jobbers, wholesalers, or subscription agencies.
POSTAGE & HANDLING _____	
US: $4.00 for first book & $1.50 for each additional book	❏ Signature _____
Outside US: $5.00 for first book & $2.00 for each additional book.	❏ Payment Enclosed: $ _____
SUBTOTAL _____	❏ PLEASE CHARGE TO MY CREDIT CARD:
In Canada: add 7% GST. _____	❏ Visa ❏ MasterCard ❏ AmEx ❏ Discover
STATE TAX _____	❏ Diner's Club ❏ Eurocard ❏ JCB
CA, IL, IN, MN, NJ, NY, OH & SD residents please add appropriate local sales tax.	Account # _____
FINAL TOTAL _____	Exp Date _____
If paying in Canadian funds, convert using the current exchange rate. UNESCO coupons welcome.	Signature _____
	(Prices in US dollars and subject to change without notice.)

PLEASE PRINT ALL INFORMATION OR ATTACH YOUR BUSINESS CARD

Name		
Address		
City	State/Province	Zip/Postal Code
Country		
Tel		Fax
E-Mail		

May we use your e-mail address for confirmations and other types of information? ❏ Yes ❏ No We appreciate receiving your e-mail address. Haworth would like to e-mail special discount offers to you, as a preferred customer. **We will never share, rent, or exchange your e-mail address.** We regard such actions as an invasion of your privacy.

Order From Your **Local Bookstore** or Directly From
The Haworth Press, Inc. 10 Alice Street, Binghamton, New York 13904-1580 • USA
Call Our toll-free number (1-800-429-6784) / Outside US/Canada: (607) 722-5857
Fax: 1-800-895-0582 / Outside US/Canada: (607) 771-0012
E-mail your order to us: orders@haworthpress.com

For orders outside US and Canada, you may wish to order through your local sales representative, distributor, or bookseller.
For information, see http://haworthpress.com/distributors

(Discounts are available for individual orders in US and Canada only, not booksellers/distributors.)

Please photocopy this form for your personal use.
www.HaworthPress.com

BOF04